Reminiscences and Reflections of an Old West Country Clergyman

Taken by Heath & Co. Plymouth Sept. 189-

W. H. Thornton

Reminiscences and Reflections of an Old West Country Clergyman

BY

THE REV. W.H. THORNTON

EXCELLENT PRESS
LUDLOW

First published in 1897 (Vol. I)
and 1899 (Vol. II)

This edition published in 2010 by
Excellent Press
9 Lower Raven Lane
Ludlow SY8 1BW

ISBN 1 900318 38 5
ISBN 978 1900318 38 9

THO

Designed and typeset by
Columns Design Ltd, Reading, UK

Printed and bound in Great Britain

Contents

Introduction

THIS IS A splendid discovery: a vigorous and engaging rural memoir which has lain dormant for more than a century. William Henry Thornton was born in 1830. His father was head of the Stamp and Tax department at Somerset House, in London, and he himself was brought up partly in Surrey, partly in a house on Clapham Common. But when he was seventeen he fell so ill with typhoid that he was taken away from Rugby and sent to Selworthy, in the Porlock Vale of Somerset, where the son of a friend was curate.

That stroke of fate determined the course of his life. He fell in love with the West Country and spent the rest of his days there, working as curate and rector in parishes around the fringes of Exmoor. In many ways he was the epitome of a Victorian priest, reading his Greek and Latin daily, but devoted almost more fiercely to his hunting and fishing than to the welfare of his flock. He was clearly a first-class rider, loved his horses and was surprisingly modern in his stable management. He often rode 40 miles a day, sometimes 80, visiting far-flung farms and cottages. He survived countless falls, and some appalling accidents in horse-drawn carriages. Even more remarkably, he survived his own medical treatments, one of which consisted in ramming tablets of sulphuric acid down his throat, followed by a dose of port.

His *Reminiscences,* in two volumes, were published for private circulation by a firm in Torquay. The first came out in 1897, and was evidently well received, for the publisher incited the author to proceed with a second instalment, and this appeared two years later. In retrospect, it is clear that the second volume was a mistake, for Thornton had already used up most of his good material, and, in order to produce the number of words requested, resorted to outrageous padding. This new edition is drawn mainly from Volume One, with some passages from Volume Two woven in.

It is a pity that he provided such sketchy information about his own family. He married 'Miss Furnival' – no Christian name or description – and in due course she gave birth to seven daughters, two of whom died in infancy. For a man of such robust energy, it must have been disappointing not to have a son.

His memoirs immediately invite comparison with that other classic of the Victorian countryside, *Kilvert's Diary,* parts of which were first published in 1938, and have proved so popular that they remain in print to this day. The Rev. Francis Kilvert will always be associated with the Welsh Borders, whose topography and people he described with lyrical grace; but although he and Thornton both treat of life in rural parishes, there are marked differences between the two.

The published version of Kilvert's diary covers only nine years, from January 1870 to March 1879. Thornton's memoir ranges over 50 years, from the late 1840s almost to the end of the century. Of the two authors, Thornton was by far the tougher character: whereas Kilvert walked everywhere, Thornton rode – and hard. He fished, hunted and shot all his life, but Kilvert was distressed when he once saw people shooting rooks. One cannot imagine Kilvert hunting red deer or baiting adders. Still less can one see him arming himself with a poker or a bludgeon to attack ghosts – but Thornton proved to himself beyond doubt that either weapon was efficacious against malign spirits.

What Thornton provides, above all, is a fascinating record of change in rural areas: the gradual disappearance of the traditional squires, the coming of the railways, the slow erosion of ancient customs, freedoms and language. Not only in Somerset and Devon, but all over England, country people will rejoice that the old clergyman rides again.

Duff Hart-Davis,
Uley, Gloucestershire,
2009.

CHAPTER ONE

Going West

IN THE MONTH of August 1847 I was a Rugby schoolboy, in those days well able to run. On a Saturday in
that month I was selected to be hare in company of one
John Bull, a boy rather older and more highly placed than
myself, and we started from the gates of the old school-
house for the Newbold run.

It was a glorious day, but hot, and we boys, clad in flannel
shirts, white duck trousers, and bare-headed, started away
at a slinging trot. Ten minutes' law was allowed us before
the pursuers were laid on. Down through the High street
and over the railway, then comparatively speaking new, we
went. On reaching the country beyond the station, we
broke the fence and began to scatter pieces of white paper
as we ran. Neither of us spoke, for the pace was too good to
permit of speaking. We forded the river a little to the right
of Brownsover Mill, and for the first time subsided into a
walk as we breasted the steep hillside beyond, and waded
through the stagnant waters of the canal.

Many summers since then have come and gone, and the
survivor may be forgiven if he has forgotten some little
details of the effort which he made that day. And yet, as I
write by my study fire, the memory of that day is fresh.
Once through the river, twice through the canal, we two
boys went. Saturated with perspiration, dripping with
water, one thought had possession of us both, one desire
was uppermost in our minds – the leading hound in all the
chase must not be permitted to gain on our flying steps.

Then in about fifty minutes the village of Newbold was
reached, the distance accomplished amounting to some
six or seven miles. At that time there stood in the centre of
the place a headless cross surrounded by a succession of

stone steps, and upon these we boys, breathless and exhausted, sat down to await the arrival of the hounds. Watches were consulted and the time was accurately taken by us both. And then occurred a little event which altered the whole current of my life. An old woman turned the corner of the street with a basket upon her arm, and the basket contained unripe greengages.

'Three for a penny,' cried that dangerous dame, and I bought sixpenny worth and ate them all. Then straggling, tailing, as the foxhunters phrase it, up came the field. The hares had not lost ground; we had about held our own against the best of the hounds, and well contented, wet and dirty, we all jogged home together as soon as the new-comers had recovered their breath.

That night the plum-consuming runner was attacked by cholera, as I now think, of the milder, or English type. They say that the memory of pain is short, but I do not forget the agony which I endured as, with my limbs contorted by the cramps, I lay groaning with the cold sweat of almost mortal pain upon my brow. It is a long time ago, and boys do not know much, but the medical practitioner who attended the school, and whose name was Bucknill was, I am sure, of the old-fashioned type of doctor.

These pages, as the reader must remember, are largely written to rescue from oblivion some features of the past at a time when the transition from old to new is extremely rapid and very distinctly marked. Types of English character which had existed without change for centuries have well nigh disappeared in the course of a single generation. Many causes have contributed to bring about this result, but unquestionably the most powerful is the increase in the means of locomotion. All men, nowadays, are inter-mingled, and lose in consequence much of their individu-ality. The son of a professional man , or gentleman of small income, born and bred in one of our country towns, is often educated at a great distance from his home, is familiar with London, and visits in distant countries. He frequently brings his schoolboy chums and college friends to his father's house, and the result is amalgamation and a softening-down of types of character.

In my early days it was not so, and in old North Devon we even went so far as to call such persons 'foreigners.' Many of my good companions by flood and field will, it is to be hoped, read these pages, and I ask the elders at this point to pause in order to recall to memory the old-fashioned professional man of our country towns. He belonged to his own type, and bore but little resemblance to any other. There was nothing elsewhere like him to be found. You knew him when you met him by his attire, by his strong prejudices, by his peculiar habits, and often by a certain shrewd, caustic wit, which was frequently strongly developed. Alas! He is gone, or very nearly gone, from our midst; and his successors are being rapidly ground down to a dead level of uninteresting uniformity.

Of this now fast-fading sort was my medical attendant. He wore black clothes, a frilled shirt front adorned by a diamond pin, and his face was clean shaved and rubicund. His features wore an habitual expression of solemnity, the professional look, relieved by a frequent twinkle of the eye, and his speech was as conventional and correct as his attire. His method of treatment was probably as antiquated as was the rest of him, but boys do not know much, and a dim recollection of chalk and opium may only be a survival of the ignorant impressions of my early youth. At any rate by his aid, or in spite of him, somehow I lived, but recovery was slow, and one day the door of the sick-ward was opened quite unexpectedly to admit both my father and mother, who had already settled all preliminaries with Dr Tait, then Headmaster of the School, and had come to take me for ever away. At this time I was a pale, long lad of seventeen, greatly depressed and of low vital energy. Then came a period of high feeding and much maternal solicitude; but what was to be done? My father thought me too young to matriculate at Cambridge, and it was doubtful whether I knew enough to make it safe for me to encounter the entrance examination which at Trinity, the family college, was accounted to be severe.

Now it chanced that my father was the life long and dearest friend of a certain Archdeacon Hoare, who was rector of a parish in Surrey, not far from where we resided, and to him application was made.

'If the boy is delicate,' he replied, 'you had better send him down to my son, who is curate of Selworthy, in Somersetshire. He will take excellent care of him, and prepare him properly for Cambridge;' and so it was settled and arranged.

This was not absolutely my first introduction to the West, for ten years earlier I had paid a visit to Glenthorne, and there as a nursery child had made the acquaintance of the highly-gifted, kindly, and eccentric owner, who was destined in after years to be my squire and life-long and valued friend. But it was the first visit to the west country of one who was old enough and able to enjoy its freedom. The impression produced upon me was profound, and while life lasts the Porlock Valley will ever in my estimation remain the fairest and choicest little district which exists on the face of the earth.

The railway in 1847 was already open to Bridgwater, and from thence my father took me by coach to Minehead and on in a carriage to Selworthy. In those days the Porlock Valley was generally considered to be rather isolated and remote, for it required early rising on the part of a traveller to reach the Metropolis after a long day's journey, and the fares were higher than now; but it seemed to be much more remote than it really was, because it had once been still more remote, and its people had not awakened to the actual condition of affairs. So far as the gentry were concerned there were but few inhabitants, and not many strangers had as yet begun to penetrate the recesses of its hills.

In those days the population of England was probably not more than two-thirds of what it is at present, and money was even less plentiful than people. So it came to pass that 'the happy valley,' as some called it, was at this time very much as it had been a century before. Not that I was altogether without introductions, for Sir Thomas Acland had been an old schoolfellow with my father, and he was the owner of the land and uncle to my tutor, Mr Hoare. Mr C. Luttrell, of Dunster Castle, was my father's colleague in the Exchequer Office, and the Trevelyans of Nettlecombe were ancient acquaintances of the family. Sir Thomas, however, was not often at Holnicote; Mr Luttrell was non-resident, and Nettlecombe far away. But in the valley, (distant from Selworthy by a mile and a half) is the village of Luccombe, and there at this time resided a remarkable clergyman of the name of Fisher, who had once held the living at Roche, in Cornwall, to which he had been presented by my grandfather.

Mr Fisher was a man of many gifts and striking attainments. He was also by nature well disposed towards and acceptable to lads, and his doors were open at once to the slowly-recovering schoolboy.

And now it is necessary to describe the new home to which my father consigned me before he returned to his family and his duties in town. But Selworthy is hard to describe, and it is not possible to do justice to a nook (and it is but a nook) which has not, in my opinion – and I have wandered far in many lands – the equal in the world. And by Selworthy I mean that portion of Selworthy in which Mr Hoare resided.

The parish itself consists of a long strip of land, which is bounded by the Bristol Channel on the north, and Luccombe, with Dunkerry Beacon overshadowing it, on the south. Porlock meets it to the west and Minehead on the east, while Grabhurst Hill intervenes in the direction of Dunster.

The village of Selworthy is called Allerford, and is situated on the high road which connects Minehead with Porlock. Eastward from Allerford by half a mile is Sir Thomas Acland's beautiful cottage of Holnicote, around which semi-tropical plants and gorgeous flowers blossom and thrive under the protection of such evergreen oaks as are nowhere else to be found. The arbutus in its glossy, red-berried luxuriance there rivals, if it does not surpass, its kindred at Killarney, and out-tops even that which adorns the old house of O'Connell at Derinane, in a sheltered recess in the County of Kerry.

Long, low, and thatched, covered with roses and jessamine, in my day (and before it was burned) crouched the roomy cottage residence of the kind and impulsive baronet. On the garden walls around it were huge magnolias, and a wealth of pyrus japonica, while bay trees, of strange dimensions for our northern clime, flourished as if they had mistaken their Somersetshire home for their native Italy. Beyond the house, to the south-east, were the stables, adorned with the antlered heads of gigantic deer, which had shewn good sport some sixty years before, when Sir Thomas Acland was Master of the Hounds. The outbuildings were sheltered by grand elm trees, which attested the richness of the soil of the meadow beyond, where wandered a little brook, interrupted in its course by ponds which were the joy and delight of the writer's youth.

A hundred yards away from the door of the house was the lodge, situated in the midst of a hamlet consisting of three or four cottages, sheltered by a gigantic walnut tree. This hamlet went by the name of Budleigh Hill. The coach road ran hard by, and from it here branches a long lane leading up the hill to Selworthy, in the direction of a high down, which overhangs the somewhat turbid waters of the Bristol Channel. That lane is the very ideal of what an old west country lane should be, and Sir Thomas was exceedingly proud of it. The banks are high, and all the way upwards a tall growth of hazel and mountain ash positively meets and intertwines over its narrow width. A little stream of absolute purity tumbles merrily along, sometimes on one side and sometimes on the other.

That lane would probably be the despair of a road maker and the delight of an artist. Half a mile upwards another lane turns to the left in the direction of Allerford, and at the point of junction is a farm-house, pretty and thatched, and in those days tenanted by Farmer Rendell and his wife.

Above the farm house, set back into the hill, stands the cottage in which resided the nephew of Lady Acland, curate of the parish of Selworthy, and here for two happy years the writer lived. This cottage had been built for a retired servant of the Acland family who had, if memory holds good, broken his neck under the four large holly trees which grew in the lane beneath Grabhurst Hill.

It is a very pretty cottage, latticed and ornate. Two large arbutus trees stand on the lawn on either side of the porch, and the house contains six rooms of comfortable size. Behind it is an orchard on rapidly rising ground, and a long stretch of interminable wood. On the right is the Rectory House, then tenanted by an old rector of more than eighty years, a kind, scholarly old gentleman, who had once been tutor to Sir Thomas Acland. Then upwards the 'goyle' closes in, and rises rapidly, but in its mouth, and opposite to the rectory, is the salient feature of the place, consisting of a well kept lawn with a footpath around it, a number of terraced cottage gardens, gay with old fashioned flowers, and some seven or eight good cottages of artistic and careful construction. The big wood towers above to the left, and the steep gorge ascends, though the heather, up the hill to the north.

Such is the scene, and we must not forget the church which, with a farm house at the foot of the churchyard, stands above the cottages, while the lane, as if tired of its previous ascending exertions, turns sharply away to the right, along the hillside, in the direction of Minehead. That little narrow valley is surely one of the fairest spots upon the face of the earth. I have often wandered about Amalfi, and the nooks and corners which are to be found between it and Salerno come next; but this is the choicest of all, and if you would see the place at its best I think you should visit it on some bright day when the sea fog which covers the hill is creeping down to the valley below, and contending with the rays of the sun as to which shall fold in its embraces the quiet residences of the cottagers below.

And the inhabitants were well suited to the scene. The curate and his two pupils (for soon from Eton came Charles Turner, destined to ford the waters of the Alma with the colours of a regiment of the Guards in his hands) perhaps formed exceptions to the rule; but the rest were of old-world type. The rector, kindly, reserved, and now mostly confined to the house by age, still studied his Greek and Latin authorities, or pored over heavy volumes of antique theology. He was a bachelor, well cared for by two maidservants as punctual and correct as himself, and in a shy nervous fashion he would play on a violin when he thought that he could do so without being heard. Very precise he was, and very particular. It was said that he once had ventured upon a horse, when John Hobbs, the sexton, held his leg to save him from falling off.

This John Hobbs once said to the writer, 'They do say, mister, that the world goes round. Lord, how can they tell up such lies? Why, I have looked out from here every morning for more than fifty years, and there has stood Dunkerry Beacon, and I have never once seen it whiskered away.'

In the farm-house below the church lived Farmer Stenner and his wife, who were, as will presently be seen, devout believers in witchcraft. Then came the cottagers of the green, old men and old women, who had been born far back in the previous century, at a time when elementary education had not been provided for their class, and these old people were looked after by a young woman , who was still there in 1891, and probably to the present hour retains her long kept place. Forty-five years had come and gone, and when I last saw here she had not forgotten me.

'Mind you, sir!' she said, 'indeed, I mind when the hunted stag came up by the cottage, and you jumped out of the study window without your hat and runned up over the hill to Meon in carpet slippers, screeching like a mad thing in among the hounds, and old Rawle, you'll remember old Rawle, sir; well, he said he did hope they'd make a parson of the young gentleman, it would be a thousand pities if they did not, when he could give it out like that, the old folks would be able to hear *him* in Church, yes, that he would warrant.' (The reader should know that Meon is a lonely farmhouse which hangs betwixt air and water amid the cliffs of the Bristol Channel.)

And then there was an aged couple (of somewhat superior class to the cottagers), who were both very feeble, and tottered about in the sun with a little dog behind them, which was seventeen years old, sans eyes, sans ears, sans teeth, sans everything – for nothing, it would seem, wore out at Selworthy. Mr Rendell and his wife, in the second farm-house, completed our society.

Down below, at Allerford, lived old Mrs Gould, the widow of a former rector of Luccombe, and at Allerford House, across the way, was her daughter, Mrs Fortescue, wife of the Rev William Fortescue, rector of Wear Gifford and old George Nympton, but resident at Allerford on account of ill-health

Holnicote was occupied only occasionally by Sir Thomas Acland, who usually came for the shooting of the black grouse in August, and for the cover shooting in December. He used often, however, to lend the house at other seasons of the year to the married members of his family. There were, of course, many farmers and small traders in the neighbourhood, but the gentry were few and remote. Such as existed were, however, known to our tutor, and distance was disregarded; it was nothing accounted of in those days.

My father gave me fifteen pounds on parting, and bade me buy my first horse. In those days, and in those parts, fifteen pounds went far; and as this book is one of reminiscences, a few words upon prices may not be amiss.

I often wonder at the complaints which now in the nineties I hear made by producers about prices, for everything is very dear when compared with what it was when I went to Selworthy. *Then* cows and calves were selling for ten pounds, ewes at a sovereign each, beef and mutton cost fivepence a pound, geese five shillings, and ducks and chickens two shilling and sixpence a couple. Oats were sold for one shilling and sixpence a bushel, and other things corresponded in value to these prices.

So fifteen pounds was a fine sum, and making the acquaintance of Mr Robert Farramore, of Hynam, I rode with him one day to his off farm at Oareford and bought my first horse, or rather mare, for the money. I shall have much to say about horses further on, for I am a man of stable mind, and should have been christened Philip had my godparents known their duty. It is enough to say now that my purchase was a long, low, brown filly, not quite four years old, fourteen hands and an inch in height, unbroken, and as green and wilful as her owner.

A more unfit animal never was selected. Mr Hoare knew everyone from Williton to Glenthorne, and they all made both of us welcome. I was always, moreover, inclined to be a sportsman. There were seven rivers to be fished, over which, in those days, few flies were thrown. There were four packs of hounds within reach. People, as I have said, were inclined to be friendly, and above all Glenthorne, ten miles away, had its hospitable doors ever open, and a delightful company within; therefore Polly, for so the young mare was called, would have had enough to do if she had been eight years old instead of four, and her purchaser lighter than he was. But she turned out well, and for many years served one member or another of the Thornton family.

I was always very fond of animals, and when Polly had had enough I would jump off her back and we two would run along side by side until we quite understood one another. Nevertheless I would here record my opinion for the benefit of all young lads, that if they want a working horse they should have an old one, and that babies in brown skins are like babies in white ones, things only fit to be played with.

I was continually at Glenthorne. At all hours of the night, that poor pony was traversing either the lower path through Ashley Lodge and Culbone Wood, or the lane through the farms above, or the high road by Hurlstone Rocks. Mr Halliday was kindness itself, and an old friend of the Thornton family. He was the son of a Scotch doctor, who in company with a friend named Farquhar (head of the Farquhar family) had gone out to India in the days of Warren Hastings, when the Pagoda tree still grew to be shaken. He was in deacon's orders, and had become known to our family when acting as curate in the Isle of Wight.

On the death of his father and of an elder brother, he had acquired much property, married a Scotch lady named Gardiner, dropped his profession, purchased the parish of Countesbury, and built Glenthorne. He was a very remarkable man, of shy and retiring habits, very plain, with a marvellous play of countenance, full of wit and anecdote, a great traveller, and very hospitable. Mrs Halliday was always kind, and I had the run of the house.

Glenthorne, moreover, possessed another attraction. It was continually being visited by people of distinction. Old naval officers, who had fought with Nelson and Dundonald, would there hold me enthralled with tales of the great war in which they themselves had played a distinguished part. Conspicuous among these was one who, when he died, was Admiral of the Fleet, Sir Fairfax

Moresby, GCB. He had, as he said, 'commanded every-thing afloat from a cockleshell to a Fleet of Line of Battle-ships.' He had cruised with Cochrane in the 'Speedy,' and had been with Nelson at Trafalgar. He honoured the Rugby boy with a friendship which for thirty years never flagged or failed, until I stood by his open grave in Littleham churchyard and reverently helped commit to the earth the ashes of the veteran of ninety-one, who had served his king and his country for seventy-eight long years.

To Glenthorne also came the Knights from Simonsbath – Frederic, Charles, and Lewis – and there I made their acquaintance. Sir Frederic still survives, and it is necessary to be careful, but I will venture to say that for wild and reckless daring I have never known the equals of that triumvirate. Age may by that time have cooled them a little, but if they were cool when I first knew them, what must they have been at an earlier date, ere the eldest had married and entered Parliament; the second been much crippled by a fall in the Roman Campagna; and the third tossed nine times by a buffalo cow in the depths of remotest Abyssinia!

The Hallidays had no children of their own, but their house used often to be well filled with young people, more especially in the summer, when Lady Cosway (born Halliday) was wont to bring down her four daughters from Cowes, and the two Miss Moresbys would be there. The supply of rough ponies was apparently inexhaustible, and the young pupils from Selworthy, ten miles away, frequently assisted the ladies to explore the whole wild Exmoor Forest, and other places besides. I, at least, was often in the company of the girls, with whom, as far as the Cosways were concerned, I was already intimate, as they had been in Surrey the playmates of my infancy.

CHAPTER TWO

Glenthorne

MUST I HERE pause to describe Glenthorne itself, this bright resort of my opening life? No, it is now well known to the over-increasing stream of strangers who throng our west country lanes from June to October, and I will content myself with narrating that it is a good country house, built on a little meadow some forty feet above the shore of the Bristol Channel, and three miles by road from the lofty crest of a hill which extends unbroken from Countesbury to above Porlock. It is seven miles from Lynmouth.

The house, facing to the east, is surrounded by good gardens, and from it ramify and spread upwards many paths and trackways which conduct the traveller to varied scenes of marvellous beauty. Admiral Moresby used often to assert that nowhere in the world, save only on the coasts of Catalonia, can you find such long stretches of luxuriant wood clothing the steep hillsides right down to the water's edge.

Besides Glenthorne, many houses were open to Mr Hoare and his pupils, some of which were occupied by people who, from one cause or another were interesting or remarkable, but it is enough to chronicle that we three dined every night at Holnicote for weeks together when the Aclands were in residence, and at this time I made friends with all kinds of celebrities who visited the hospitable Baronet in his Somersetshire country home.

Once Southey was there, and Dr Brown, the great African traveller, made a lasting impression upon the author's recollections. He came up from Holnicote to stay with Mr Hoare at the cottage, a large, untidy man, but before he left the Aclands' house there occurred a laughable scene.

Admiral Jenkinson was a fellow guest, and at breakfast he said something which pleased the famous explorer and linguist. 'Ah, Admiral, I will kiss you,' shouted Brown, who so saying rose from his seat.

'I will be hanged if you shall,' said the sailor, and taking one of the dining room chairs, he held the four legs against his antagonist's face, and retreated round the table amid the merriment of us all, but in vain; he was pinned in a corner, overpowered, and *kissed*.

It so happened that I was present, and I walked up the long lane with the conqueror to show him the way to the cottage. Under the arbutus tree, close to the porch, down sat Dr Brown, and then I, who now think that I must have been a remarkably cheeky youth, began in this way –

'Dr Brown, they tell queer stories about you. They say you wrote to Lady Olivia Sparrow, from Zanzibar, to send you out a wife, and that Lady Olivia read the letter aloud at her breakfast table, remarking that you were a ridiculous man to make such a request, and that no one would go. Upon which Lady Selina Hawker remarked that you were not ridiculous at all, and on being further questioned said that she would go, and went. Doctor, is that true?'

But the Doctor said it was not true, and told me a wonderful tale of his courtship, which had been carried on at Mr Holland's house in Sussex (once the abode of my grandfather.) He told me that, having inconvenienced the lady, he offered to teach her Hebrew, and after a few lessons had been given he informed Mr Holland of his intentions. That gentleman then offered his assistance, on the ground that Dr Brown was a foreigner, and not used to the ways of our aristocracy.

'No, no, my dear Holland, but I will do my own jobs myself,' said Brown. 'See, I have written my letter to propose to her thus:

Dear Lady Selina,

If you love me, write back by return of post: 'Dear Brown, nothing shall prevent our union,' and be sure you put three dashes underneath.

Well, two days after I cried out at breakfast, 'Aha, my good friend, here is my letter, and here are the dashes! Aha!'

The doctor that evening was very amusing and full of anecdotes. He told me he was once under the tuition of the Jesuits in the College of the Propaganda in Rome. He was there taught that if he ever should be nonplussed in argument with a heretic he must draw himself together, and exclaim, 'Dear friend, is it possible that a sensible man should advance so feeble and argument?' Then assuming an indignant expression of countenance he should instantly change the subject.

'One day,' continued Dr Brown, 'after I had become Protestant, I met and argued with an old Jesuit father, who presently pushed back his chair and regarding me with a pained expression of surprise, began, 'Dear friend, is it possible that so sensible a man. . . ?' – when I cut him short by saying, 'Father, Father, I have been at the College of the Propaganda as well as you,' and the poor man cried out, 'Oh, boo!' and ran away as fast as he could.

On one occasion he never went to bed, but slept on the floor, and frightened a poor housemaid very nearly into fits as she stumbled over his body when she opened the windows in the morning, but with us he left his room, barefooted in his dressing gown, went into the garden, and lighting a great pipe, sat down under the arbutus tree. Old Mrs Tibbs, our housekeeper, who had been sent from Winchester by Mrs Hoare to look after her bachelor son, a little energetic woman of fifty years, with a continual face-ache, espied him from her window, and saw the rain come down. She descended, not much more fully attired than the traveller himself, and much to the amusement of her master, began to remonstrate violently, lugging, meanwhile, at the great recumbent figure on the grass. 'Get up, get up, sir,' she said, 'you will catch your death of cold, you are already wet through.'

'Yes, I am wet, madam, I am wet, and when I am wet I sing one of the songs of Jerusalem until I am dry,' he replied. But the little woman would not allow him any peace, and ultimately he had to return to his bedroom and dress, after which operation he peacefully smoked in the rain on the grass until breakfast was served. Then one of our neighbours, Mr Chilcott, R.D. of Monksilver, came to take him

away to speak on behalf of Foreign Missions at Wiveliscombe, and brought with him for that purpose a fly from
Minehead.

The doctor turned disconsolately to me and said, 'Ah,
my young friend, but I have no moneys. I lost all my
moneys last night.'

Now it is not pleasant to be told by a guest that he has
been robbed in your house, and to spare Mr Hoare at once
I rose and begged Dr Brown to return with me to the
bedroom which he had occupied, and this he did, staring
and looking about him with lack-lustre eyes. Down I went
on my knees beneath the bed and pulled out a sovereign,
the washing stand yielded two more, and three were
unearthed in the grate. Half-crowns and sixpences were
everywhere, and I gathered together what I could find.
'Now, doctor, have you recovered *all*?' I asked.

'My dear friend, I do not know. Lady Selina, she gives me
the moneys, and when they are gone she will give me
more.'

And so he left, and the inhabitants of the cottage were
inclined to believe that the report was true which said that
when Thompson and Grey had perished at Cabul, Brown's
life was spared because the Afghans considered that he was
entitled to receive the consideration at their hands which
is due to the mentally afflicted; and yet in good truth he
was not insane, but only very eccentric.

There was a great deal of eccentricity in those days in
many of the people at Selworthy, or so it seemed to some of
us. Mr Fortescue was peculiar. He had in early life been
engaged to be married to the lady who eventually became
his second wife, and who at fifty was perhaps the youngest
looking and most beautiful woman of her age whom I have
ever known, but the match was broken off by his friends,
and he married another lady and had one son, Mr Archer
Fortescue. On becoming a widower he had returned to his
first love, and they were at this time living in Allerford
House, and were friendly with Mr Hoare and his pupils.

Mr Fortescue was a pluralist rector of the old sort, and he
would sometimes ask me to a great dinner at one o'clock,
and then produce a bottle of port wine, perhaps on an

August day. I did not want the wine, and I did want to go out, but it was useless to resist.

'Come, come, sir, none of this infernal new-fangled nonsense, if you please. My wine is all right, sir, and you need not turn up your nose at it.' And down that bottle had to go, no shirking or heel-taps! The old gentleman, moreover, used to wink his eye sometimes, and say that he had some excellent cognac in his cellar.

'I found one morning that both my horses were gone,' he would say, 'but James Dadd (his coachman), James knew which way to search, and we found them loose in the lane beyond Exford, and there was a keg of this cognac left under the manger too. Will you try it?' Now in all my intercourse with smugglers, illicit distillers, and such like people, I have remarked the peculiarity that their wares either were, or were honestly deemed to be, of extra quality. Was it that the sense of irregularity added flavour to the dram, or were the smuggled spirits really particularly choice? I do not know; but years later on in my life I sat by the death-bed of a very old smuggler, who told me how he used to have a donkey with a triangle on its back, so rigged up as to show three lanthorns, and how chilled he would become as he lay out, winter's night after winter's night, watching on the Foreland, or along Brandy Path, as we called it, for the three triangular lights of the schooner which he knew was coming in to land her cargo where Glenthorne now stands, and where was the smugglers' cave. 'Lord bless you, sir,' and the dying man of nearly ninety chuckled, 'we never used no water, we just put the brandy into a kettle and heated it, and drinked it out of half-pint stoups, us did, and it never did us no harm whatsomdever, it was of that quality it were.'

And there is another phenomenon which here I would also like to chronicle. There is a certain Dean of one of our Cathedrals, now living, who in old Rugby days was introduced by men to a blacksmith at Great Harborough, near Rugby. The man had forty brace of living partridges in a bedroom when we called, and putting our purses together, we bought a brown terrier dog, parted with because, as our friend of the forge told us, he could not be depended upon to work the hares *mute* into the nets at night. It has even been the same, and at the very time when my father, who was head of the stamp and tax department at Somerset House in London , was interviewing the fine Constabulary of Galway, and receiving their solemn assurances that illicit distillation was a thing of the past, I have been guided by Betty and Kathleen to the still or store used by them in the bog, and treated to potheen or mountain dew, the rough men mistrusting me no more than did the joking girls.

When I returned to England I roasted my father well upon the subject, withholding, of course, all mention of names and places, not but what the old man was as safe as the young one, for as soon as he knew how the secret became known, he cried out, 'Don't tell me! I will *not* be told. God bless me. I should have to make a disturbance, and perhaps get those poor girls into trouble.'

Mr Fortescue's manservant, James Dadd, was also a character.

'James,' said I, 'James, how are you?'

'Better, sir, better, thank you kindly. I had a little pepe (pipe) in my mawbag (stomach) chucked (choked) yesterday, but I have been a-shaking of myself, and I have shucked it out.'

James was a great believer in the efficacy of shaking. One night at this time (and I remember that Mr Archer Fortescue was on the occasion home from the Orkneys, where he had a Government appointment), James Dadd was driving Mr and Mrs Fortescue home from dinner from Dunster, and Mr Archer Fortescue was on the box of the carriage. They were in a cutting in the main road, just before they came to Budleigh Hill, when a clatter was heard, and next moment there was a violent collision and a fall. When Mr Archer Fortescue got down he found a well-bred mare, *stone blind* of both eyes, quite dead, impaled on the point of the carriage pole, and her rider lay insensible in the road.

Next morning James was sent up to inquire how the sufferer was progressing, and I saw him in his stable later on in the day, when the following conversation ensued:

'Well, how did you find him when you rode up?'

'Nicely, sir, nicely, he just put out his hand from under the clothes and gave me a shake, and he said he would never forget it. He said, sir, he knowed that I had saved the life of him, for I had killed the growth of the inside of him.'

Now this, good reader, requires explanation, and you should understand that the eccentric young man, who, himself blind drunk with gin, had urged a mare, blind of nature, to her destruction and his own detriment the night before, was under the impression that he had some polypus or tumour in his inside (he probably, after imprudence, had occasionally felt indigestion), and he thought that the shock of the collision had detached this incumbrance, and cured him.

One morning I went bareheaded to the yard above the Selworthy Cottage, to see the boy groom Polly properly. It was early, let us say about half-past eight.

'Good morning, sir,' said the boy. 'Do you know that Mary Stenner has seen a ghost, and is well nigh mazed this morning.'

Up the hill I went at full speed, highly delighted, and ran unceremoniously into the kitchen of the farm-house by the church.

Mrs Stenner was at that time perhaps thirty-five years of age, stout, ruddy, and free from fancy. But there she sat by the kitchen fire, 'in the vapours,' as our forefathers would have said. Burnt feathers, fans, cold waters without, and a taste of hot waters within, all these remedies were in full requisition, and others besides them.

'Oh, Mrs Stenner, is it true you have seen him?'

A sigh, and a sip, and a shake of the head were given or taken, but there was no reply.

'Oh, Mrs Stenner, *do* tell me what he is like?'

'Mr Thornton! My dear soul! Why – *did* you not hear me screech? I screeched that loud! Oh dear, oh dear! I thought you would hear me! I'll never again come up from Budleigh Hill after dark alone, no, never, never!'

'Well, but my dear Mrs Stenner, what *did* you see after all?'

'I hadn't left Budleigh Hill by two gunshots when there it was, the nasty thing, running at my side. 'T'was awful. It had four legs, and it was black, and had great fiery eyes as big as saucers, and it ran on until it came to where the water crosses under the road, and they things, of course, never can abide running water, so it just couldn't get across, and off it went up in the air like a flash of fire.

'I screeched, oh, I screeched, and I thought that the parson and you would surely be down the hill to me, and they from Budleigh would come upwards.'

I was young then, and so I made a mistake by remarking that no doubt it was her sheepdog that had come down to meet her, come 'against her,' as they say in Somersetshire, and given her a start. That suggestion, however, would not do at all, and I had to beat a hasty retreat.

Presently I met the sexton, John Hobbs, and made eager enquiries again.

'I know all about it,' said John, "tis exactly twenty-five years since we was bringing the corpse of —— from Horner Mills to Selworthy, and the handle of the coffin against the head came loose, just exactly to the very spot where Mary Stenner met with the ghost last night; I picked up a stone and knocked it in again, and no doubt it went into the poor thing's brain, and let the spirit out. Oh, yes! I know all about it.'

And some of the clergy were just as superstitious as were their flocks in those days. One scarcely dare tell tales of his fellows, but there was 'one parson in that country then as was so strong as he could lay any ghost. But there! It took so much out of him that he was obliged to give up and go. You see, sir, they *would* fetch un, and he didn't like to refuse, and so he was no better than skin and bone.' So the people would speak of a clergyman who was then well known to me.

The evening of Mrs Stenner's adventure I dined with the Fortescues alone, without my tutor, and on leaving their house about eleven pm I had a choice of two roads, one by the turnpike to Budleigh Hill, and so up the lane; and the other by the back of Mrs Gould's cottage, creeping round the covers to Selworthy. For some moments I stood irresolute, until a happy inspiration came upon me, and I wrenched a heavy stake from out of the fence; it was pointed and sound, so with it I faced the lane and the ghost, and reached home unmolested.

Once or twice since that night I have been confronted by these ghostly dangers, and I have ever met them promptly with the poker, and still believe with a firm belief in the efficacy of such carnal weapons on such trying occasions, if only they are previously and properly advertised. No Cock-lane or other ghost that ever I heard of will face a charge of shot.

If the reader will pardon a slight digression, I will tell another tale, true and to the point. The Knight family ordinarily wintered in Rome, but one winter it was not convenient to send the ladies so far away. Two of the brothers, (Frederic and Charles, I think) went, therefore, to Jersey to look out for a residence, and found what they required close to St Helier. The house was good, the gardens ample, the rent exceedingly moderate, but the house was haunted; no one could live in it.

The brothers took it at once, ordered in some provisions, and announced, what was strictly true, that either of them could depend upon putting a bullet into a penny piece at a distance of twelve paces, and that they meant shooting. They heard no noises, saw no sights, and left, and the ladies came.

Now many years before this time a sort of shrewd, half-witted lad had followed Mr Knight from Killarney, and had remained with him as groom. Peter the Irishman, he was called, and I myself have had an adventure or two by his side. Peter was devoted to the Knights, he was as faithful as a dog, but he had one great fault of which he could not be cured, that of spasmodic drinking. He would be perfectly sober for weeks or months, and then he would break out and drink for days, and be quite useless.

Well, Peter was left in charge of the ladies, and the brothers returned to England. As soon as they were gone night became hideous. The basement of the house was apparently converted into the prison of the damned, and the ladies wrote to Mr Knight to say that they could not remain for their servants were frightened to death. Such was the result of the first night's experience, and next day Peter was missing.

Mrs Knight was very angry. She did not doubt that he had broken out into a fit of intemperance, and she said that he ought not to have done so while she was depending upon him to support the household against a ghost or, for what she knew, a company of ghosts. The cheap brandy shops of St Helier were searched in vain, and when darkness came the house was locked up, and Peter locked out.

At the witching hour of twelve the ghostly crew recommenced with clanking of chains, rattling of bones, sobbings, howlings, groans and peals of demoniac laughter. Then came a sound of whack, whack, whack, and an Irish yell: '*Yrorawhist! Yah! Yah! Yah!*'

Down trooped the household, and there in the cellar was Peter, flourishing a big stick over the prostrate form of the gardener and custodian of the house, beside whom lay a lanthorn, a chain, and some bones upon a string. This good man was permitted to sell the fruit and vegetables when the house was not occupied, and lost his profits when it was.

My own only proud adventure with a ghost, or misadventure, will be narrated presently, but it belongs to the 'fifties, and we are as yet in the 'forties only. Suffice it to say that I got through it successfully, thanks to the aid of a poker.

Allusion has already been made to one or two of the clergy, and certainly in the Porlock neighbourhood in 1847 they were different to those who succeeded them, and to such as are now to be found. What a contrast, for instance, exists between the present rector of Porlock, Mr Hook, and old Mr Boyce, upon whom I called in company with Mr Hoare half a century ago.

Mr Boyce was verging upon ninety when Mr Chilcott, the rural dean, and Mr Hoare called upon him in order to induce him to accept the incumbency of the well-endowed parish of Old Cleeve, so as to enable them to sell the advowson for the benefit of the widow of the late rector, and I went with them. The old man had for years been secretary to the hunt, and was reported to have been accustomed to give out the meets of the stag-hounds after the second Lesson.

Mr Knight had a story that one Sunday the congregation was addressed by the clerk in this way: 'I do hereby give notice that there will be no service in this church (Brendon, probably) this day, 'cause why? Because Parson

Boyce has lamed his hack, and has gone therefore over-
night to Barnstaple a-stag hunting.'

There were plenty of clergymen in the Selworthy neighbourhood who were fond of sport, and among them Mr
Robert Gould, son of old Mrs Gould at Allerford, was
conspicuous. He was born at Luccombe, in the rectory
house, and he knew all the country from his childhood.
He made his own fishing flies and was a wonderful fisherman. On one occasion he caught so many trout in Badgworthy water that he had to charter a boy and a horse to
carry them away.

He was quite as good with the gun as he was with the
fishing rod, and in the use of both he gave me many a
lesson. Once in those days he walked from Ilfracombe,
where he resided, to visit his mother at Allerford, taking
probably Hangman Hill and Shoulsboro' Castle, Cheriton
Ridge and Badgworthy on his way, and on that occasion he
brought in forty snipe to his mother at Allerford, a snipe a
mile, as he said.

Robert Gould shot two bitterns, probably the last in
England, in Porlock Marsh. Those were stuffed, and in his
sister Mrs Fortescue's possession. I wish I had them, but I
know not where they are now. In Gould's company was
ever Joseph Jekyll, rector of Hawkridge and Withypool,
who was lighter, tougher, even more hardy than his friend,
and quite as keen a sportsman. Jekyll rode to hounds, also,
and was, like Gould, exceedingly fond of whist.

It would be easy to tell many tales of these men, and of
George Owen of Tiverton, who was much cleverer than
either and quite as peculiar, but one story will serve to
illustrate the country and the times.

Jekyll was from home, and Gould was at Hawkridge
doing duty for him during his absence. There was to be a
wedding at Withypool, three miles away, and Gould,
mounting Jekyll's horse, rode slowly up the valley towards
the church. In a wood he met with a man who told him
that the would-be bridegroom had been boasting at the
public-house that he would 'do' the parson out of his fees.

'All right,' said Mr Gould, 'hold your tongue,' and he
rode on.

The service proceeded in orderly fashion until the rubric was reached which directs the bridegroom to place the ring *with the accustomed offering* on the book.

'The ring,' said Gould, and it was produced.

'Five shillings.'

'Never,' said the bridegroom. 'I'll never pay it.'

'Hush, hush, my good man, do not brawl; you need not pay, but you are not married. I am going into the vestry.'

There he went and sat down. Presently the best man came in and paid him five shillings, upon which he returned and, taking up the thread of the service, secured the happy pair in the bonds of holy matrimony. Then the bells rang out, and the bride, taking her husband's arm, encountered the youth of Withypool who, lifting up their voices with an accord, exclaimed, 'Thee do the parson? The parson's done thee!'

There was another clergyman of a different type, with whom the author was very intimate. This was Mr Anderson, usher in a school at Minehead, and curate of Stoke Pero and of Culbone. He was a highly-educated, quiet, and most exemplary Scotchman and used, for the sake of economy, to walk from Minehead to Stoke Pero, thence to Culbone, take the services at both places, and go back to his work at Minehead at night.

It is almost incredible that he should have done this, but the recollection of the performance is vivid, and I was then, and afterwards, very friendly with the Anderson family, which consisted of three sisters and this brother. They afterwards lived together at Porlock Ford. It was with Mr Anderson that on Oare water I had my first day's trout fishing. It was on the 9th of March, 1848, and I caught seven fish that day. One of the Miss Andersons had lived for years in Russia, at Moscow and St. Petersburg, and had much that was interesting to tell of the country and the people.

Before leaving for the present the subject of the West Country clergy and their parishioners I would mention that there then lived a parson who was most notorious, with an evil notoriety. I must not mention names lest I should get myself into trouble; but this man and his doings were well known, and he was a terror to the countryside.

One day in the spring of 1848, mounted on the long-suffering Polly, I was at the meet of Mr Stoate's hounds, at Luccombe. A young farmer was also there, who said, 'There was queer going on at Hawkridge on Saturday. Parson Jekyll was writing his sermon, and he heard hounds a giving of it down in his wood; then they stopped, and he, mistrusting something, took his hat and went out, and sure enough there was old Mr Choune a-digging out of a fox. They two had not been chummy like for some time, and so Jekyll he goes up to the other and says he: 'Mr Choune, I should have thought you knew better than to dig out a breeding earth in another man's country in the month of March. Now, you call your men away, or I will prosecute you for breaking ground.'

'I have brought my fox from Anstey,' said the other, 'and I mean to have him out; and as for you! You dare quarrel with me, do you? Don't you know that I have only to say 'Bones, bones' at Hawkridge, and name no names, and there are those about me as will take care that your carcase is lying under a hedgerow before the week is out?'

'And with that,' said the farmer, 'he got on his horse and rode down to Dr Mitchell, at Winsford, and swore information against Jekyll for stealing his terrier dog; so Mitchell gave him a warrant, and sent the constable to search the rectory, and then was not parson Jekyll in a rage? Besides, there *was no terrier*,' added the farmer, 'after all.'

In those days I first made the acquaintance of John Russell, and kept it up until the old man's death in 1882. Russell was simply ubiquitous; but his life is too well known to be here enlarged upon. One of his stories is, however, worth repeating, as illustrative of the manners of old North Devon. Russell used to tell it somewhat in this wise :

'It was somewhere in the 'twenties, when I was curate of Iddesleigh,' he would say, 'that a parishioner of mine was apprehended on a charge of sheep-stealing, tried at Exeter, convicted, and hanged. Shortly after his execution I met the foreman of the jury, and I thus accosted him: 'What did you mean, you rascal, by hanging ——? Don't you know he was the best earth-stopper in the country?'

'There, now, Mr Russell, and why could not you speak up in time? If us had only known that your honour wanted him, us would never have brought him in guilty, not on no account whatsoever, and that I do assure you.'

There were two very eccentric yeomen who kept hounds in the Porlock Valley at that time. Mr Stoate, at Meon, and Mr Phelps, at Porlock. The story ran, whether true of false I know not, that the owner of Dunster Castle inherited his estates on condition that he kept hounds, and that being non-resident he did it by deputy, through Mr Stoate. The latter was very impulsive, and used to amuse the young men at Selworthy by first beginning to holloa at some offender who was well out of earshot, perhaps a mile away or more, and then checking himself. 'You toad fool,' he would cry across the valley to the man who had headed his fox; and then he would shake his head sorrowfully, and keep the rest to himself. He was of the fat, ruddy, jovial type, and required a strong horse to carry him.

Very different was Mr Phelps, a broken-down, melancholy man, mounted on the relics of a noble horse (upon one hundred and fifty guineas reduced to the level of fifteen pounds), who generally came out late, and after blowing a melancholy note in the street of Porlock, where he lived, would collect around him the mangy members of what was then called 'a trencher-pack,' for Tom kept one, and Dick another, and a third poor hound, perchance, had to keep himself. Then on they went. Polly in those days was wanted for nobler work, and often I ran afoot. The hungry hounds would sometimes kill and eat a cat on their way through the town, for they were *very* hungry and, like wolves, their numbers made them bold; then through Hawcombe we would go into the wildest and most lovely of all deep-wooded valleys, and so upwards by the brook to Exmoor.

In those days the country was wild and unfrequented, and you could hardly tell what game the hounds would find; they ran, moreover, like the wind when they did find, for they ran for their supper. Mr Phelps never attempted to go a yard to them, nor could he. The field was generally small, and I was afoot; but there was nevertheless a wild excitement connected with the hunt, for a red-deer stag might easily crash through the coppice, or a fox be unkennelled, or a hare kicked out of her form, or a badger be intercepted on his way home to his lodgings, or even a marten cat sent jumping from bough to bough along the oak coppice on the steep hillside, while the hounds were screaming in transports of delight over her strong musk odour as they tumbled, raced, or stood on their hindlegs below.

The marten cat is extinct, but it was not extinct in 1847, and I have since seen two of them in captivity at the Manor House at Lynmouth. These belonged to Mr Locke, another eccentric gentleman, who used to put honey upon his cheek in order to encourage these fierce blood-suckers to mount upon his shoulders and lick his face, a thing they would do with avidity.

Then Mr Phelps would go home, for the field, as he knew, would take the hounds back and inform him of their performances. Sometimes an unkind practical joker would tell him that he appeared to be unwell, a remark which was likely to consign him to his bed for a week, as he was an exceedingly nervous man. Remember that I am telling of old-world people and of old-world ways, ways which already in 1847 were fast lapsing into oblivion.

In those days I was very intimate with Mr Abraham, who was practising as a doctor at Dunster. He was a man well versed in the manners and customs of the country, and he told me the following story.

Many years before this time, so he said, there was a certain Archdeacon residing in this part of the world, a man of seventy years of age or thereabouts, an old public schoolboy, an old-fashioned, orthodox clergyman, fond of theology, and not averse to port wine, a man vigorous for his years, and a general favourite. Well, this venerable gentleman, while riding in a lane in the Milverton direction, encountered a string of donkeys laden with ruddle, to sell to the hill-country farmers for sheep marking purposes. The donkeys were thin and over loaded, and behind them walked a wretched, dirty, emaciated old man with a heavy knobbed stick in his hand. The last donkey had a large open sore on one of its quarters, and just as the archdeacon rode by, down came the knob of the stick right on the running sore.

'You cruel old rascal!' cried the Archdeacon, 'if you beat that poor brute like that, I'll beat you.'

'It will take a better man nor you to do that, I reckon,' said the other, and whack came the stick again on the sore. The Archdeacon said no word, but rode to the first gate, tied up his horse, returned, and went for the donkey man with a will. No one was there to chronicle the encounter, but it got wind, and report said that at seventy, beef, port wine and science had prevailed over poverty and potatoes. Very soon all the gentry and farmers when they met him winked, nudged each other, and liked the Archdeacon exceedingly; but who was the donkey man?

Mr Abraham unearthed him. He had come from no one knew where, with his donkeys, and had squatted outside Luxborough churchyard where, in an angle of the wall, he had erected a one-roomed cottage, of which the church-yard walls formed two sides, and the roof was roughly thatched. When Mr Abraham first called he found a wife there, dirty, taciturn, and old as her husband. They did not mix at all with their few neighbours. One day the carpenter at Dunster said to the doctor, laughing, 'I have had an odd order today, sir. A living man, an old fellow from Luxborough, has been to my place and has ordered his coffin. I told him to lie down on the floor that I might take his measure, and then I chalked around him. 'A little more room for the shoulders, sir,' he said, 'if you please, I might grow a bit stouter before I die.'

Shortly afterwards the old man came with a donkey and took the coffin away, and when Mr Abraham next called at his house he discovered that some of the stones had been shifted from the wall, the earth (which was higher inside than out) had been removed, and the aperture lined with slabs. There the coffin was thrust in, and was used as a drawer to contain bacon, old nails, twine, mouse-traps, and other sweetmeats, as I used to see written on a shop front at Wandsworth in my infancy.

Mr Abraham, who was a great lover of queer people, used frequently to call on this old couple. One day, about my time, he was riding through the village and saw the old man at his cabin door, smoking his pipe.

'Good morning, John, and how is Mary?' said he.

'Mary's ago, sir, dropped off about twelve o'clock.'

'Do you mean to say your wife is dead, John, and that you have not called in the neighbours?'

'They keep theirselves to theirselves, and I keep myself to myself, so I have just put two penny pieces on the old woman's eyes, and laid her out myself, tidy.'

The news quickly spread, and up went the doctor, and found the woman still alive, though exhausted.

'Run, you villain, run for your life, and get me a drop of spirits. You have laid your wife out, and she is still living; run quick, or I'll have you hanged.'

When Mary got the spirits, to which she was not used, she spluttered and came to. She survived the old man, and died at last in Williton workhouse.

'You rogue,' Mr Abraham used sometimes afterwards to say to the dirty, emaciated old donkey driver. 'You rogue, you know you had some fine young woman in your eye when you laid out your poor old wife like that.'

'Well, master, I considered her dead, surely; but when your honour rode up I *was* just a-thinking of Susan Floyd; I was a-thinking that the old woman's clothes would fit to her exactly like, and wouldn't require alterations.'

CHAPTER THREE

Country Folk

THE POOR PEOPLE were very poor, and very primitive in their ways. I was young at the time, and what with the amount of Latin and Greek, of Euclid and algebra that I read of a morning, and the extensive and varied shooting which old Sir Thomas Acland most kindly gave me; what with an occasional day with the hounds; what with the general hospitality shown to me by every gentleman within a radius of many miles, I had not much time to take notice of parochial concerns. There must, however, have been a village school of some sort at Selworthy, because I remember assisting Mrs Arthur Mills and Mrs Leopold Acland to arrange a treat for the children. There were also several parochial charities, but the children in those days were very shy, and their parents were very poor and destitute of comforts. Less than fifty years have elapsed since then, but throughout the country generally the condition of the poor in our rural districts has wonderfully improved.

This improvement may bring with it great calamities at home and abroad if troublous times should arise, and find us dependent for food upon the foreigner; but even if we have to pay eventually a heavy price for our cheap provisions, for the consumption of our over-teeming town populations, at least we have had some compensation in the increased happiness of two generations of Englishmen and women; aye, and of English children also who, in 1847 (only too often blue with cold and pinched with hunger) laboured excessively out of doors at an early age.

The farming people were, in those days, very primitive, although there were a few big farmers in the Porlock valley who took in *The Times* and talked about guano. But the smaller people were very primitive in their ideas, and yet there was already a little of the modern spirit of scepticism in the soft mild air which floated above the thatched roofs and whitewashed walls of the house which nestled low in the 'happy valley.'

I myself had been brought up in an enlightened Evangelical family among Wilberforces, Hoares and Venns, and I was, consequently, horrified when the miller's wife at Horner Mills (where I had gone for cider to drink with my bread and cheese while engaged in fishing the brook), anticipated the criticisms of Bishop Colenso, as follows. I had been telling her something about Mary Stenner and the ghost, and she exclaimed: 'Lord! Sir, I really thought that such tales could *not* be believed; I thought they were like Jack and the Beanstalk, Moses and the bulrushes, and all such-like.'

In those days everybody was hospitable. No one ever begrudged you anything. You could eat, drink, sleep, shoot, fish, ride, or walk almost anywhere you pleased, and the pleasure afforded by your company was thought to be payment enough. The truth is that the country was not at that time opened up, and people were glad of the companionship of anyone who was a little different to themselves.

The strange creatures who sometimes now emerge from our large towns and scatter themselves broadcast over the face of the poor country, have much to answer for. They are apt to corrupt our simplicity; they diminish hospitality; they curtail freedom. I have entertained grave suspicions that some of them are rather idiotic. They occasionally seem to be under the influence of a delusion. When they walk though our well-cultivated corn-fields they imagine themselves to be pioneers in a trackless wilderness. I have seem them holding on firmly to the pavement of our country towns by aid of alpenstocks. They have come to my house along good turnpike roads provided with compasses. They will stare into the entrance of a rectory house, inhabited by a graduate of Oxford, under the delusion that it is the wigwam of a savage. They will flatten their noses against our drawing-room windows the better to observe the manners and customs of the aborigines within. All this it is very easy to smile at. But when they

enter a time-honoured temple of God, apparently to discover what strange superstition forms the worship of the
place, and on learning that it is only Christianity after all
that is believed in, clatter out in the middle of a prayer to
chatter loudly outside, it is difficult to refrain from reprov-
ing them,

These people are apt to leave gates open, so as to allow
cattle to wander. They grub up our wild plants by the roots,
light fires in dangerous situations, trample on crops,
bestrew nature's loveliest scenes with scraps of most greasy
paper, sing very vulgar songs very much out of tune, and
make themselves generally disagreeable. They have caused
much of the old Devonshire hospitality to disappear.
When they come in large numbers, simplicity goes, and in
our watering places virtue is apt to go with it.

Of course, there are very many excellent, cultivated,
charming people who travel about, people with minds and
manners; but no one who has groaned as I have groaned
over the havoc wrought by an indiscriminate rush of
summer visitors to places such as Lynmouth, will wonder
that I feel strongly and write strongly on the subject.

The tourists did much to corrupt the people of Lynton.
But in 1847 they were not numerous in the district, and I
was, therefore, permitted to have a fling which could not
now be obtained, and which was peculiarly acceptable to
me. The winter of 1847- 48 was a singularly wet one, and
the Porlock Valley is very subject to rain. Sir Thomas
Acland owned in that neighbourhood many thousands of
acres of arable, woodland and moor, acres which ran on
from Selworthy to Luccombe, over Horner to Winsford,
and from thence towards Killerton, and he was generous
with his shooting, as he was generous with everything else.

For my part I was rarely dry, but wet agreed with me, and
I was welcomed everywhere. In those days it really did not
matter if you did trespass with rod or gun, for nobody
minded. A man could not now walk away from Ilfracombe
and wander over every acre of wet ground, looking for
snipe, until he came to Allerford with forty in his pouch, as
then did Robert Gould. A man could hardly now ride into
the court of a strange farmhouse, greet the good wife, put
up his horse for ten hours in the stable, return to tea and,

leaving a few trout behind him, ride off amidst the entreat-ies of the household that he would soon come again to visit them; but this could then be done, and in a few of the wilder districts it can still be done.

As a rule, however, the tourists have spoiled the country for the residents, spoiled it in every way. It cannot be helped, but old Devonshire is gone, and it only remains to record its former opportunities and its ancient ways. To me in my teens every river now closed was open. There was a reach certainly in Dunster Park, another half mile at Holnicote and a stretch at Castle Hill, to fish which permis-sion was required, but it was not worthwhile to ask for it when the other numerous waters of a well-watered county were open to the rod.

Sir Thomas Acland's youngest son, now in New Zealand, and a Mr Jenkinson were the constant companions of my youth upon all the rivers. Dawn of day would often see us off for Exford for the Exe, or for Withypool or Dulverton for the Barle, and night would be falling before we returned. So keen were we then that each of us carried a notebook and a pencil, and scales to weigh the larger fish which we caught, before we consigned them to the basket; but the fish were very small. They averaged about eight to the pound, and the best nine that I ever caught in one day I gave, in 1854, to Mrs Roe, at the Manor House, Lyn-mouth, and they weighed collectively three pounds and a quarter.

The shooting was almost equally free. Many and many a day have I ridden over the Dunkerry country, with fleet setters held in reserve to be used as their fellows became exhausted, by reason of their long range through high heather, looking for black-game. Then the dogs would drop, and the riders, leaving their ponies, would close up to the leading setter, and not infrequently in those days have I put down my hand and taken up the plump bird from under the rigid nose of the panting dog. I have always been something of a sportsman, but I have never known any other bird, except occasionally a snipe, thus caught by the hand, uninjured; but I have seen a hare in like fashion taken up from her form.

The gentry were, also, very hospitable, and Mr Hoare's pupils had in all ways an excellent time,

In those days there was a very charming young lady, who resided at Old Cleeve with her brother, who was engaged to be married to one of my former schoolfellows, a lad who had written a famous prize poem at Rugby, and was afterwards destined to lead the way in the production of what may be termed very muscular literature. As a general rule it is only ladies who imagine fifteen-stone guardsmen on thoroughbred horses flying the Thames below Windsor, or chasing tribes of wild Arabs, with the aid of a French *vivandière* standing four feet six inches in her stockings; but Mr Lawrence was quite capable of similar feats of imagination and was, moreover, undoubtedly clever.

The young lady was Irish, very pretty, and mischievous as well. It is a long time back to the winter of 1847–48, but if she survives and reads, does she remember still how she dropped the hot coal into the boot of the Reverend Joseph Jekyll after the dance at Dunster, and what the reverend gentleman said before he extracted his foot from the burning boot? And there was another young lady, equally charming if somewhat less vivacious, who was engaged to be married to the son of one of England's most famous Lord Chancellors, while her brother was serving in the Rifle Brigade, with which he went to the Crimea.

Up to 1848 the outside world had been nothing to me. I had cared for nothing beyond my home. But with the spring of 1848 my education began. In the intervals left between reading for Cambridge and sporting, I suddenly became aware that crowns were falling, revolutions occurring, and that the political situation at home was not very safe.

It was in those days that a king of France arrived at Newhaven, with a carpet-bag and a hat-case, and called himself 'Mr Smith.' It was then that I saw my old father sally forth at the head of some hundreds of special constables to hold the Clapham Common against the Chartists, who were coming from Kennington towards Clapham Common. It struck me at the time as being rather funny that they should not be allowed to go out of London to air their grievances on Clapham Common; for they could not

well hurt the gorse bushes, and they would certainly be
further removed from the shops and from temptation. But
no! The sacred precincts of that goose-green were not to
be trodden by sacrilegious feet, and so my good father
barred the way.

There were, I believe, five points to their Charter that
day. Four of these have been peacefully adopted since
then, and are now buried and quite forgotten amid the din
of existing strifes. But they stirred up my blood at the time,
and I listened eagerly to my father's reminiscences of
1798, and the great riots which had then been enacted in
Dublin, and I longed to be sworn in also, and to be allowed
to go and help to keep the pass.

It was in this spring of 1848 that I first began to read the
newspapers, and I have read *The Times* through, I believe,
every day since that time. I had my eyes opened, also, in
another direction, for I now made my first acquaintance
with the Spiritualists.

Everyone, it is said, has an aunt who resides in Bath, and
I myself was exceptionally well provided with friends and
relatives in that ancient and beautiful city. So it came to
pass that when I journeyed between Selworthy and
Clapham I used frequently to break my journey at Bath,
and stay with my mother's cousins, Miss Nisbet, or Mrs
Mount, or with Mr Ross, who long before had married a
Miss Gould, of Luccombe, and now resided in the Combe
Down Road.

Well, one night at Mr Mount's house, in Camden Cres-
cent, I was told that the ghost of somebody's grandmamma
was certainly confined in the drawing-room table, and that
if I would only lay hold of the table in concert with the rest
the appalling fact would be proved to demonstration by
reason of the table turning round. I am not, of course,
responsible for the logic of this; but these spirits are not
logical, and their devotees resemble them. Well, on to that
table I held, and as I was not allowed to remove my hands,
a very pretty young lady cousin, since then twice married,
fed me with ices from a spoon. While this exercise was
continued the table was obdurate; but when the ices were
all done and the young lady looked expectant, that table
revolved like a mad thing. Of course it was quite fairly

done; but the spiritual power was at that time very strong in my arms, and I would have smashed any kind of table at the risk of hurting my imprisoned grandmamma, rather than have caused disappointment to so pretty a cousin. Everybody, I remember, was thoroughly satisfied, and considered that the old lady – (Miss Nisbet, who was very evangelical, suggested the 'Old Gentleman') was certainly present.

The country people generally were very Protestant, and although their Protestantism was peculiar, it largely manifesting itself in opposition to anything new and unfamiliar, yet it was genuine and deep-seated. Fifty years, however, have changed all this, and farmers' sons and daughters, and young country people generally, have come quite to like rather High Church ways, and their elders have given way to them in this, as in other and much more important matters.

Another great revolution of feeling and practice has taken place in the last half century. The country people, generally, do not now come to church as regularly as of old. Many of the farmers have grown cold and indifferent, and the labourers attend very badly. But the change is more apparent than real. Modern scepticism, no doubt, has in this matter something to answer for; but there was a great deal of latent scepticism in the old days among people who came to church. The fact is, that they attended then because they were obliged to do so. There were more labourers in our rural parishes than there was work for them to do; they were most miserably underpaid, and were largely dependent upon doles, and the squires and the farmers supported the church.

It is now hard for an employer to obtain a good workman. In those days it was hard for a good workman to obtain employment. A labourer did not dare to risk his situation; and in sickness and old age he was, also, much more dependent upon his superiors in wealth and station than is now the case.

Old Sir Thomas Acland had an eagle eye, and he used to look round Selworthy Church and take notice of those who were present. The poor people were very poor, and Lady Acland was very benevolent. The farmers were

Conservative, and stood up for the church and old customs. So the poor people came to church. If by so doing
they got but little good, at least they received no harm, and
some sort of reverential spirit was maintained in them.
Now every good man is worth the money that he earns.
The working people are comparatively rich, and the world
is open before them. They go more easily to America than
their grandfathers went to London, and they are no longer
afraid to leave home. The upshot of it all is that in this
matter secondary motives have ceased to play an important part, and if poor people do not wish to come to
church, they stay away.

It is becoming very much the same with the family.
Children and servants in former days were ordered to
church as a matter of course, and were punished if they
would not go; but now we live in a lawless age, and
everyone, rich and poor, young and old, does pretty much
and says very much what he pleases. We lose in uniformity,
we lose in discipline, perhaps we lose also in opportunity
for doing good; but we gain in sincerity, and our churches
are no longer places of *rol-call* and of drill, as are, or in old
days were, our college chapels.

People are better educated and, becoming more intelligent and more cultivated, many of them like church better
than did their predecessors, who attended with greater
regularity much duller services than those now rendered,
because they thought it advisable to do so. We gain in
quality if we lose in quantity. On such comparative matters
as these it is, however, very difficult to speak, and therefore
I will content myself with merely describing old West
Country church life as it existed in the Forties.

It was very primitive. A clerical friend of mine, feeling
exhausted, asked the parish clerk to read the Lessons. One
of these was from Daniel, and the clerk stammered hard
over 'Shadrach, Meshach, and Abed-nego,' but when the
names again occurred, he paused, drew himself together,
and said, 'These three chaps with the long names again,'
and went quietly on with the chapter.

Selworthy Church was bare, the seats were high,, and the
Aclands had a sort of special box with a fire-place in it, all
to themselves. The services were simple, and the choir, if I

remember rightly, brought their own musical instruments
to church, and generally sang Tate and Brady's Psalms.

When Sir Thomas was at Holnicote, he came twice to
church on Sundays; and in the afternoon he would bring
with him two or three favourite dogs, shut them up in
Farmer Stenner's barn during service, and then, letting
them out, would start with Mr Hoare and his pupils and,
perhaps, some of his family, for the most glorious of all
earthly walks, up through the Coombe and over the hill,
and away to Hurlstone Point, the place from which in
ancient days the Devil pitched two great stones, called
Whitstones, across the valley and well up on the crest of
Porlock Hill, some four or five miles away. There these
stones still remain pointing backwards to the Point, monu-
ments of diabolical skill and strength and dexterity.
Thence the party would return, skirting the glassy, slippery
slopes leading precipitously down to the cavernous recess
which pierces the Point at its extremity, and through which
the waves toss and tumble in stormy weather.

We generally walked home through the woods by 'Agnes
Fountain,' the dear old baronet keeping us alive with
impetuous declamations on any conceivable subject,
moral, religious, scientific or political, which at the
moment came uppermost in his fertile mind. He was
always interesting, always fresh, always – as Mr Halliday
used to say – inclined to talk about three things at once.

Then we would dine together at Holnicote, and have a
bottle of Cockburn's port. Old Sir Thomas always gave his
friends very good port wine, and on one occasion, just as
the bottle was put upon the table, he was called out of the
room upon business. He had at Killerton a chaplain
named Bond, who afterwards was appointed to the living
at Mariansleigh, and this gentleman was present. When
the baronet returned, he said at once, 'Where is the port?'
and the reply from a witty guest was prompt and appropriate, 'Well, Sir Thomas, to tell you the truth, I believe it is in
Bond.' Those were happy Sundays, and I should like once
more to attend service in Selworthy Church, shake hands
with a few surviving veterans, and then in company of
children and of grandchildren, walk that dear walk again.

The spring of 1848, like the previous winter, was mild and wet and I, the only pupil of Selworthy, for Turner had not left Eton to join me yet, took to fishing as if I had been born a heron or a kingfisher. I always had a liking for small and crabbed waters, for no one fishes them; in them the good fish live, and are unsophisticated withal.

We were never in those days particular as to poaching, but, whether or no, I filled my pouch like an otter, and I often now think of my own early and great performances with the rod, and in saddle on the moors. I liked to visit the very topmost waters, fish with a short line, fine gut, and a single fly, often a red one with a white tip to the body. I would throw myself down quite flat, and wriggle up the brookside like a snake, throwing my fly into the small pits and narrow stickles most successfully.

In those days I generally carried a basket which held fourteen pounds weight of trout, and after learning to fish, I did not consider that I had done well if I did not succeed in filling it. No one in these latter days, on those same upper waters, could do as much. But dearly also did I love the woody, tangled brook which runs down from Holnicote, through Bossington, to the sea near Hurlstone Point.

Sometimes with a worm, sometimes with a bluebottle, sometimes with infinite pains with artificial flies, I would fish that tiny brook, and its trout, if not numerous, were large and fat. When it rained hard, and thunder was to be heard, several of us would make a clot with worms and worsted, and go down at night with a bag and a lantern to catch eels, and an occasional trout in the brook.

From some cause or other the clear streams in the north of Devon are much more tenanted by eels than are the rivers in the south; and great was the scrambling of pupil and farm boys as at midnight, and in streaming rain, the eels would disengage themselves from the worsted, and glide about in the long grass of the meadow, endeavouring to escape and get back to their homes. At other times I would go down to the ditches in Porlock marsh to catch eels with an eel spear, ever so many at a time. Really I scarcely know how I found time to get at all these rivers, but in 1848–9 it was my custom to fish the Timberscombe

brook, Chalkwater, Exe, Barle, Lyn, Horner and Hawcombe brooks, and last but not least the little stream of
Holnicote. No one ever said me nay.

Polly was ubiquitous, and really I liked fishing for trout
better than I liked reading Thucydides, *much better;* and
even now, when old age is coming upon me, and should
bring wisdom in its train, I do not know that in this I was
much mistaken. For what would Thucydides do for me,
and what did I owe to Thucydides? No, I preferred

> Tongues in trees, books in the running brooks,
> Sermons in stones, and good in everything.

I look around me today and I see my grandchildren, chips
from my own block, good young fellows enough, and my
heart sinks on account of them, for the world is not what it
was in the Forties. They have the inclinations, but they
have not the chances which I had.

What is to be done with the present generation of
active-bodied, well-conducted, perhaps rather dull-witted
lads? Fifty years ago they could go out with my own three
brothers of India, and there make fortunes; or with Sir
Samuel Baker to Ceylon, and shoot elephants and grow
rich; or with Mr Harris, of Hawkmore, to New Zealand,
and in twenty years turn £5,000 into £50,000 and so return
to their native land; or to Australia, with many of my
friends, and live a life of adventure, and make money.
They could emigrate to America, or to Africa, and prosper
and do well.

But now they can no longer range with rod and gun
through Devonshire or Somersetshire unchallenged, nor
buy for £5,000 twenty-five thousand acres of good land in
some temperate climate and, at the same time, settle down
among friends and live beside brother Englishmen. Those
days are gone, and to men of their class life is in some
respects harder than it was, while sport generally is not so
good, and is certainly less easy to obtain. But notwithstanding this change in the times, really it often seems as if the
grandchildren wanted more indulgences than the grandfather required. Life is full of such anomalies.

The Selworthy pupils, however, were very simple in their
ways. If they could not ride to hounds, they would run with

them. If they could not get a seat in a carriage, they would go in a cart. If meat and wine were wanting, they would do equally well with cider and bread and cheese.

Mr Acland and Mr Tripp at this time went to New Zealand, as did also Mr Harris; Mr Browne and the two Collyns to Australia; while the elder Thorntons had already long before gone as writers to India. They all did well and prospered, and as they were simple in their habits, manly, and of good character, they succeeded in life. No man ever asked them to square the circle, or to lecture learnedly upon Aristotle, and yet there then was room upon the earth and a living for *them* as well as for those who were scholars.

The truth would seem to be that modern life is reducing social inequalities. Surely this, if true, is an argument against Socialistic enterprises, for time is doing rapidly that which the Socialist desires to be done. The general mass of the poor is much less poor than formerly, while it is harder than of old for gentlemen's sons to obtain even so much as a gentlemanly competence. Of course, there is behind these two classes the starving, unhealthy, drunken, dishonest residuum of the nation, to cause us disquietude and alarm, but for the most part we seem to be settling down to a general dead level in mind and training, in habits and wealth, in opportunities, and in everything else.

The old sportsmen are nearly gone, the old clergy are gone, and so are the old-fashioned country gentlemen. Indeed, the highly polished gentleman himself has become scarcer than he was. There are other good types coming up in his place, no doubt, very good; but if you look through the House of Commons today you will find only a few, comparatively speaking few, specimens of that high type of accomplished gentleman which gathered round the coronation of our Queen. The rough uncultivated poor have in truth gone up immeasurably, while the others have come down to meet them; and what will be the end thereof? Surely at best a somewhat uninteresting uniformity?

But it was not so at Selworthy, and as a boy I was privileged to know several of the military companions of

Wellington, as well as some of Nelson's sea dogs of captains. I knew many, also, of the tough fellows who, often unable to read or write, fought under these great commanders – men who, against great odds, had held Hougoumont for twelve hours, or made one Spanish line-of-battle ship a bridge whereby to get at another.

I knew some of the highest class of civilians also, men who did not care much, either in public or private life, for material interest, but who would have gladly sacrificed life and child, laud and gold, to uphold the honour of the flag. They are mostly gone, and with them have gone, also, flogging in the services, and cockfighting, and much of rough barbarity.

A cottage girl is often now really far advanced in cultivated intelligence, and little resembles the village maidens of my days at Selworthy, while the boys are better mannered and better instructed than they were; but many of our politicians are not what they used to be. They do not look forward. They are not so statesmanlike as were their fathers. Some few of them, I believe, would willingly consent to become altogether subservient, to lower the flag of old England for ever in the dust and merge her with the already overgrown United States of America. They would, indeed, do almost anything to gain money, and to avoid danger, for verily they are quite cosmopolitan in sentiment.

Our country gentlemen, I say, are mostly gone, and as for our bishops and clergy, you would often hardly know that they belonged to the same order as of old, either by their habits or by their appearance, or even by many of their aspirations and views. So great has been the revolution effected in one short half of a century.

CHAPTER FOUR

Deer, Foxes, Snakes

IN THE SPRING of 1848, while out shooting with Sir Thomas Acland, I accidentally discharged my gun, and although young Larcombe, the under-keeper, with more readiness than veracity, roared out, 'Mark hare, gone back!' his father saw what had happened, and told the Baronet.

I shall never forget the scolding which I received, for the old gentleman was energetic with his tongue as with everything else, and he was very angry with me. However, he concluded by saying that although he would not allow his friends or himself to be shot by a careless youth yet, for my father's sake, he would not altogether stop my amusement. I might still continue to go out, but only with a keeper and old Mr Hoare, the head of the brewing firm, who happened just then to be staying at Holnicote, as being nearly related to Lady Acland.

Mr Hoare was a dear old gentleman, and I never quite understood the principle on which he was selected to be my victim, but he made no objection whatever to the arrangement, and we had many pleasant days together looking for pheasants in the hedgerows near to the coverts. After a time I was again allowed to shoot with the rest of the party, and my carelessness was forgotten.

It was at this time that Mr Hoare, who was about seventy years of age, was attacked by a savage ram. At first he thought that the assault was ridiculous, but changed his mind when he found himself repeatedly knocked down as fast as he got upon his legs. At length he contrived to clamber up on a gate, and was truly thankful to be out of his woolly assailant's reach.

Thirty years later a ram attacked a poor woman at Sandy Park, near Chagford, and after knocking her down and breaking her leg, stood sentry over her for hours. She could not crawl away until the neighbours came to her assistance, as the ram butted her immediately if she moved.

It was now that, while hunting with Mr Stoate's hounds, I noticed that they were marking at an earth on Lucott Moor, beyond Horner. I tried hard to get them away, but old Larcombe, the keeper, came up on his pony and, declaring that by the smoothness he knew the hole was used by foxes rather than by badgers, insisted upon digging. Presently he came upon a one-eyed vixen and five cubs, only a few days old. I put one of these little things into my pocket, and the Dunster saddler took two. The other two were killed, and the mother very cruelly turned down before the hounds. She gave us a good run, and we lost her at Exford or in its neighbourhood.

I then rode back to Selworthy and fed the small cub with a spoon. At night it slept in a basket on my bed, and soon learned to suck milk through a quill with a nipple attached to its extremity. That fox grew very tame, and I used to let her run into the long wood which stretched for miles from the back of our cottage. Often I have searched for her in vain, and when at last I have desisted, she has poked a little sharp nose out from under a dock-leaf and come gambolling round my legs. But she always kept an eye on my hand, and would never allow me to catch her. The only way to accomplish this was to walk into the house, when she would follow, and then if I was very quick I could shut the door and pounce upon her.

That summer I went to see my friends, and I took my fox with me in a basket. At Bridgwater a porter asked me if I had a dog, and that I must take a ticket for it to London. I told him that I had no dog, so he went and fetched the station master, and the following conversation occurred:

'You have a dog there, sir. You must pay its fare.'

'I have no dog,' I replied. 'I have a fox, and you have no tariff for foxes, and I will not pay. You had better take care, too, or it will bite you.' For he was opening the basket.

'Now, young gentleman,' said he, 'you must pay, for as everyone knows, a fox is a dog, and is to be paid for accordingly.'

'You are very ignorant, my friend, of natural history,' I replied. 'These animals are of a different species.'

'But it is a dog fox,' he urged.

'No,' I replied, 'it is, on the contrary, a vixen;' and the train coming up, I jumped into it with the basket, delighted and victorious.

When I got to Clapham the fox ran away and took refuge in a lunatic asylum. I fetched her back and she ran there again. So, as I was going to Scotland, I gave her to the mad-house proprietor, who also allowed her to run loose even as I had done, until one night she killed about twenty prize fowls belonging to a neighbour, after which performance she was chained up, and I used to see her endeavouring to catch the fowls in the yard where she was confined.

This fox would put a bone just at the very furthest limit to which she could spring, and then she would lie down with her head between her paws waiting for some incautious fowl to come within range to peck at the bone. But the birds seemed to be as wide awake as the fox; and just, and only just, avoided the snare.

That summer I went to Scotland, and visited Lord Leven, at his place near Cupar, and then went to the Grants, at Glen Moriston, and across from Inverness to Loch Alsh to stay with a family of the name of Livingstone, who were related to the Spooners, and resided on the mainland, just opposite to the southern end of the Island of Skye.

After remaining with them for a few days, and making the acquaintance of Gerald Spooner, afterwards destined to be my parishioner on Exmoor, I went across the ferry, and then on foot for thirty miles to Sligahan, at which place I arrived after dark, tired and hungry. The one inn was low and small, and the landlord, seeing in me only a youth with a knapsack, told me that his house was full and that he could not take me in, or even so much as give me dinner.

I replied that dinner I must have, and that I would sleep in the straw of the stable, but that I would not be driven away. Then a door opened, and a gentleman asked me to come in and dine with him and his daughter. This I was glad enough to do, and he proved to be a Mr Currie, of one of the great shipbuilding firms, Member of Parliament for Guildford, and well known to my father.

Seeing me thus befriended, the landlord grew civil, and said that two young gentlemen had for some nights past been occupying a room with two beds, and that he would ask them to sleep together so as to give up the second bed to me. The boys were, I believe, actually in bed at the time, and one of them good-naturedly turned out for me. I had walked some thirty miles without food, and I was tired and exhausted. The next morning, while we were dressing, I learned from my companions that they were only just recovering from a severe attack of scarlet fever, and were travelling to recover their health.

I had walked my shoes off my feet on the previous day, so I returned to the Livingstones in a boat, through rocks and stormy seas. When I told my kind host that I was probably fever stricken, he said that I must go and stand before the kitchen fire so as to roast myself thoroughly, and this I did, to the complete satisfaction of himself and his wife, who really thought such treatment efficacious.

While staying at Loch Alsh I went out fishing with Mr Spooner and roused, I remember, the first roe deer that ever I had seen. Afterwards, on returning to Melville, Lord Leven's house, I found that my sister was there, and that she was very ill. She had arrived during the time I was in Skye, together with my mother and father, and was taken ill with a mysterious complaint from which, although she is still living, she has never recovered.

After a few days, and in company with my cousin, Lord Balgonie, who together with Turner soon was destined to fall a victim to the war in the Crimea, I returned to London, and from thence to Selworthy.

It was now that I saw my first run with the stag-hounds, and I shall never forget it. The red deer upon Exmoor were few in numbers, and greatly harassed, for in 1848 the hunting men were also few, and nobody took much trouble to preserve the deer. It was said that their estimated number on all the Exmoor Commons at this time was but thirty, with thirty more, perhaps, in Haddon and its neighbourhood, and a few on the Quantocks.

Red deer are mischievous animals, and there was probably no damage fund, for there was then no money in the county. So it looked as if they would soon be as extinct upon Exmoor as they were already in the Dartmoor Country. Being constantly dogged and harassed, even, perhaps, fired on by the farmers, they were very wild, and were acquainted with a vast extent of country, as, as all sportsmen know, hunted animals run well or badly according to the extent of their knowledge of country.

Matters are now very differently managed. There is an ample damage fund. Riders are numerous, and the deer are plentiful. So sport is more certain to be had, but the runs are generally very inferior to what they were when the deer were for the most part lighter, younger, and much more often disturbed than is now the case.

On an August day in 1848 I rode Polly up to Cloutsham. Sir Arthur Chichester had the hounds that year. He was a heavy man, with a fancy for riding thoroughbred horses which seemed to me quite inadequate. Already, when I arrived, he was there with Jack Babbage, his huntsman, and the riders, few in number, were collecting on the spot The hounds were shut up in a barn at Cloutsham, and the old huntsman, on foot, took me into the garden in front of the picturesque farmhouse and, pointing across the valley to where Sweetery Combe runs up into the heart of Dunkerry, shewed me two fine stags lying down lazily in the heather. I could see them throw up their antlered heads to drive away the flies which teased them. They were close together, and about half a mile away from where we stood.

The deer had been harboured, or marked down, by Blackmore, of Larkborough, the 'Red Rube' of one of Whyte Melville's novels. Sir Arthur now told the huntsman to rouse them, and he, taking with him a couple of old hounds called 'tufters' crossed the valley and ascended the hillside towards the stags. They parted, and one ran rapidly to the south-west, along the side of Dunkerry, in full view, with the tufters after him .

Then, as soon as the huntsman could return to us, the hounds were let out of the barn in which they were confined, and we all galloped hard in a body up the Exford road to the summit where it passes over a lower point of the Dunkerry range of hills. When we had reached nearly to the top, all of a sudden the hounds swerved from the road and, for a moment throwing their tongues (stag-hounds are mostly silent), raced away to the right for Tomshill and the Exmoor forest. We had crossed the line of the stag, and the business of the day was begun.

Alas, poor Polly, a pony indifferently fed, but four years old, and out of condition, was quickly nowhere. It is now forty-eight years ago; but I can well remember my chagrin and despair when, in a few minutes' time, do what I would to the contrary, I was alone, and two dark specks in the distance showed where 'Tory' and 'Commodore' were racing in sight of the hounds.

It was a dangerous, boggy line of country, and one with which as yet I was but little acquainted, but I was all right, for we were in front of the tufters, and I came along with them. They were slow *old* hounds, and the scent was somewhat foiled by the pack ahead. I was, therefore, able to keep them in sight. So on I went, past Tomshill and Larkborough to Oare Common, through Badgworthy wood, and away to Scob hill, though the Lyn river by Malmsmead, and down to Wiltsham. There I found the field gathered together by the side of a big black pool. They had killed the stag and performed his last funeral rites, so I, after a long look at my first dead stag, rode back to Selworthy.

My memory is good, and I could tell of the details of any an after gallop, but I remember none better than those of that bright August day, when poorly mounted and alone, I struggled forward for many a mile over the open country of Exmoor.

There is in the Museum in Exeter a case which contains the head of a red-deer stag; the horns are those of one aged seven, and beside it, in the same case, are those which the same deer carried at six, five, four, three two and one year successively. The stag that bore them had been cap-tured whilst a calf by Mr Clarke, the doctor at Lynton, and was kept by him in a paddock. It was living at this time, when a party was organised at Minehead to spend the day at Lynton, and many young ladies determined to go.

There was a second usher at the Minehead School, a powerful young gentleman whose name I have forgotten, and he also joined the expedition. The party went by sea, and in due time landed at Lynmouth. They presently walked up the Lynton hill to see the stag. One young lady remarked that it was graceful, and the second said that she should like to see it run.

The usher was gallant, and at once clambered over the fence, rattled his hat, and shouted, but the stag did not feel at all alarmed and assumed a threatening attitude. Then the invader retired, but too late. The stag was upon him, a nimble beast, and the usher, taking him by the horns, was forced back over the fence in a moment, but in a terrible condition.

Of course, nothing improper was intended, but it is awkward, nevertheless, when a young man is unceremoniously returned to a party of nice young ladies with no clothes at all upon him worth the mentioning. The good people of Lynton, however, pinned him together, and lent him a shawl for a petticoat, so that with great care he was able to sidle into the boat; and, sitting very still, did not, I believe, come to pieces again before he reached home, and could send for the doctor to attend to his scratches.

I do not think that that stag was ever again subjected to intrusion. I am not acquainted with the manner of his sad end, but probably the beast became elated with his victory and dangerous, and was shot. You can see his horns at any rate in Exeter Museum to this day.

The current in the channel off Minehead is very strong, and I remember going with Mr Hoare and George Ross to bathe there in the summer of 1848. We took a heavy boat, rowed out for a mile and then jumped overboard, leaving the boat to herself. When we were tired of swimming, one of us endeavoured to get in, but found that he could not succeed. The boat was heavy, her sides were high, and the swimmer could not lift himself in. Here was a pretty mess. A storm was brewing, we were perhaps a mile and a half from land, and the tide was running up channel at the rate of five miles an hour.

We were all naturally naked and growing cold. We could get hold of the side of the boat, but our united weight and strength would not suffice to bend her over sufficiently to enable us to get in. So Ross and I held on together to make a bridge for the tutor, who was ten years our senior and stronger than we were, but we were horribly slippery, and he could not get an angle out of us to stand upon. We were much scratched and kicked, but somehow or another at last he dug his knees into the neck of one of us and, scrambling in, pulled us up into the boat.

We then had a hard and heavy pull back to Minehead through such a thunderstorm as I have rarely seen. In one minute we were as wet as if we had been in the water in our clothes, and the thunder and lightning were simultaneous. I do not think that anyone spoke as we trudged back through Hynam to Selworthy, or dared to open an umbrella, for awe of that fearful lightning.

I bought Polly from Mr Parramore, of Hynam, and he had an old lady living with him, his grandmother, I suppose. This old lady gave a tea party, and took down her best china in honour of the occasion. She left the room for awhile; one of the party made the tea, and then old Mrs Parramore returned. When she found that the tea was made, she said to the maker, 'Emily, my dear, did you take anything out of the teapot before you made the tea?'

'No, Aunt. I only warmed the pot.'

'Then, my dear, you have made an expensive pot of tea. I had two five-pound notes in that pot.'

And now Charles Turner came from Eton, bringing with him a bull-terrier. He was a heavy, indolent, good-tempered fellow, who had been used to much more self-indulgence in school than was allowed to us at Rugby. My impression is that I used to take back a sovereign when, after the holidays, I returned to school, and he took twenty; but nevertheless we agreed very well, and never, indeed, had a quarrel. I lost sight of him when he joined the Guards, as I at the same time went up to Trinity, and although he succeeded to an estate at Tandridge in Surrey, where my aunts, the Miss Parrys, resided, yet I never once saw him after his return invalided from the fatal trenches before Sebastopol.

In 1848 we both had dogs, and sometimes we used to go out at about ten o'clock on summer evenings, and let these dogs roam. After a time we would hear them bark and howl, and on running up would discover a hedgehog rolled together, upon which the dogs were pawing and pricking their noses. We used to carry the little beasts home and turn them out in the kitchen, but they generally managed to escape into the woods, and we saw them no more.

A gipsy girl in Horner wood told me that her people liked hedgehogs better than game. She said that she never skinned them, but rolled them up in clay and baked them in the ashes under the kettle. She kindly offered to cook one for me if I would come into camp at dinner-time.

They are busy little routing things, with funny actions peculiar to themselves, but although they are innocent of many of the crimes imputed to their charge, yet I am afraid that they must plead guilty to the allegation of being fond of eggs. I think they would eat eggs if they met with them, and they have sharp, inquisitive, prying little noses of their own.

The Happy Valley was full of them, and we could always catch two or three of an evening if we pleased to do so. It is said that hedgehogs kill snakes and eat them. West Somersetshire used to abound with vipers. Farmer Rendall told me that one of these reptiles had flown at his head, and this story induced me to make many experiments. I came to the conclusion, after long experience, that a snake can only throw itself the distance of its own length, in short extend itself, but it can do this with great rapidity. Allowance, however, must be made for many circumstances if you would judge of the powers of a snake properly. For instance, these animals are most torpid when gorged, or very cold, or when just about to shed their skins, and generally they are most active when they are near their strongholds.

If you meet with a snake in the open, it does not progress very rapidly, but if it is within a few feet of a clitter of rocks, lightning is not swifter. I never have been able to irritate a viper into striking at a distance greater than its own length, say three feet. The poison is like treacle in appearance, and is concealed beside the tongue in long glands. I never could get a viper to strike more than two, or at most three times. After the first attempt, the discharge is very slight.

It is a curious fact that snakes skin their eyes as well as the rest of their bodies. I have killed these reptiles and found loose skin over their eyeballs, which partially blinded them. You may find all shades of colour, from bright copper to black, and again to grey. Something depends, probably, on their habitation at the moment, for animals assimilate themselves readily to their surroundings; but more depends on the length of time that snakes have worn their skins for, like ourselves, they grow grey with age, and are brightest in youth.

I have known many people bitten by snakes. Mrs Larcombe, the keeper's wife, nearly died from snake bite while I was at Selworthy. She was bitten on Dunkerry when gathering whortle-berries. Her husband went to a wise woman, who hung an amulet on her neck, and told her to place her bed so as to point due north and south. The poor woman nearly died, and the white witch declared that the bed had not been set true to the north.

I once lost a favourite mare with her foal by adder bite – the same good mare which had on a memorable occasion carried me seventy miles between dawn and noon. Cattle and sheep are often bitten, but hounds are the most frequent sufferers. There must, however, be something in the canine constitution which enables it to resist snake poison, for I have never known one die; the suffering nevertheless is apparently very severe.

The only snakes in England are the common snake, the viper, and the slow-worm. The viper of these alone is poisonous. It is, I believe, quite true that vipers, in order to save their young, swallow them. The late Mr John Ponsford, of Ford, and Wm Bragg, of Furlong, both witnessed such an occurrence, little snake after snake disappearing down the throat of the mother, and I have myself opened a dead viper and liberated a whole colony of most interesting little snakes. The viper produces her young alive, but the common snake lays eggs. I do not know much of the habits of the slow-worm, but it is very brittle and will break up into half a dozen short lengths if you strike it hard.

CHAPTER FIVE

Cambridge

I LEFT THE PORLOCK valley in October, 1849, for Trinity College, Cambridge. During the two years which I had spent in Somersetshire I had made many friends, and had grown from a sickly lad into a strong young man, so strong as to be able on one occasion to row from Minehead across to Wales. Mr Hoare was with me, and either Turner or Ross. We landed at some little place near Cardiff, and we dined – the only time in my life – upon roasted curlews, which were served up like wood-cocks, but were not very good to eat. Then we pulled back in safety; but I do not think that these long expeditions in small rowing boats are to be recommended.

I have rowed from the Cumbrae Islands across the Clyde to Rothesay at night before now, and have nearly been drowned for my pains. I did the same in the Bay of Naples, rowing, by deputy, for twenty miles from Capri to Ischia. My companions and myself in the Bristol Channel did not well know where we were going, and we took the chances of wind and tide. As it happened, we got ashore at some little place to which the people of Cardiff were wont to boat for picnic purposes.

And now, endeavouring to sell Polly, I encountered my first horse-dealing difficulties. As a rule you can readily buy horses, but rarely sell them. Few people understand horses, although most people think otherwise; most people also delight in teasing, and all want to cheapen the sale. I was driven wild. I had a very good pony, six years old. I wanted fifteen pounds for her, and I was told that I had ridden her to death, that her wind was gone, and her eyes were going etc, etc, and that I should be fortunate if I made ten pounds of such a poor, worn-out animal.

So I hardened my heart and, wishing Mr Hoare goodbye, rode off at about twelve o'clock on an October night, meaning to reach as far as I could towards Bristol, before I put Polly and myself into the train. It was a showery moonlight night, and we arrived at the Carhampton gate about one o'clock. There in those days resided an old woman, who was about eighty years of age, and was well known in London, for she regularly supplied Fortnum and Mason with laver, as the edible seaweed is called.

A shower was falling, and Betty was in bed, having previously locked the gate. I was furious at the delay, and abused the old woman roundly for detaining me. She did not dress much before she came downstairs, and I remember vividly how, when I told her that she really might make more haste to unlock the gate after keeping me so long in the rain, she exclaimed, 'Drat the man, cannot he let me get my slipper?' and looking down I saw her fishing about at the bottom of a puddle with her poor old dirty naked toes in the endeavour to recover the submerged slipper. Then I paid her one penny, and she returned to her bed, quite satisfied and none the worse for her outing, for even the old women were hardy in those days.

Then I rode on, and catching a train at Bridgwater, was dropped at Reading, where I remounted Polly and rode by Stratfieldsaye to Basingstoke, and on to my brother's house at Candover. He took charge of the worn-out mare, and drove her in harness for several years until, indeed, I went to Exmoor in 1856, when he returned her to me. I gave her to Mr Robert Smith, of Emmett's Grange, and she became a mother of many colts.

And now for three years I quitted the West Country, enjoyed University life, and made friends, but I did not forget the 'Valley,' and as my parents wished me to be a clergyman, I left a request with the Hallidays, begging them to remember me if a little later on they should hear that any West Country rector required the services of a curate.

In October 1849 I matriculated at Trinity College, Cambridge, and as it was impossible to obtain rooms in College, my father took lodgings for me at Smith's, the third shop from St Mary's, in King's Parade, and there I remained until after I had taken my degree.

An old Brighton schoolfellow named Torr unexpectedly turned up. I knew two more undergraduates named Cornwall and Babington, also of Trinity, and Newton of Magdalen, who has since won fame as a naturalist, is a cousin of mine; with these exceptions, I had my friends to seek.

From the first I did not read much, partly because my family said I could never take a good degree, and I did not care to work hard for a bad one, and partly because I was idle; but I attended the Union Debating Society, read a certain amount of English literature, walked a great deal, boated a little, and rode to hounds whenever my purse was full enough to enable me to do so. Alas, alas! My friends of those days are now mostly gone to their rest.

I was at once admitted to be a member of 'the Synagogue.' This litle society was composed of rather distinguished men. Van Sittart, Hort, Brimley, the Butlers, the two Macmillans, Whymper, and Hardy, with others, met every Sunday evening at Howard's rooms in Sidney Sussex College. Van Sittart and Hort were New Testament revisionists and famous scholars. Brimley was librarian of Trinity, and author of some Essays which had a reputation in their day. One of the Butlers was afterwards head master of Harrow. The Macmillans were the well known publishers and booksellers; Whymper and Hardy were fellows of their respective colleges and famous mountaineers; Howard was afterwards one of H.M's early inspectors of schools.

Our plan was to assemble with pet dogs, artfully concealed in our gowns, at Howard's rooms in Sidney, at about seven p.m. Then the learned me fought over Greek Testament readings and differences of MSS. Afterwards we had supper, drank much audit ale, and finished with the reading by one of the party of some difficult sermon, generally by Archer Butler, and free discussion thereon. All the time we smoked, and went back to our rooms by midnight.

It was a great privilege to me to be allowed to be present, and the discussions, though free, were always conducted by men who were believers. Nevertheless it was a mistake, so far as I was concerned, to send me to college at all, for I had no great head for mathematics, and I never saw the practical value of any very deep knowledge of the classics. I knew enough to be able to pass an examination without difficulty, and I desired no more.

There was the making of a good soldier in me, I believe, but in those days the wise men, with their usual unerring sagacity, said that there never again would be war. My dear mother barred India, to which country she had already sent three sons; and there was a prejudice at that time against medicine, although Sir Thomas Acland was breaking through it at Oxford with his third son, Henry. I would have gladly worked at medicine as something which pays and is practical, and I now regret that I was not, at any rate, better instructed in secondary subjects, not then in vogue. I knew quite as much Latin and Greek when I went up as I did when I came down, and in mathematics never proceeded further than Euclid and algebra, statics and hydrostatics, with a little trigonometry of a simple description. If only I had been taught modern languages and to draw, the knowledge would have been of great advantage to me in after days, but a soldier's life would have suited me best.

If I had a boy of my own I would teach him handicrafts. He should be not only well read, but able also to turn his hand to all things practical, but that was not then the training of gentlemen. Boat racing was too hard for me, but I rowed in the first Trinity second boat, and had friends in our racing boat, notably Henry Wilkinson, who pulled a strong bow oar, and was my dear friend until nearly forty years later, when stern death took him from me.

An old schoolfellow named Torr kept a horse and, when I could afford it, I used to hire and ride with him. He and I had a friend of the name of Tyler, a nephew of the Bishop of Worcester, Pepys. He was a little fellow and plucky. One day we rode together to the steeplechases at St Ives, and to finish the proceedings there was a scratch consolation steeplechase over the principal course, with catch weights and a two-guinea entry. Tyler asked Torr to lend him his mare, and the owner consented, saying that he did not know whether she had even been jumped in her life. We turned Tyler's jacket inside out to serve for colours, borrowed a cap, and away they went, Tyler leading and taking the first fence at full speed, but he could not hold the mare, or keep her on the course, and soon we saw him disappearing in an erroneous direction, crossing the country and fencing in first-rate style. He is now a quiet West Country clergyman. I wonder whether he remembers the day when he thus rashly imperilled his neck.

Early in my college days I became a disciple of Dr Harvey Goodwin, who was rector of St Edward's Church, in Cambridge, and I always, when I was able to do so, attended his church. He continued to be my most trusted leader until his recent death occurred at Carlisle, of which diocese he was bishop. I also often went to St Mary's, and rather sympathised with the sentiments of the old verger, who remarked that he had heard University sermons preached for thirty years, and thanked God he was a Christian still.

My manner of life led me to cut early chapel, rise rather late, go to lectures or read until about one p.m, then row on the river, walk or ride until about four p.m., when we dined together in hall, Then either give or attend a wine party for dessert and conversation, play billiards for an hour, attend evening chapel and, returning to my rooms, close my outer door, to read something or other and, I am afraid, smoke immoderately. Before examinations, when I was slightly roused to exertion, I would do nearly all my reading between seven p.m. and about two a.m.

We were mad in those days about colouring clay pipes, and I once challenged a friend called Lysley to colour one better and more quickly than myself. It was near the time for the previous University examination usually called the 'Littlego,' and I smoked strong shag tobacco, pipe after pipe.

At that time I always finished the day by reading a chapter in the Greek Testament, and on this occasion when I took up my small copy of that book, at about three a.m., I found that I was suffering from narcotic poisoning. I was not ill, but my hand shook so much that I could not hold the book, and sleep was impossible. Every nerve in my body seemed to be preternaturally awake, and I could have heard a watch tick in another room. Next day I recovered, but I have never again smoked so much, or experienced similar sensations. My pipe, however, had made great progress, and really might well have been worth a halfpenny.

I may here say that neither my friends nor myself were addicted to drinking. I have a strong head and a good digestion, and once or twice in my life I have shared in a heavy drinking bout, on some special occasion, but never so as to be apparently the worse for the excess. That, I think, was the way generally. Men at college were very moderate until some great temptation arose, such as occurred at the supper when they went out of training after the boat races.

There was a Trinity man, a coxswain, who had a club foot. No one knew that he was nervously sensitive about the matter of his infirmity until one night after the races. About midnight the Dean was on the grass plot in the great court, when the gates were opened to allow the Trinity crews to come in from their supper in the town. The telescope with which the Dean was observing the heavens was a large one, and the deformed man who, being short of stature, steered a boat, took it into his tipsy head that the Dean had planted himself in that position to examine *him,* and he remonstrated, 'Mr Dean, Mr Dean, I am very lame and I am very small, but I am not so lame nor so small as to justify you in staring at me through your confounded microscope.'

How well do I remember the Dean's mild reply, 'Take him away, gentlemen, take him away. I fear that the poor young man is intoxicated.'

But there was not much hard drinking at Cambridge in my day, although I think that the fermented liquors, port wine and audit ale were somewhat powerful. What a change has taken place since then in this respect. We now drink Anglo-Bavarian beer, light Bass ale or claret. Then, the ale was brewed sweet and strong. Audit ale would burn like brandy; it was kept for years until it grew hard, and had a biting twang: it must have been good for the production of gout. Cannington, near Bridgwater, was famous for this kind of ale in the days when I travelled frequently through on my way from Selworthy to Bridgwater. If we did not drink beer, we drank port and sherry, but we did not drink much of anything.

I remember a great night at the Union Debating Society when Fitz-James Stephen, the future judge, so exasperated his principal antagonist that he proposed to resort to fisticuffs. I can see Stephen now welcoming the onslaught on the platform, with both hands extended, crying, 'Come on.' I remember, too, a great debate on 'The Capacity of Women,' in which a special friend of mine took the ungallant side.

I knew Whymper,[1] a scholar and, since then, a great Alpine explorer. He was an adept with the gloves, and much interested in the prize ring, which at that time was a flourishing institution on the land. He lent me *Fistiana* to read, a book which contained a record of all the great encounters.

I was at Cambridge before the days of athletics, and my record will look small, but I was a good walker, and made a wager and won it, that I would fairly walk eight miles within ninety-six minutes. I was also umpire when two dear friends of mine, Edward Luard and Norton, afterwards rector of Wellow, walked a twenty-mile match against one another. Horton won, doing the distance on the Ely road within four hours.

One day Tyler was playing cricket on Parker's Piece in flannels when Pepys, his cousin, rode up on a newly-purchased horse. Tyler began chaffing, and said that he could run faster than the horse. Presently they wagered that the race should be for one hundred yards, over ten flights of hurdles, and then Tyler, the impromptu steeple-chaser of St Ives, borrowed the horse and rode him with a will at the high quickset hedge, which guarded the private grounds of the Governor of Cambridge Gaol from Parker's Piece. The horse jumped the fence and landed in an asparagus bed.

Loud shouted the gardener and gave chase. Tyler rode through the vegetables, turned his horse and came back crashing through the cauliflowers in the endeavour to

---

[1] He made the first ascent of the Matterhorn in 1865

jump out on to the road, but the ground, spongy and soft, was lower inside than out, and the horse would not take the leap. Then warders rushed into the garden, and Tyler worked wild havoc as he repeatedly faced the fence, but it was in vain, for he was caught and taken, horse and all, to prison. I well remember Pepys's face as he lost both his horse and his cousin, immured in that dread abode. The Governor, however, was good-natured, and I dare say thought that the jump was a plucky one, for he let man and horse go after an hour or two, and did not complain or prosecute. Perhaps he had once been an undergraduate himself. When the match came off, the horse was nowhere, as he could not pick himself up between the fences, and the man won easily.

I got into a town-and-gown row on November 5th, in the company of Babington, Horton and Luard. We were all biggish fellows, and we thought we could face the roughs, but we were smashed in a moment. I never understood until then what it is to be wholly overmatched.

We went in pluckily enough. I hit out right and left at a man in front of me, and was knocked down from behind, and from both sides at once, by people I did not see. Then the townsmen let me get up, and I saw all my companions down. I had a blow from a turf or piece of peat slung on a string, which curled round me from behind, and filled my eyes with dirt. The crowd opened and we fled, gowns extended in the air, dirty and bruised, with two hundred men and boys in full chase, enjoying the fun. I do not know how it may be when a few determined men, with firearms in their hands, make a stand against overwhelming numbers, but it cannot be done in the open unarmed. There was a good deal of bad feeling at that time between town and University, and I have known some serious encounters take place. The undergraduates were supercilious in their manners, and this was resented.

I remember a man named Wodehouse, (some relation of Lord Kimberley's, I suppose) who was hustled by several townsmen in a passage in Green Street.

'Do you know who I am, sir?' he asked. 'My name is Wodehouse.'

'I don't care if your name is Wodehouse or Woodlouse,' was the reply, and a battle ensued.

But as a rule no great harm was done, because the combatants never attempted a general engagement, but only skirmished in small parties. The bargees on the river were the most pugnacious opponents of the gownsmen. Their Christian charity is well instanced by the story of a Cambridge student who was stretched on the banks of the Cam. He overhead one bargeman say to his mate, 'Who is that bloke on the bank?'

'Don't know,' was the reply.

'Then heave half a brick at him,' said the first.

I myself have seen two undergraduates seize a bargee and fling him headlong into the river. He got out and neither said nor did anything, but there was a look about him which boded ill for the first collegian whom he might meet alone.

It seems difficult to me as I write in my study, an old clergyman, to believe that I was reckless in those days; but I remember well how, when I was playing with singlesticks in Babington's rooms, in the old court of Trinity, I slashed his face all down with the point of my weapon, for we were playing without masks. After we had patched him up somebody said, as he leaned out of the window, which looked into the bowling green behind the chapel, that it was a high drop. On which I offered to run and jump out for a wager of five shillings.

It was taken, so I ran swiftly across the room and, doubling myself together, jumped out of the open window and alighted on my feet and sustained no injury. I do not know the height, but the rooms were on the second storey, and I ought to have broken my back.

Then we all went down to the boats, and behind Jesus College, in the marshes, a horse was apparently asleep, and I offered the loser of the previous wager that for a similar amount I would jump the horse. The wager again was accepted, and sidling gently near to the animal I made a rush and cleared him. I fancy now that I can feel his backbone going up against my body, as the startled animal hastily rose. If he had caught me the fall would, I imagine, have caused a very dangerous accident, but I was young then.

The music at our chapel was good, and the service on Sunday evenings very imposing. The fact that attendance was compulsory made irreverence, I fear, not unknown, and there was a most abominable custom of making the chorister boys sing at St John's, and then taking them away in the middle of the service to sing the same Psalms again at Trinity. They were, inconsequence, perfect imps of mockery.

After service, we often gathered together round Newton's statue in the dim antechapel to hear the voluntary, and on one occasion it was reported that Walmisley produced a marvellous effect by sitting down upon the keys of the instrument. No one knew what had occurred, but the crash was said to be quite sublime.

One day several of us ran over to Ely, and as we delayed on our way to see some coursing, we hurried at the end in order to be in time for the afternoon service in the magnificent cathedral, which was then being restored. We were hot, the cathedral cold, and Luard next day was attacked by marsh ague. I have never seen the malady save only that once, and it is a very sad one. Dear fellow, he died soon afterwards at his father's house at Witham, in Essex, and I was with him at the end. Ely must, I think, be fourteen or fifteen miles distant, and we frequently ran there and back.

At Cambridge I knew three brothers who combined, as I believe, the occupations of dog-stealing and poaching. It is a fact that I bought of them the cleverest dog that I ever owned, but evil communications corrupt good manners, and he had become in their company a sad blackguard of a dog, who would drink gin with avidity. Indeed, he liked his gin and water very sweet, and hot and strong.

The brothers who sold him to me were said to have establishments at Oxford, Cambridge and in London, and they sold dogs at one university to students at the other, and when that game was played out the poor dogs were sent to town. They were smart, stylish, fashionably vulgar young men, and they kept a roomy dog-cart and a spanking, fast-trotting mare. Their system, I believe, was to work in pairs. One brother took the reins and drove slowly through the well-preserved country in the neighbourhood of Cambridge, while the other sat by his side with a short gun in two pieces (the stock in one pocket, the barrels in another), and under the seat was a rather small but very perfect dog.

On reaching a favourable spot, the gun was put together, and into a wood or into a turnip field the poacher went. He was a crack pigeon shot, and he generally managed to get in with right and left barrels; then the dog retrieved, the game was thrown into the well of the cart, the gun was again concealed , and away went the mare at sixteen miles an hour through the level lanes of East Anglia. Three miles further on, and after a hasty glance around, the operation was repeated, and so on towards home.

Gentlemen did not sell their game in those days, and it was therefore more valuable than it is at present, and I have seen as many as twenty hares in one field in the neighbourhood of Newmarket. A good hare was worth five shillings, so the trotting mare paid for her oats, and the excitement of the sport was something additional.

In the spring of 1850 my brother-in-law, Mr Rogers, took me to Paris, together with his son Reginald, who is now vicar of Cookham. I shall never forget that visit, my first to Paris.

Mr Rogers was a very clever and intelligent companion, but much given to neglecting the body. He used to take us sightseeing before breakfast, and would have forgotten the meal altogether if I had not insisted upon being fed by about eleven a.m. I have often seen him wretched and exhausted from having allowed his mind to overbear his body.

At the French Opera we saw a play called *L'Enfant Prodigue,* and to my dying day I shall never forget it. The scene was laid at Memphis. The time was that of Moses. The prodigal son had run away from Goshen to Memphis. The mysteries of Isis consisted to secret eating of beefsteaks by the priests who worshipped the sacred ox. '*Mangeons le boeuf apis,*' they cried. The Israelite had, however, in the temple unsuspiciously gone to sleep, and was discovered. The priests endeavoured to murder him to avert his culinary disclosures, but he escaped by throwing himself into the Nile. There Arabs captured him and took him into the desert. He fainted, and they left him to perish in the sand. Then he dreamed, and you saw his dream, an avenue of angels, with his home in Goshen at the end. The first angels were young women hung up by invisible wires, these were succeeded by paintings, and the spectator could not tell where nature ended and art began. Then the dreamer woke to repentance, and arose and went to his father. I have never again seen anything like the scenery and gorgeous rendering of that piece, and the music was excellent also.

In the summer of 1850 I went with my father and mother to Ems, near Coblenz, and while there we heard of Sir R. Peel's death, caused by a fall from his horse. My father had known him long and felt his loss greatly.

One day I wandered away and got lost in the pine woods at the back of the little town. Presently I came upon a kind of pavilion in the forest, and out of it issued some twenty girls and a few young gentlemen. They took a knotted cord, and putting a clothes ring upon it joined the ends. Then a fine handsome young fellow stepped inside and the girls passed the ring. The young man kept slapping their hands in the endeavour to have the ring, and they all laughed heartily. That young man married our Queen's eldest daughter, and died of cancer in the throat – Emperor of Germany.[2] How little we can foresee our fate!

I caught some carp in the Ems river with cherries for bait. Then my father took me and my elder sister to Switzerland, and he was taken ill of lumbago at Lucerne. I left him, and proceeded with a knapsack on my back to Fluehen, at the end of the lake, where I caught an Italian diligence [coach] and ascended the St Gothard Pass. On approaching the summit I left the conveyance, and obtained the services of a guide to conduct me over the

---

[2] Frederick III, King of Prussia and Emperor of Germany, married Princess Victoria, the Princess Royal in 1858, but died of cancer of the throat on 15 June 1888, after a reign of only 88 days.

snows to the little hospice of the Grimsel. When we were on our way, very near to the Lake of the Dead, a snowstorm came on, and I well remember how instantly lost I was. How the guide kept his head I do not know. Mountain, air, lake, guide, everything was in one moment enveloped in whirling mist, and I lost all reckoning, but the guide held on.

When we reached the wooden shanty, which in winter time is abandoned, I found one visitor sitting down to his dinner. He was just about my own age, twenty years, and he asked me to dine with him, and this I was glad to do. He proved to be an American. Next morning he and I proceeded to walk the thirty miles down the pass to Meiringen; prresently he began to disparage the English.

We were but two boys, and when he talked of frigate actions, I retorted with repudiations. He asked whether if the Americans were displeased we should ever dare to put to sea again, and I, mindful of Sydney Smith, enquired whether his small clothes really were his own, or obtained on loan, never to be returned to their true, but defrauded English owner.

So we grew warm, and our conversation snappy. Presently we came to the Falls of the Aar at Handek. I have never since then been at the place, but it is clear in my memory still, for I ran a fearful risk. My recollection tells me that there is a frightful gorge, very narrow, and that from its throat the Aar river jumps suddenly down some three hundred feet into a dark abyss; as the water falls, another stream, coming at right angles, makes the same leap, and the two torrents intermingle halfway down. Across the Aar, exactly above the fall, a wooden bridge is constructed, which leads to a ledge of rock on the further side, from whence you can see the second stream come down and obtain a further and better view of the boiling chasm.

The bridge was gone, and some workmen had lowered two small pine trees across the passage, the small ends resting on the further side. The trees had been squared above and below. More were to be added, and double rails were to be attached, but only the two little trees that day were there.

To them down we came at well nigh duelling heat, and my companion at once said that he should cross, meaning to shake me off. I replied that of course we should go over, and there was no need to make a fuss about trifles, but I was horribly afraid. The trees were saturated with spray from the waterfall, were slightly apart, and slippery in the extreme, the roar was frightful, and the spectacle generally bloodcurdling to the last degree. There was no hand-rail, no stay of any sort, but, with his nose in the air, straight at it the Yankee went, and crossed. I followed, although the workmen held my arms, and screamed their remonstrances in German Swiss, a peculiar patois that I could only very generally comprehend.

But shaking myself free I also crossed. We then both pretended to look at the view, but in our heads I am sure there was but one thought, viz., how we should even return alive.

Then as he had previously led the way, I held it to be for the honour of England to go first on the return journey. The very narrow ends of the trees were towards me. I longed to throw myself down, clasp the planks with arms and legs, and swarm to the other side, but honour forbade that I should seem to be uneasy. So I crossed, never daring to look at my feet lest I should grow giddy at the sight of the turmoil below. I remember that just under the parted planks the water ran green and swift as it curled over the lip of the precipice.

Well! I am alive today, and I have seen danger since. I have had a loaded pistol snapped at my head at five paces, and incurred other risks, but I never have been, I believe, in such great the imminent danger as when on that August day I literally walked the plank.

We went down to Meiringen together, and I on to Brienz, but we did not quarrel any more. We were sobered. We had proved each other's pluck, and had felt what it is to have the vital force die absolutely down in one's inwards.

In 1851, after growing exhausted at the Crystal Palace Exhibition, Hyde Park, my father took me to Ireland, and it was near to Sligo that I was shown the poteen while my father was haranguing the preventive men. I can still call to memory the shy, startled look of the girl who guided me. It is only in Ireland, and I fancy only in old Ireland, that people will show you something to keep you from knowing anything about it. I caught the only salmon I ever have caught at Ballina. A very large one broke away, but I landed another of seven and a half pounds weight.

The famine was then in the land. It was terrible. 1847–48 had been the worst years; but I saw people dying in the roads in 1851. At Outerarde a curious event occurred. We were to spend Sunday at the place, and after we had dismissed our car on the Saturday afternoon, I took my fishing rod and went to the river; as usual a ragged boy attached himself to me and assumed at once the duties of factotum.

Very soon I was horrified by the sight of a great many women, who were standing near a place where men were hauling in nets full of salmon. These fish were in some instances opened on the spot, and the starving women eagerly devoured the raw offal; the result was frightful, for their skins were red and diseased. After a little while a small boy came to me and said that he had left his mother starving in the mountains, would I give him something. I appealed to my self-constituted factotum, and he confirmed the story, so I gave the boy half-a-crown, and told him to lay it out on food, and to return at once to his mother. Soon afterwards I gave up an attempts at fishing, and turned backwards sick at heart. As I drew near to the inn I saw my father talking to a small boy, and discovered that encouraged by his success with me, the boy had determined to wait and beg again. I took him by the throat, made him disgorge what my father had given him and, abusing him roundly, sent him home to his mother.

Next day being Sunday, I had nothing to do, as there was no Protestant service at Outerarde, so I chartered the factotum to guide me across the mountains to the cabin of the destitute woman. The country around was exceedingly barren, and after a long walk we came upon several cabins. On entering an uncultivated piece of garden ground I saw two girls eating raw seaweed. They had just returned from the shore with a basketful and were eating. Unless the reader has seen famine, actual famine, he will not be able to realise at all the appearance of those girls. They were blue, they were emaciated, they were wild.

In the garden were mounds. In reply to my enquiries they said that these mounds contained the bodies of their father and others of the family, that they could not pay the fees, so they had buried them one after another, as they died in this terrible year of famine, in the garden.

Then I went to the cabin. It had no window, and no chimney, at any rate, the smoke from the peat fire within broke forth as I opened the door and stifled me. I drew on one side, and the woman crawled to me on her hands and knees from her bed of damp straw hear the fire. She could not stand. She was quite naked, save for a strap and a piece of sacking round her loins. I offered to take her to Galway workhouse, to pay for a conveyance, but she refused, alleging that the change would kill her, which was true. She had received the half-crown, but I gave her an additional ten shillings, and left her and her's *to die*.

We had a fine month in Ireland, and drove everywhere in the cars of the country. One day we had a kicking mare. We had gone thirty miles or so with her and she kept on kicking. In an Irish car the driver's legs are in the way of a kicking horse, and our man displayed much agility in getting them out of the way. Presently we came to a long steep ascent, and the driver, taking advantage of the ground, began to thrash the mare very severely indeed. The animal plodded on. Near the summit the man desisted, and spoke sweet words of encouragement. The mare in reply never said a syllable, but waited until she began the descent, and the driver, father, luggage and myself, she kicked us all out into the road, and stood still.

'Does your master allow you to behave in this kind of way?' asked my father.

'Faith, your honour, he says we are well matched, the biggest pair of blackguards in the place, and that he always sets a thief to drive a thief, so the mare and I just go together.'

My father had once been guardian to Lord Clonmel. He was a long-backed man, with prominent teeth. One day in

Dublin he upset some apples from a store, and the owner, a woman, abused him. 'Ah,' she said, 'but you're no better than a comb, anyway.'

He turned round and told her that he would give her a shilling if she could prove to him that he resembled a comb. 'Faith,'she said, 'and are you not all back and teeth?'

I do not feel sure whether it was during my visit to Ireland in 1851 that I had the following conversation with a driver, or whether I have heard it since.

'Pat, who lives in that house?'

'The man who lives in that house is dead, your honour.'

'And when did he die?'

'If he lives until tomorrow he will have been dead a month.'

An Irish inspector of police told me a beautiful story of a sermon. He had gone to a chapel, and the priest whilst preaching enquired of his parishioners, 'What is it that makes you bate your wives?' 'Whisky.' 'And what is it makes ye neglect and ill-treat your poor children?' 'Whisky.' 'And what is it makes you shoot at your landlords?' 'Whisky.' Then, screaming with excitement, he cried: 'And what is it makes you *miss* them?' 'Whisky.' 'O, boys, what more can I say to convince you of the evils of drink?'

In 1852 I was present when the old Duke of Wellington was buried in St Paul's Cathedral, and the scene was very impressive. At that time many of his former companions in arms were still living, and it was a great spectacle to see these veterans in full uniform, adorned with crosses, and medals, and decorations, sorrowing around the coffin which contained all that was left of their famous leader. Most of them were old, and many were maimed and crippled, but they had a splendid appearance, and the hearts of all England were with them in their grief. They were at that time shrinking in number very rapidly, and the annual Waterloo banquet had shortly after to be given up as it became too painful to the survivors to sit down to the ever-shortening tables, and take note of the widening gaps which each year made in their gallant company.

I remember that on one of the last of these anniversaries Mr Popham of Littlecote sent two trout from the Kennet which weighed more than sixteen pounds, as his contribution to the banquet. On the day of the funeral the crush in St Paul's was terrible, and I was fortunate in being able to assist a stout lady to rise, who had fallen literally between two stools, and was in danger of receiving most serious injury.

Then I went to Scotland to stay with my uncle, Lord Leven, who was renting an estate at Moffat, on the border; and there I had the best day's shooting of my life, for I was never a good shot. I brought home that day seven and a half brace of birds, a red grouse, a black grouse, and a snipe, besides two or three hares and some rabbits.

During the same summer I went with a reading party to Rothesay, in the Isle of Bute. Two Cambridge friends of mine, named Evans and Orpen, were of the party, and we read with a Fellow of Trinity Hall, who was engaged to be married to a Miss Morrison, of Rothesay. I took with me a retriever dog, which I had purchased of a dog-stealer of Cambridge, and this dog during its visit to Scotland acquired a taste for whisky, which proved fatal to him in the end. We had a happy summer among the Isles, and one or two adventures, which are worthy of record.

Mr Morrison, brother to the young lady, possessed a line which was two miles long and had hooks attached to it at intervals of a fathom. This line he would lend to us, and we employed two boatmen, named Alexander MacKendrick and Willie MacNaght, to bait it with pieces of herring. It took the men a whole day to bait, and even when herrings were selling for very little the cost was considerable.

Then at about nine o'clock of the night, accompanied by the two boatmen, we used to row away through the Kyles of Bute to some retired arm of the sea, and there we would sink our line with a buoy and a heavy stone at each end, and another buoy in the centre. Then we would approach the shore stealthily, at the same time preparing our splash nets, which were provided by the men and were intended to catch salmon on the sandy shores. Some of the party used to land and hold on to one end of the net, while with muffled oars we let down the remainder in a semi-circle, and landing at the other end we hauled it to shore. Sometimes we caught a salmon in this way but not very often. Afterwards we gathered sticks in the darkness, lit a fire, roasted eggs and potatoes, boiled water and coffee, and supped. Once we burned down a shed under which we had incautiously lighted our fire, but generally we were more careful.

The boatmen had a bottle of whisky provided for them, and they always drank the whole of it *neat*, and apparently did not suffer any inconvenience from the fiery draught, but when, in the interests of sobriety, we substituted beer for the spirits, I remember that they became somewhat intoxicated with the milder but unaccustomed beverage.

Then breaking our shins and risking our necks we used to clamber to the summmit of the nearest cliff in order to see the sun rise, but as soon as the first streak of dawn appeared in the east we generally raced down again to the beach and, leaping into the boat, rowed for the nearest buoy and began taking in our line. It was marvellous to see the quantity of fish that we caught, fish of all sorts and sizes; but the principal excitement occurred when a large conger eel was brought to the surface of the water. We did not care to take him into the boat uninjured, so when the gaff was into him, and as he was being lifted over the gunwhale, one of the party would chop at him with a hatchet. If he hit too hard the body fell back into the sea and was lost, and if he did not hit hard enough to sever the spine the fish would go snapping along the bottom of the boat, and I have seen all legs swung overboard out of the way while each man did his best to kill the poor creature. Then we pulled back into Rothesay with our knees buried in gasping, slimy fish.

We were exceedingly popular, we were civil, and easily pleased. We owned the line, we bought the bait and paid for it being put upon the hooks. Then we hired the boat, and paid the men for being out all night, besides giving them supper, plenty of whisky, and nearly all the fish.

Our popularity stood some of us in good stead, for one night one of our party heard the sound of music and dancing, and came and told the rest. They went into the street and saw, though the blinds of an upstairs room, the revolving forms of dancing couples. They applied respect-fully for admittance, and were refused. Some Glasgow or

Paisley artisans had brought down their sweethearts for a jollification: they were literally paying the piper, and naturally did not wish to see their young women monopolised by Cambridge undergraduates, who would only be too ready to call the tune.

One of our number was a long tall Welshman, and presently he reached up to the balcony outside the ballroom and, with assistance, hoisted himself in; he then helped up a couple of his companions who, after breaking the glass of the balcony door, entered with him cap in hand with an expression of hope that they did not intrude. The girls giggled, the men scowled, and the rest of the reading party coming in, sent for half a dozen of champagne, and ere long had almost a monopoly of the young ladies, who possibly were not unwilling to pique their admirers. The men, meanwhile, remained silent and sullen, until in the early hours of the morning we withdrew, to seek our lodgings and repose.

Our party had not gone far down the street when they heard a rush from behind them, then in another moment they were engaged in a serious hand-to-hand encounter with the men whom they had annoyed. It was really serious: the long Welshman, as I am sorry to narrate, ran away; but one of our party, taking a Paisley man by the throat, dashed his head through the window of a cottage in the street. I remember that in so doing he cut his own wrists most severely with the glass. The Cambridge men were, however, getting the worst of the fight, when their cries brought our boatman, Willie MacNaght, from his bed. They did not know or remember that they were near his house, but he heard them and, armed with an oar, he rushed to their aid.

A great gaunt, sallow man, he must have been very powerful, for with long sweeps of his oar he soon turned the tide of battle, and our party pursued the retiring artisans right back to the gates of their fortress, where they left them to patch up an angry peace with their fair but inconstant sweethearts.

We had some adventures during that happy summer. Once we took a large cutter, very light in the water from want of ballast, and sailed to the neighbouring island of

Arran. Here we spent the night, after ascending the mountain called Goatfell. Next day we were becalmed, and were unable to row by reason of the height of the decks above water, so we drifted about in cloudless sunshine amid shoals of porpoises, which flapped and rolled like great black pigs in our wake, and all around us. We had no provisions and no water on board, but we had a case of beer and plenty of tobacco, and it was then that, one of our party breaking a bottle accidentally, I first learned the intemperate nature of my black dog, 'Sailor.' He greedily lapped up the liquor.

Presently a gale came on, and we raced through the Kyles of Bute, and reached Rothesay in safety late at night. I remember how a seal that evening popped her head out of water, and looked at me quite closely through her large melancholy eyes. She was just like a dripping woman, and in a moment I understood how the tales of the mermaids came to be told and believed.

After supper one of my companions gave my dog a tumbler full of sweet strong whisky-toddy, and this he drank even as he had drunk the beer. It was the beginning of the end, for I was never able to restrain my friends from giving him wines and spirits until the poor dog died of drink, and of eating copper coins, at Cambridge.

Once we lost our tutor, Mr Walton, and having no one to read with, started in search. We were much amused when we discovered him, with his young lady by his side, perched upon the top of a high stone wall, with a little black bull rampaging below. They said that they could not get down on the safe side on account of a fall in the ground, but we did not believe that they desired to do so.

On my return to Cambridge, one day Mr Grant, who was rector of Hellions Bumpstead, asked me and one Brownlow (he had known us formerly at Rugby) to dine with him. We accepted; and Brownlow and I tossed up to decide who should drive. I won the toss. Hellions Bumpstead is about twenty miles from Cambridge, a village which boasts of having been the birthplace of Dick Turpin, and has in it the largest oak tree in England,

We reached our destination, and remained until about ten p.m. On going out we found that snow had fallen, and

Brownlow refusing to drive on a dark night in snow, I again took the reins. We had a spanking sixteen-hands-high mare in a dogcart, and there remained only two hours in which to get back before college gates were closed. All, however, went well until I was sending the long mare at best pace down the slope of the Gog Magog Hills, just after leaving Linton. Here the snow balled in her feet, and while going at the rate of some twelve miles an hour, down she came. I do not know how the exalted ecclesiastic, now at Clifton, felt at that moment, but I well remember how I grasped at the mare's ears as I went over her down the hill into darkness, going well, like a man, to the front!

Brownlow and I had shared the same study at Rugby; we both belonged to a special debating society, and were intimate with each other. Some time afterwards he turned Roman, and we parted company, but that night he and I had together about as 'imperial a crowner' as has ever come in my way.

Was it then that the Dean of Trinity distinguished himself by issuing the notice, 'Thornton to call on the Dean at eleven a.m. Out after twelve on Saturday night. Such irregularity cannot be allowed on a Sunday morning.'?

And now, in 1853, I took my B.A. degree, but I did not go in for honours. When I went up to the Senate House to take my oath, and obtain my degree, an official handed me a copy of the foolish oath which made me declare that I abjured the Pope and the Pretender, the Khedive and the Mahdi, or some other quite impossible conjunction of people. I had never seen that oath before, and as it was in Latin, and I had scruples about oaths, I was endeavouring to translate it to find out what it meant, when James Payn, the novelist, who was of my year, and a friend, snatched it away, remarking, 'Never mind! It is in a dead language and ought to be dead itself to boot; as the boys say, it does not count.'

CHAPTER SIX

Countesbury

IN JANUARY 1853 I left Cambridge. My kind aunt, Miss Selina Parry, gave me one hundred pounds and told me to buy a good horse, as I was, no doubt, mentally overworked, and a judicious course of hunting would do me good. I bought a chestnut of Quartermaine, in Piccadilly, for seventy pounds, and spent the remainder of my aunt's present upon saddlery, purchased of Wilkinson and Kidd. Wonderful saddlery! I use one of those bits still in 1897, and it has been in the mouths of various horses for many tens of thousands of miles. The leather was also as good as the steel. There is no leather like it to be found nowadays. We have advanced downhill from such a standard of excellence.

I took the horse at once to my brother's house at Candover and rode him for two days a week with the H.H. and Hambledon hounds. He did not turn out very well, so I sold him again in April, and he was, I believe, killed in the cavalry charge at Balaclava while carrying an officer up to the guns in the Russian batteries.

This horse opened my young eyes. When I bought him he was a thorough-bred cob, and in a fortnight, after I had heedlessly ridden off his dealer's condition, he was a thorough-bred weed – more than one half of him was gone. Great care should always be taken of horses that are bought of a dealer. They are fit for nothing for a month, and no one can say what they will turn into. That horse was nearly killed by being asked to gallop too soon, and in my opinion it is generally far better to buy a rake and to build him up, than it is to pay a long price for good looks and dealer's condition.

Iron wire was rare in those good old days, though now it is too common; but I remember that in a run near Alresford, while I was riding this horse, we came to a wire fence. A Mr Knight of Ropley then kept the hounds. He and his huntsman got down, hung up their red coasts on the wire and kindly allowed the field to ride over their coats, which was done by all of us without accident. This reads as a trifling incident, but only he who has known what it is to be hung up on a fence of wire has any idea of the exceeding danger and horror of the situation. A well-bred horse so caught is transformed in one moment into a raging demon, and is regardless of all consequences either to his rider or to himself.

In April my father gave me sixty pounds, telling me to take my sister to Paris, and to return when the money was gone. Miss Stainforth joined us with thirty pounds more of her own, and the money was entrusted to my keeping. After we had worked really hard at sight-seeing, and were tired, I asked the ladies whether they would like to visit the Lake of Geneva in the early spring; and on hearing that they would be delighted to go there if the money would hold out, I took tickets for Dijon, where the railway ended, without troubling myself as to how we were to get on from thence.

We left Paris at ten a.m., and reached our destination by dinner time. At the hotel we were told that the vehicle which carried the letters started from the railway station at one a.m., and that it carried three passengers. We therefore drove out of the town at midnight, and our conveyance deposited us at the terminal and returned to the town.

It is difficult to believe, but the station master actually refused to allow us to go inside the enclosure, and with that want of politeness which frequently characterises French officials, he thus compelled two ladies to sit on their trunks in an open road at midnight, until the train came in from Paris. It was behind its time, and out of it sprang a man who was armed with a through ticket to Geneva. I begged him to allow us to proceed. I said I would sit on the luggage or occupy the banquette with the driver, but he was violently rude, and refused to sanction any stretch of the rules which governed the use of the vehicle.

We were left, in consequence, outside the station, a mile from the town, and with no means to remove our luggage, as everyone had gone to bed. There was nothing for it but to anathematise French rudeness and see out the night, which was fortunately fine. The ladies, however, trudged back to the hotel and spent the time in a sitting room.

When the morning came, a man drove up to the railway station in a very dirty carriage which was drawn by a gaunt old horse, in conjunction with a small pony. This conveyance I engaged to take us to Dole, and after picking up the luggage I drove into Dijon to tell the two ladies what I had done. We were all very miserable, and we started at once in the early dawn. We crept, we crawled, but we reached Dole in time for dinner, and obtained places in the Besançon diligence at about eleven p.m., or later.

Then on we went over the Jura mountains, climbing higher and higher until at last we became embedded in deep snow. It was dark, and the wind was blowing hard, but the men quietly took out the horses and went away, leaving us passengers alone in the cold to speculate upon the possibility of being attacked by wolves. After some hours of absence the drivers returned with sledges, to each of which two horses were attached, and in this fashion at early dawn we rattled down to Lausanne, where we arrived about three p.m. The ladies had travelled from ten a.m. on Thursday until three p.m. on Saturday without being able to undress, and we had not tasted food since we left Dole on the previous evening. However, none of us suffered, and I well remember the grand sights to be seen as the day dawned on the snowy mountains, and we glided in our sledges into the low country of Switzerland.

The lowlands round Geneva were covered with wild flowers of all kinds, and resembled a beautiful garden. I have never seen the Lake of Geneva since that spring, but I am told that the little villages have grown into great towns, and that the pleasant apple-covered slopes bristle with huge hotels.

That summer I spent at Cambridge, reading for what, by a pleasant fiction, was called the Voluntary Theological

Examination, which the bishops required Cambridge men to pass before they would ordain them. My old friend Babington, who had rooms in the Great Court of Trinity, lent them to me, and I occupied them from about June until the end of October. Two other Trinity men, already acquaintances, also came up on the same errand, and I made the firm and lifelong friendship of them both. They were Richard Kindersley, son of the Vice-Chancellor, and Henry Wilkinson, of boating reputation, bow-oar of the first Trinity eight.

We were inseparable. We read the Greek Testament twice through together. We ate, drank, read, rode, boated together, and examined each other in theology. Kindersley was a wonderful pool player, a dead hand at a winning hazard, and he and I had our game together every evening before we settled ourselves down to read church history.

Kindersley kept a horse, and my father, towards the end of the vacation, allowed me to have one. So I bought Fisherman for fifteen pounds, a bay with broken knees, and he was the first horse I ever jumped a five-barred gate upon. We were rather fond of riding to Audley End, Lord Braybrooke's place, and of ordering and eating our dinner at the inn. One day we walked round outside the park and were unable to find the bell, which hung pendant inside an iron gate near a lodge. Some little truffle-dogs (for truffles grow in the neighbourhood) were playing with each other on the grass, and one of them, after watching us as we fumbled fruitlessly at the gate, left his companions, jumped up, caught the handle with his teeth, and rang the bell violently as he swayed to and fro in the air.. The lodge-keeper came out and told us that the dog often thus rang the bell for visitors; and then the little beast went back to his game, apparently unconscious that he was a rational animal.

One day in September I had a letter from Mr Halliday to say that Mr Mundy, the vicar of Lynton, wanted a curate, and that I could have the curacy, but that there would be no pay with it. My father, however, kindly said that he would allow me two hundred pounds a year. I was enamoured of the West Country, and therefore agreed with Mr

Mundy to take entire charge of the little parish of Countesbury, and to assist him sometimes also at Lynton, for the modest stipend ot twenty pounds a year.

In October I passed the Voluntary Theological Examination, sold Fisherman, bought of Death and Dyson (Diesoon) a big bay mare named Cochin China, and said goodbye to Kindersley and Wilkinson, who went from Cambridge to Wells Theological College.

I, on the contrary, took the new mare to Candover, to my brother's parish, and rode her hard with the Hampshire hounds until it was time to go down to the West in December, to be examined and ordained by that redoubtable prelate, Henry of Exeter. He was by far the most formidable man with whom I have met in my life, the only man of whom I have ever been afraid; everyone was afraid of him. He did not, however, altogether gain my respect, for he warned us young deacons against dancing at a time when his own son, a clergyman, possibly unknown to him, was giving a ball in Exeter, while he was at Bishopstowe.

After my ordination on a Sunday in Exeter Cathedral, I went to stay with Sir Thomas Acland at Killerton, until Thursday, when, in floods of rain, I went to Crediton by raid, and there took a coach for Barnstaple, driving on from thence to Lynton in a private conveyance. Mr Mundy took me in until I could secure lodgings. He was a married man, with a niece and a nephew residing with him. He had taken a high degree at Oxford some years before, but had, as I considered, somewhat run to seed, and was not so able a man as in youth he had promised to be. He was, however, very kind, and kept me until a few days later, when I had, ambitious young man as I was, taken a whole house called Island Cottage, consisting of two furnished sitting and five bedrooms, a kitchen, back kitchen and flower garden.

I had at that time an income of two hundred and twenty pounds, of which the Bishop or his secretary, together with Exeter expenses, consumed annually twenty pounds. Cochin China came down, together with a favourite white terrier with one black ear named Crib. So I hired a stable and engaged a young shoemaker to groom the mare. She cost me another forty pounds, so that I had one hundred and twenty pounds to keep me in food, drink, clothes and travelling.

I was never so rich in my life, and I have never lived so well. Mrs Bevan [his landlady] delighted in me, for I allowed her to do whatever she liked. I breakfasted late and heavily, at about half-past nine, and then required nothing more until I returned to dinner at about eight. Soon she became famous for her dinner parties. I left all the arrangements to her, and old Lord Castlereagh, Foreign Secretary of England, in all his glory, was not dined better than the curate and his friends; only, it was too magnificent.

If the women do not want to marry the men, at least they like to spoil them, especially curates; and with Mrs Bevan at my back, with her excellent cuisine, youth and good health on my side, a crack blood mare beneath me, keen professional inclinations and instincts, tempered by a strong love for rod and gun and hound, fondness for bird and beast and plant, with Glenthorne always open to me, and a wealth of friends in the dear old Selworthy district, twenty miles away, with a liking for solitude, and an aptitude for men and possibly for women, I was petted and made too much of.

In those days, at three-and-twenty, I knew no fear and scoffed at fatigue, bad weather and exposure. Nothing came amiss, and I would walk, ride, shoot, fish and drive with anybody. I was great, moreover, on the cliffs, and was never tired of risking my life, often alone, hanging and clinging in mid-air on the Foreland, seeking for eggs. The boatmen were fond of me, and many a stormy trip I made with them to Ilfracombe and elsewhere. The wild shooting over the Glenthorne property was at my disposal. My basket would hold fourteen pounds weight of trout, and I thought scorn of the day on which I could not fill it.

I was keen in my parish work, also. But what did I know about it? Countesbury was handed over to me absolutely, week-day and Sunday alike, with its school and two hundred and fifty inhabitants.. As to Lynton, with its two thousand, I might do what I pleased, much or little; but Countesbury was my own domain, and I was twenty-three – *i.e.,* absolutely ignorant.

Is there any other profession in which such a state of things would be tolerated? I know not, but at that time I took it all as a matter of course. Kindersley and Wilkinson were learning something of their business at Wells, but I – well! My assurance now seems to me to have been quite amazing.

Bishop Philpotts said to me, with the satire natural to him upon his lips: 'Young man, I suppose you will be wanting to preach. I wish for one year I could silence you altogether, but I cannot, as there are two churches to be served. You would like also, I daresay, to preach your own sermons, and this, no doubt, would be excellent practice for you; but think, sir, of the inconceivable sufferings you would inflict upon your unfortunate hearers.

'No, for the first year I command you never to preach if you can help so doing, and when you cannot, select one of Bishop Andrewes' sermons. It would take an hour to deliver, translate it into modern English, cut it down to twenty minutes, and however much you may bungle it, you cannot do much harm by your clumsiness.'

But, as I wrote before, I was in high wrath with him about his apparent inconsistency in the matter of dancing. So I gave him no heed.

And what did I know about elementary education; or what did I know of the wants of the dying? Everybody, too, patted me on the back; everyone had a kind word for my youthful assurance. So, like the green fool that I was, I plunged boldly in where angels would fear to tread. And I did not do so badly after all. I had some money, some influence, popularity, energy, and aptitude for children.

At once I laid my hands upon the school. It was two miles away, on the summit of Countesbury Cliff. It was kept by Mrs Elworthy, the widow of a butcher of Lynmouth, and she knew positively nothing. It was never inspected, no one cared for it, and few children attended it.

Well, I bought some books and I asked a Miss Hollier of Lynmouth to help me. She was at the time engaged to be married, and therefore was safe. She was of resolute turn of mind, and she wanted occupation. Mrs Elworthy was not averse to having her school quadrupled. So to work we went. Miss Hollier started on foot up the mountainside in all weathers and every day by half-past nine a.m.. By ten I followed, sometimes on Cochin China, more often on foot. Soon we had some forty children, and we taught them by might and main. We knew nothing of the tricks of the trade, but every child was of burning, living interest to us both, and we grudged the school no hours. On most days I taught until nearly one o'clock; I engaged competent amateur examiners, and before an examination we would often teach in the afternoon as well as in the morning. We lent books, we made friends of the children, and I can truly say that never, in after years, and with the aid of trained, certificated, paid teachers, have I turned out a better lot of children than were those old Countesbury youngsters of 1854–55.

Where are they now, those children of more than forty years ago? I do not know; but I hope that somewhere or other there are still intelligent, middle-aged men and women who think kindly and speak kindly of the untrained efforts of the uninstructed but eager curate and his first lieutenant, Miss Henrietta Hollier.

We created a sensation, for good education was not in lonely places general in those days, and I think that the older people liked us, but were amused at what I dare say they thought was our eccentric and Quixotic enterprise. I feel sure that this was the view taken by our old Squire and his Scotch wife at Glenthorne.

The wind blows so hard upon the top of Countesbury Hill that I have, before now, waited for the children to leave, formed them into a string, and personally conducted them under the hill before I parted from them, fearing lest I should otherwise see some little scholar going away at the height of a thousand feet, head foremost towards Wales. This may sound absurd, but I have tales to tell of the power of moorland wind which will rob it of all its absurdity.

And I was equally audacious in other matters of clerical life. I never felt nervous; my parishioners spoiled me and turned my head, so I little thought then, as I thundered away at the visitors in Lynton Church with all the wisdom of my twenty-three years, what I have often thought since in my maturity – viz.: how extremely likely it was that in the congregation in front of me there were those who were much more fitted to teach me than I them.

In those days I use to think that anyone who did not agree with me was, must be, a fool, pure and simple; and here again I lay the blame upon my parishioners, who, instead of treating a great, green boy with a kindly sympathetic wisdom, would frequently address me with the remark, 'What a beautiful sermon that was of yours yesterday. I only wish we could have you always.' Oh, ladies, ladies! You have much to answer for.

And it was just the same with the sick and dying, I knew about as much of sickness or of death as does a strong tom-cat. Bursting myself with health and energy, I could not properly sympathise with either, but I was kindly, and generally carried with me a good book, so that elders of eighty years and upwards actually often submitted to my crude ministrations.

Lynmouth was then a small village, with few permanent residents, and those few were horribly divided into cliques and sections. I had, of course, the entry into all houses. The more exclusive set associated with certain regular summer and sporting visitors, among whom was Captain West, who brought with him his stag-hounds from Bath. Outside, and away from the parish, I knew everyone, nearly down to Taunton on one side and to Barnstaple on the other. So Cochin China, like Polly, her predecessor in the west, had enough of it. But she was a big blood mare, nearly sixteen hands, and in after days she once carried me seventy miles before noon, when I rode to detect a murderer. Like many a good horse of mine, both before and since her time, distance never made the least impression upon her. She was absolutely indomitable.

My curate days were days of fishing. I had been sufficiently keen on the rivers while residing at Selworthy, but now I was almost an otter. There was not in that country a brook with which I was not intimately acquainted, from Heddon's Mouth to Dunster, aye, even to the Williton Water. Many and good were my fishing allies. Among them, first in excellence came Robert Gould. He once caught more than three hundred trout in one day, and hired a horse to convey them to Ilfracombe, where he resided. Captain Leeds was nearly as good – almost the only man I have ever known who would say, 'Do you see that fish? He is a good one, and feeding. Now, I will go home, fetch my rod, and catch him.' And catch him he would.

The fish were not large. I once sent nine trout, which I had selected out of twenty, to Mrs Colville Roe, who was giving a dinner party at the Manor House. These fish weighed collectively three and a half pounds. I caught them with a natural fly in some deep pits below Wiltsham. On one occasion, in three successive days' fishing I caught ninety-seven, one hundred and nine and one hundred and thirteen trout respectively. This could not now be done.

Those were happy years. Often I met with Captain Moresby when he was ashore, and Captain Gore was my frequent companion on the river. He was the youngest son of an Irish Earl of Arran, one of a very large family. His nose had been broken by the fall of a block which was cut away by a round shot during his first naval action, at a time when he was, I believe, only eleven years of age. He told me that when that day the cannon balls began to whistle over the deck, they caused him and one or two more midshipmen of like childish age to duck their heads. This being observed from the quarter-deck, the Captain roared, 'What are you bobbing for, you boys? Did you never see a round shot before?' A minute later another shot came singing close over the captain's head, and involuntarily and unconsciously he bent before it, and was ever afterwards named 'Old Bob' by the boys.

I was very intimate, also, with the Hollier family, who shortly before my arrival had migrated from South Wales to Lynmouth. They were closely associated with Mr Babbage, the mathematician and inventor of a calculating machine. I had been at college with one of the sons, and when he came down to stay with his parents, we read the Greek Testament together diligently, and talked much of theology. By him I was introduced to a Mr Snowden, who every year arrived from Bath to spend his summers at Lynton.

Snowden was a kindly bachelor of fifty-six years, with ample means, and we all became very intimate with him. He was a great walker, so we would sometimes breakfast together, take a boat, sail down the coast to Ilfracombe or to Minehead, and run home some twenty miles, to dine with him at Mrs. Blackmore's lodgings, which he always occupied in the season. There we had a grand entertainment, and a full supply of first-rate wine, for our host was a famous judge of brands and vintages. Sometimes I gave a return entertainment, and as Mrs Bevan, my landlady, had been cook to a Foreign Secretary, and I let her do as she pleased, my dinners were perfectly sumptuous.

Snowden introduced me to Captain West, who brought his pack of stag-hounds from Bath and hunted the Exmoor deer. West himself ran like the stags he hunted, and loved so to keep down his weight. I can almost see him now – as the rest of us, Snowden, Hollier, Bush and myself, plodded our way over Hangman Hill on our return from Ilfracombe – running down the steep inclines again in front of us, traversing the country backwards and forwards like a hound, the better to work off his superfluous flesh and energy.

Snowden was very kind; if there was a case of distress, he would assist most liberally. I remember that at this time I adopted an idiot child named Mary Marshall, whose widowed mother actually died in the act of committing her to my charge. I promised the poor woman to take care of her daughter until she was old enough to go into service, unless she should prove to be incapable of earning her own livelihood. This was rather rash of me but Mr Snowden came to my rescue, and between us we boarded the child out until Mrs Hayes thought fit to interfere and induced us to send the little girl to an asylum in Bath. There she grew worse rather than better, and after five years her uncle took charge of her, and finally sent her to the workhouse. Snowden had pensioners all over the country, and our long walks were often taken to see some crippled boy or bed-ridden woman who owed much to his kind liberality.

So time wore on. In the morning I read a chapter of the Greek Testament, breakfasted, ran up to school at Countesbury, returned and, mounting Cochin China, rode far and wide visiting my parishioners, often with fishing rod in hand and basket at back. Then I returned to dinner and went out in the evening to one or other of my friends' houses, if I did not dine at Glenthorne, as was the case very frequently.

I do not think that I read a great deal. Old Bevan had the Weir, and at night I would accompany him with Crib [the dog] by my side, and, provided with a lanthorn and a walking-stick, I used to knock down and bring in the fish that were stranded by the receding tide. Many a hot chase I have had after a fine salmon, Crib swimming and yapping, I wading with uplifted stick and lanthorn held aloft, stumbling over the great boulders and occasionally extinguishing the light.

It was at this time that I first became acquainted with the working of the Temperance Movement. Mr Collard, a retired solicitor from Wellington, was its apostle, and I remember how surprised I was to find that the boatmen, who at his instigation had taken the pledge, would drink spirits if they were given to them. 'What?' I said to Ned Groves (who is still living) when Captain West had given him a brandy flask to drain. 'Are you not a teetotaller?'

'Of course I be; but this don't cost me nothing, do it?', he replied.

In after years I saw much of this kind of thing, and it has made me somewhat mistrustful of the value of the movement. After all, if conscience, self-interest, religion and regard for family will not restrain a man from intoxication, is it likely that a signature to a paper will prove effectual?

In the summer of 1854 Mr Knight came down to lodge, and I was introduced to his charming wife. They both took a great fancy to me, and exercised much influence over me. The Knight family were bearing rather hardly on Mr Knight. It was an instance of the old case where a father over-estimates the value of his property, and, leaving an

undue proportion to his younger children, too much
impoverishes his eldest son. Mr Knight, however, still
clung to the land, overburdened with charges though it
was, and at this time he was engaged in an attempt to
induced the Guests from Merthyr Tydfil to take up iron
mining on his Exmoor property. I was fairly carried away
by enthusiasm, and espoused my friend's cause with heart
and soul.

He was a hard rider, a dead shot, a man of many adventures; and she was witty, unfortunate, very beautiful, and
twenty-two. They made me their friend, they told me their
troubles, they asked me to be guardian to their boy in the
event of the father's death, and in return I ransacked the
hillsides of Exmoor in search of iron ore, and rode long
and late with one of the boldest riders who ever crossed a
horse.

I remember on one occasion having breakfasted with Mr
Knight at three on an October morning, we mounted our
horses as soon as we had finished and cantered away up
the Watersmeet Valley. I rode on Cochin China and he was
on a big brown Dongola horse, with four white feet and a
white nose, of his own breeding – for the Knights believed
in Arab blood. Our objective was Bampton, where he had
forty or more ponies for sale by auction. He told me that
his Worcestershire friend, Sir Thomas Sebright, wished
him to send up two good ponies for his wife, and he asked
me to help him select them. They were all unbroken and
perfectly wild, and he had never seen them before,
although they were his property.

When we reached Cheriton Ridge he began to gallop in
the starlight over the broken ground, and it was hard to
keep up with him on the Chains. Through the deep
ground, however, we went, and on reaching Simonsbath
we found his old servant Sam Harwood, with two horses
saddled, awaiting us on the road. We changed and cantered on, reaching Bampton before eight o'clock. We had,
I suppose, ridden thirty miles or thereabouts. I remember
well how that morning I despised the Bampton people,
who were only just leaving their beds and peeping at us
from their windows as we rode by. Then we breakfasted
again and walked out to the paddock to see the ponies.

We chose two, say Nos. 13 and 27, and he requested me to buy them for him at the sale. This I presently accomplished, but I had to pay about sixty guineas before I could secure them. Mr Knight was wondering how his friend would like the price, when a tall man approached us and bitterly complained that he had come all the way from Birmingham to buy ponies, only to find the best bought in by the owner. He said that he was a horse-dealer. Mr Knight replied that there was reason in his complaint, and that he might have the ponies if he pleased, at the price. The man took them, and, as I afterwards heard, lost them in Birmingham, where the little beasts broke away from the station and were only with infinite trouble recaptured.

The ordinary price of an unbroken four-year-old pony was about ten pounds, so I congratulated myself upon my good judgment in selecting beforehand the two longest-priced ponies on record. That day at Bampton I made the acquaintance of Mr Leech, the artist for *Punch,* who was accompanied by Mr Higgins, the terrible 'Jacob Omnium' of those days, and the friend of Thackeray. Then we rode back to dinner at Lynton, picking up our second horses at Simonsbath.

My life as a curate was naturally very uneventful. I was nearly ubiquitous. Nothing came amiss to me. If I could not drive, I rode, and if I could not ride, I ran; and forty miles, more or less, were nothing to me whether with a horse or without one. I was only engaged to take one Sunday service, that at Countesbury, and the clergy for many miles around took advantage of this circumstance, and of my bodily activity, to get their churches served gratuitously when they were unwell or absent from home.

I have before now taken three full services, with christenings and funerals between, have been wet to the skin before I began the first of them, and have neither changed clothes nor taken nourishment until I returned home, after riding perhaps twenty or thirty miles and experiencing three or four separate wettings, one upon the top of the other, and I have never taken a guinea from anyone in all my life.

The younger generation of clergy will think I was a fool for my pains, and few of them would care to follow my example, yet even now, in my sixty-eighth year, I am often similarly worked and greatly exposed.

Naturally my willingness in these matters made me popular, and I had the run of all the houses within some twenty miles of my residence, and could shoot or fish wherever I pleased. Two nieces, daughters of my brother Edward, who was then a Commissioner under Government in the Punjab, kept house for me during the summer months, and my parents and other relatives visited me from time to time. These nieces were with me when I met with an accident, from the effect of which I have never entirely recovered.

On my way to Glenthorne I was chased by a bull, and, running for my life, I leaped down from a wall which skirted the cliff behind the Foreland. There was a clean drop of about ten feet, and as I jumped I turned to see how close was my pursuer, with the result that my body was twisted at the moment when my feet touched the ground. My back was ricked, and I lay disabled while the bull regarded me with anger from above. He was, however, far too heavy to care to follow, and was satisfied to have driven me away. After a while I managed to walk on to Glenthorne, but the Hallidays being absent from home, I returned to Island Cottage to dinner. When afterwards I endeavoured to rise from my chair, I could not do so, but was carried off and put to bed by Mr Bevan and his wife.

I then sent for Mr Clarke, the Lynton doctor, the man who kept the tame stag whose horns are now in the Exeter museum. He was a very rough, old-fashioned doctor, and exclaimed, 'What made you send for me? Get Mother Bevan to rub in some hartshorn and oil and then to iron you down with a very hot flat iron. You will feel the effects of this accident so long as you live.' And truly, ever since that time I am apt to get crippled in the back at certain seasons of the year.

The spring of 1854 was one of the coldest on record. Wild ducks, wild geese and wild swans were on the coast. The snow lay deep, and on a snowy night in March a barque from Bristol ran ashore below Glenthorne. As soon as I heard of the occurrence, I set off, and after wading through drifts five and six feet high I arrived at last at the smugglers' cave below Glenthorne. Here the vessel lay on the rocks, partly out of the water, hard and fast. The crew had left her and were quartered in the cave. Never did I see such rubbish as her cargo consisted of: Calico brightly striped, all shoddy and dressing; tin swords, beads, muskets which shot round the corner, if indeed they could be discharged at all; rubbish of all kinds, on its way to South Africa, to be exchanged with the poor natives for ivory and gum. If I remember rightly, this vessel was ultimately floated off and assisted into dock.

During that great snow I walked to church on the summit of a high wall, with my congregation behind me. We balanced ourselves and felt our way with sticks, for if we had stepped aside we should have been buried either in the field or in the lane below. My people were very good, and many of the men came to church. They knew that I had waded often waist deep in snow up from Lynmouth, so they turned out from their firesides to support me.

I sometimes think that this old loyalty of feeling is weaker than it was. The sense of duty, also, is less strongly developed nowadays than formerly, and although my parishioners in North Bovey behave well to me on the whole, yet they do not stand by me as did the men of North Devon. 'What does it matter to him whether we attend or not? He has a stiff journey to Doccombe, no doubt, but why on that account should *we* take cold?' So they say. Years ago the poor may have been sometimes driven to church, and otherwise treated inconsiderately, but now the tables are turned, and I think they often neglect to do their part in that sacred but unwritten contract which exists between man and man.

In some respects our country people have improved, but they are not now, I fear, as loyal to either church or state as were their forefathers. 'Nothing matters,' so they say. I see this tendency to carelessness exhibited in a thousand ways, and I am sorry it is so. Times were harder then than now. It was better worth while to take pains, and more necessary to work hard in order to obtain a livelihood. Most people were trained to be self-denying.

Machinery has displaced hard labour, and the very men who in my boyhood broke out into riot and burned machines because they interfered with labour, will not now do the work which they then coveted. Cheap jam, cheap bacon, cheap lace, cheap stockings, cheap shirts and dresses have displaced old household industries, and thus enabled working men and women to find time to read the cheap and often objectionable literature of the day.

Their political power has increased, they travel about and see more of the world than formerly, and the general result is that they are slacker in their habits and more easy-going than they used to be. The change is not, however, all in the wrong direction, for they are more intelligent and gentler in their ways, as well as far better off and more comfortable than were their forefathers when I was ordained.

In the autumn of 1854 the Crimean war broke out, and great was the general excitement. I shall never forget the impression which was produced upon the people of Devonshire as the stories of the Alma and Inkerman were told, and when they became acquainted with the sufferings of our men in the trenches before Sebastopol. My nephew, Mr Rogers, was with the 33rd Regiment. Charles Turner and my two cousins, Lord Balgonie and Captain Haygarth, were in the Guards. The former escaped without injury. Turner carried the colours of his regiment, if I remember aright, at the Alma. He and Balgonie both lived to return to England, only to die of their privations.

Haygarth still survives, although he was shot through both shoulder and thigh as he went up the steep slope above the Alma. A certain Captain Villiers came wounded from the war to Lynmouth. He had been spitted on a Russian bayonet as he leaped down from the parapet into the Redan or the Quarries. He had a great ghastly wound in his side when he dined with me at Mrs Bevan's somewhere about this time. He had a brother, a major in the same regiment with himself, and he could not keep quiet, but got up from his chair and walked about during dinner time declaring that he had no business to be at home, and that he felt sure the Russians would do for 'Charlie' before he could return to him.

The family had formerly lived in Bath, and when they left for Tours had bricked up their wine cellar, but an ex-servant burrowed underground, and when the Colonel returned, at the close of the war, to console himself with the excellent wine which his father had purchased in large quantities, he found nothing but empty bottles.

The next winter, the famous Crimean winter of 1854–55, was even colder than the last. The severe weather did not set in until after Christmas, and then its severity was appalling. Our poor soldiers suffered terribly in the Crimea, and the season brought me an adventure or two which I have not forgotten, and which I shall never forget.

I was sitting in my room one stormy morning when a great cry was raised in the street, and I was told that there was a wreck in the bay. I hurried out under shelter of the low wall of the pier, and my heart grew sick within me as I saw a small vessel come round the rocks from the westward. She was about half a mile from land, her two masts were broken off short, and four human beings were lashed to their stumps. The top hamper was clinging to her side and causing her to heel over to leeward. A strong sea was running, with the current up-channel, and two miles in front loomed the gigantic mass of North Foreland, stretching far across the head of the bay. White foam was flecking its steep and murderous sides well nigh to the summit, one thousand two hundred feet above.

One thing was manifest. No one could doubt the doom of crew and of vessel when those two short miles should have been traversed. Lynmouth at this time possessed no life-boat, but many stout, broad-bottomed boats were in the river, or hard by on the shore. The coastguard lieutenant, Hodges by name, was in bed with low fever, and I was sick with impotent benevolence. Presently from out of his bed, looking pale but dressed very smartly, came the lieutenant and called for a crew. Eight men volunteered and stepped into a boat, as also did Mr Hodges, with the tiller in his hand. The men showed no signs of excitement, they were only rather more grumpy in their manner than usual, for they meant to risk their lives, and to do so with as little civility as possible, after the fashion of true-born Englishmen. There was no kissing of wives, no hugging of children, no hand-shaking with friends.

'Now, men, get into the boat, can't you?' from Hodges.

'No cause for you to be in such a darned hurry, neither,' for reply. And then: 'Shove her off, and never mind those blazing fools on the bank above you', as away they went to sea.

I shall never, never forget how that boat looked when the first wave caught her as she left the partial shelter of the pier. She stood up like a horse, and I thought she was gone, and all nine with her, but she righted, and the men pulled strong. Often we could not see anything of her in the trough of the waves, and then she would rise and ride over some great rolling pillow of water, only again to disappear.

Presently we saw her pass the wreck and come to on the further side. Then she returned, bringing with her two men, one woman, a boy and a shaggy dog. They were all nearly dead, for they had been drifting for a long time, and the human beings had been lashed to the masts and continually water-washed. Then the wind moderated, and a second crew went out, and caught the derelict. They rigged up a jury mast, set a table-cloth or something of the kind, and after cutting the top hamper adrift they actually succeeded in getting her into Porlock Bay, where, just in the little harbour's mouth, she sank.

The Lieutenant took off his wet clothes and went to bed to finish his fever comfortably. Dear old fellow, he was living a year or two ago, and I could wish him immortal. The man, the woman, the boy and the dog remained at the Rising Sun on Lynmouth Pier, but the half-drowned, frozen skipper went back with the salvage crew. Then I went about with my hat in my hand to gather money to give to the men who had risked their lives to save the lives of others.

I went to my chief, Mr Mundy, and I received a rebuff for my pains. He had not been a witness of the wreck; he did not fully estimate the peril of the crew; he under-estimated the sacrifice of the lieutenant; he had been misinformed; and above all he did not approve of the initiative being taken in such a matter as this by a young, independent curate.

All this I resented. I was only receiving twenty pounds as salary, and it was an understanding from the first that I might earn a guinea where and if I could. I was only responsible for the one Countesbury service on the Sunday, and I was doing any amount of work gratuitously at Lynton both on Sundays and on week-days. This labour I did not begrudge, but if he would not help my gallant friends of the boat, why then, I would not help him so much in the future as I had done in the past. Thus I determined, and moreover a little extra money would not, I thought, be unwelcome. So I wrote him a note in high wrath to say that I had done a large amount of extra work for him for a year and a half, but that now I meant to take any paid duty that I could meet with and could arrange for.

I do not think that he and I were ever really friendly after this, and I began to inquire diligently after duty. Presently it was said that the rector of Stoke Pero was at Ilfracombe, and in ill health. Stoke Pero was not more than fourteen miles away over the moors, and what in those days were miles to me or to my mare Cochin China? So I determined to go to Ilfracombe and endeavour to obtain duty.

It was during the thick of the Crimean war, in February 1855. The thermometer was below zero, and bitter indeed was the blast. I did not care to face the forty miles on horseback, so I went to the Lyndale Hotel and hired a horse and gig for the modest sum of ten shillings, and drove myself. Flocks of wild geese flew over my head as I crossed the Parracombe Commons, and on reaching Ilfracombe I put up the horse at the Globe and went in search of the rector, but learned to my dismay that he had left the town.

By the time that I had dined it was growing dark, and the evening was one of the coldest on record; but after wrapping myself up as warmly as was possible, I took the reins and drove slowly up the hill. The Lynton road winds for some miles along the sides of ravines, and crosses very high ground before it begins to drop into the valley of Parracombe. On one side is the hill, on the other is a low parapet wall.

Darkness came on before I reached the summit, the thermometer marked zero, and I had no lamps. Suddenly the post horse which I was driving stopped and began to snort. I listened, heard a succession of low groans, and,

straining my eyes, thought that there was something loom-
ing in the darkness ahead. So I descended from the gig,
and after stroking and encouraging the quiet old horse,
which still objected to go forward, I left him and began to
explore the road in front.

Soon I came upon the Barnstaple coach which carried
the mails. No one was with it, the fore wheels were jammed
against the wall, over which the pole projected, and hung
up to it on the far side were two coach-horses, their
hindquarters resting on the sloping edge of the precipice;
they were nearly strangled, and were groaning horribly.

My first thought was that the driver of the coach was
beyond and below them, so I sprang over the parapet and
began to search the steep hillside, but I could find nothing. Crawling back to the horses, and keeping my footing
as well as I could, I opened a large clasp-knife and began to
cut the harness away in order to set them free. Only those
who have endeavoured to cut old coach-harness which has
been hardened by exposure to a thousand storms can
understand the difficulty of the task. The leather resisted
the knife as if it had been made if solid timber, but I
worked hard and liberated the poor beasts from all but the
pole chains by which they were dangling, and these, in the
darkness, and with the weight of the horses upon them, I
could not manage.

It was therefore a great relief to me to hear a shout from
the road above and to be joined by a stranger, who told me
he was Mr Avery, a cab proprietor returning to Ilfracombe
with an empty carriage from Barnstaple. On hearing what
I had done, he took one of his lamps and my knife, and
cutting some strap which in the darkness I could not find,
freed one of the horses, which fell rolling and crashing
into the ravine below. Then he did the same for the other,
with similar results.

'Now then,' I said, 'where is the driver?' and he told me
that his horses had shied at something a few hundred
yards further up the hill. We left our respective conveyances to take care of themselves and ran upwards until I
stumbled over the body of a man. On feeling his head I
stained my hands with blood, but the man neither moved
nor spoke. Mr Avery took him by the shoulders, and I took

him by the legs, and we carried him down to the conveyances. Then we opened the door of Mr Avery's carriage and bundled him in, neck and heels, all of a heap. I told my companion that I would remain until he could send assistance, and that he had better drive first to a doctor, taking with him the injured man.

When he was gone I went to the coach and took from it all the mail bags. These I piled up in a heap in the middle of the road and sat down on top of them. It was cold work, but I had not to wait very long before I heard the sound of a mass of people, who came tearing up in hot haste from below. I felt uncomfortable lest some of the letters should be stolen, so I made one man identify another and took the names of all before I would part with the bags. Then I got back into my gig and drove on to Lynmouth.

The driver recovered, and I frequently saw him, but he had no recollection whatever of what had occurred to him after leaving Barnstaple that night. He remembered subsequent occurrences, but he was almost unconscious of the events of his life before the accident.

Those drivers of North Devon were wonderful men. There was one Warwell, who drove the coach from Lynton to Bridgwater. I once started with him very early in the morning to meet my two nieces from London. We left Lynton at about six a.m., and Warwell had beer at Countesbury, beer again at Porlock, Minehead, Dunster, Williton, Putsham and Cannington. What he consumed during the couple of hours during which the coach waited, I do not know, but on the return journey he had spirits at every place where in the forenoon he had called for beer. We reached Lynton at about ten p.m., and he congratulated himself on his self-restraint in the matter of drink. He never took spirits before he turned backwards, as some people did; but he never could abide their drinking ways, so he said.

It must have been about the summer of 1855 that Lewis Knight lost his wife and all his children in the steamship *Ercolano* off Civita Vecchia. He himself lost a thumb and two fingers, which were jammed off, but he saved the rest of himself by clinging to the rigging below the bowsprit of the vessel that ran them down. The shock to his nervous

system proved to be so great that he never ceased to shiver
until a year afterwards, when he was tossed nine times by a
buffalo cow near the third Nile cataract. This truly
Knightly exercise sufficed to again warm and put him
right, and on his return he married secondly my charming
neighbour at Lynton, Miss Sandford, who brought him
several children.

When old Mr Hollier died, and the family prepared to
leave Lynmouth, their departure would of course deprive
me of my school teacher. I was, moreover, no longer very
cordial with my rector, so I told him I would leave at the
end of my two years' service.

When I informed Mr Knight of this contemplated
change, he asked me if I would accept the first presentation to the incumbency of Exmoor. His father had bought
the forest in 1812 of the Duchy of Cornwall, and an
arrangement had been then arrived at by which Mr Knight
should give twelve acres of land for church purposes, and
that the Duchy should endow with one hundred and fifty
pounds a year, as well as build a church and parsonage,
whenever the population should amount to five hundred.
The time had now come when this scheme could be
carried out, and as the five thousand pounds which had
been set apart from the purchase money in 1812 had been
accumulating for more than forty years, there was money
enough for the purpose.

My father would at this time have liked me to take a
curacy in his own county of Surrey, so I determined to go
to Clapham to consult him as to the Exmoor plan. When I
told him that I should prefer to remain in the West
Country, he most kindly gave way, and promised to furnish
the house on Exmoor for me as soon as it should be in
readiness and fit for occupation. I therefore told Mr
Knight that I would accept the new living if he could
procure the presentation, and he wrote to Lord Palm-
erston, who replied that he had known my father in early
life, and was glad to oblige his son, as well as to please the
owner of the property. So I returned him my thanks and
accepted the appointment.

CHAPTER SEVEN

New Church, New House

BEFORE PROCEEDING TO Lynmouth, to superin-
tend from thence the completion of my new house
on the Moors, I went first to stay with my father and
mother on the top of Clapham Common, and it must have
been whilst I was their guest that the rejoicings were held
to celebrate the termination of the war in the Crimea, and
I went to see the fireworks in Hyde Park. They were very
fine and the crowd was enormous.

When at about midnight the last rocket was discharged,
a vast multitude of people surged out through the various
gates into the surrounding streets. I was at that time a stout
young man of twenty-six, and as I neared the Albert Gate I
was jolted against a boy, a young gentleman, of some
fifteen years of age, and when I saw the seething struggling
mass of people who were being compressed in the narrow
gateway, I thought that the boy was in danger.

I asked him how he would manage, and he seemed to
think that he might really be crushed – so I stepped on one
side and told him to mount on my back. Then with my
load I took my place in the stream, and slowly moved with
the mass through the gate. Here I had intended to put
down my burden, but could not do so, and it is a fact that I
carried that big boy on my shoulders all through the
squares and down Regent Street, and never had an inch on
which to deposit him until I set him down in Trafalgar
Square. How long the transit lasted, I do not know, and
who the boy was I do not know, but I sometimes think that
as I staggered along that night in the capacity of Sinbad
the Sailor, I was doing one of the good actions of my life.

I was now naturally anxious to complete my new house
and the church at Simonsbath. The builders, however,

were behindhand with their work, and there seemed no
immediate prospect of our getting into residence. Of
course I was for ever riding over to the Moor, and I soon
discovered that great rascality had been practised by somebody. The work was being done by contract under the
Government Office of Woods and Forests, and the Com-
missioners had sent down a clerk of works. I was then
young and inexperienced, but I soon saw that there was
something amiss,

'Let me look at your specifications,' I said at last, and on
obtaining them from the clerk's reluctant hands, I discovered that the house was to be fitted with lead which
weighed six pounds to the square foot and with lead
piping to correspond, but on trial the lead proved to be
too light, and the articles supplied were generally inferior
to those which were specified; so I sternly ordered them to
be removed on pain of complaint to the office.

I had many black looks and an insulting letter or two. But
the light lead was stripped off the roof, the weak pipes
were dug up, and, so far as I was able to discover, dishon-
esty disappeared. But I was young, and where I discovered
one fraud, I missed ten others, and later suffered greatly in
consequence.

The church, for instance, was faced with Bath stone, in
itself most unsuitable to the locality, which is one thousand
one hundred feet above the sea level. But the stone was
also taken from the surface of an inferior quarry, and was,
moreover, positively thrown out of the boat which brought
it from Bristol, into the sea at Combe Martin, where it
remained until it was saturated with sea water.

When the winter of 1856–57 arrived, with its heavy rains
and still more trying frosts, that stone peeled off in flakes.
It was enough to make me cry with vexation to see my
pretty little church, my first church, not six months old,
with a cart-load of debris below each window, and great
rifts in the mullions and window-sills.

Then came a gale, and as over Exmoor the wind blows
hard at times, I saw every slate on the church and house
gaping like a sick oyster, while hundreds were whirled away
to a distance. Then I discovered that although the Government had paid for copper nails, yet iron ones had been

used. Inside the house it was the same; locks would not work, or handles turn, or if they turned they turned completely off. I was in despair. I applied to Mr Knight, who was a member of Parliament, and I obtained some redress, but not much.

My father, who was the most generous of men, gave me five hundred pounds to help me furnish the new house. Then my niece, Miss Stainforth, joined me and offered to live with me on the Moor and to keep my house. At length the church was completed, and my old friend, and new bishop, Lord Auckland, came down in bad weather from Wells to consecrate it.

I had to pay nearly fifty pounds in fees and expenses to obtain a perpetual curacy of one hundred and fifty pounds a year. The Government also left me much to do. No gardens were made, so I had to fence the house round with oak posts, and, after grubbing up rocks, to make paths and flower beds. I also built the kitchen garden wall, which was very expensive, and I bought trees and shrubs. In short, the place was handed over to me incomplete, and I not only had to complete it, to furnish the house and replace bad fittings with good, but also to pay heavy dilapidations on my own improvements when in 1860 I resigned the incumbency.

The parish is a large one, so large that I calculated that it was possible to have to ride twenty-five miles in order to visit two parishioners if they should both require my presence. It took me, moreover, some time to find them all out, hidden away as their cottages were in outlying combes and mires. They were from all parts of England, for the lowness of the rent per acre had attracted broken-down farmers from afar, and the native population was rather wild, lawless and uncivilised. A little school already existed, but I procured a new school mistress from Truro, who shared my fortunes for twenty-three years and is still a great friend to myself and my family.

In those days I was ubiquitous, and after doing my parish work I would mount a second horse and slip down to Glenthorne to dinner, or to Lynmouth to spend the evening, returning at any hour of the night and often across the open moors. It was a pleasure to me on a dark night to strike across country with the knowledge that a small error might impound me in a mire or leave me unable to get over a boundary wall. Lynmouth was eleven and Glenthorne fourteen miles from Simonsbath; but a young man who, with two good horses idle in his stable, would for the mere sake of exercise walk into Barnstaple and back, a distance of thirty-two miles, or, on returning from London would sometimes leave the train at Tiverton, and with bag in hand run home to supper, Tiverton being twenty-seven miles from Simonsbath – such a man, I say, did not make much of distances, and the habit remains; even now at sixty-seven I think less of asking a good horse to carry me sixty or seventy miles than many young men think of riding a distance of six or seven, if indeed they ride at all.

It was in 1858 that I rode out from Exeter at three pm, on a horse for which I could not obtain fifteen pounds, and dined at Simonsbath, forty-two miles away, at 8 p.m. What would most of the curates think now of three full services, with perhaps a funeral and a baptism, taken in three churches, without food or drink, sometimes in bad weather? Those churches were Countesbury, Oare annd Brendon, and necessitated a ride of sixteen miles. But we clergy were generally alike for this hardness in the fifties.

Sometimes there was a little risk attached to these expeditions, as when on Christmas Day 1856, my services being over, I cantered off in deep snow to beg for my Christmas dinner of Mrs Dash at the Manor House at Lynmouth. On Pray-a-way Head my horse and I ran into a drift and rolled over together with such force that we rolled out in the further side, but I was able to remount. The breath, however, was so knocked out of me that I lay gasping for some time, and the old mare herself looked stupefied. But we reached Lynmouth in time, and I am not sure whether it was on this occasion or another at the same house that eight guests sat down to dinner, most of them men of North Devon note and fame, and more than eight bottles of port wine were consumed, no one being apparently the worse for the excess.

My brother Reginald had taken a cottage at Ottery St Mary, and I frequently relieved my loneliness by driving the grey horse Somerset there in order to visit him. The distance was over forty miles. On the first of these visits I used a brother's privilege, and did not announce my intention, but drove up to his door about 3 pm. He welcomed me warmly, but said that he was sorry that both his wife and he were engaged to dine out, and that I should have a lonely evening in consequence. Upon my looking disappointed, he added that his host was a good-natured old clergyman who lived about three miles away, and would, he thought, be just as willing to receive three guests to dinner as two, and that he would send a man on a pony to inquire. This brought a warm note in reply inviting me to dinner, and I went.

On reaching the house, which was named Larkbere, I discovered, to my surprise, that I was already acquainted with the younger of my host Mr Furnival's two daughters, whom I had met the year before at Lynton. The elder daughter of Mr Furnival made an impression on me, and I also thought that Miss Shand, a girl of sixteen, was very pretty and attractive.

At Simonsbath I was lonely and depressed. I had a house and something of an income, and my thoughts turned towards Miss Furnival. So I wrote a letter to her father to say that I wanted a school-mistress, and should be thankful for his aid as an experienced clergyman in order the better to select one. This brought a warm invitation to myself and my niece to visit Larkbere; from whence I was to go teacher-hunting with Mr Furnival, which was just such a business as he dearly loved.

The month was March, and the weather cold, but I drove my niece down behind the grey horse Somerset in a four-wheel dog-cart, on a Monday, and remained until the following Friday, ostensibly intent upon the education of the poor, but privately courting Miss Furnival On the Friday, rather late, we started out on our return drive of forty miles, I had, also, that day, a waggon loaded with furniture, books and good engravings coming to me from Tiverton railway station.

We fed the horse at Dulverton and made our way over the Exmoor Commons as a cold, damp evening set in. There were many gates in those times across the roads, and

I had therefore frequently to get down and give the reins to my niece, who drove through whilst I held back the gate. At last we came to Cloven Rocks, within half a mile of home, and at the head of a long descent. Here my niece refused to drive the horse, on the ground that she was unable to see the gate-posts. So I had to fumble about in the darkness to find a stone with which to prop the gate open whilst I led the horse through. He was a grey, fifteen hands three inches high, and very well-bred. I fed him full of beans and clipped him close, giving him three blankets as compensation for the loss of his natural jacket.

He was, moreover, near home, and was impatient at the delay, and when I again took my seat he pranced about regardless of the fact that he had drawn a four-wheel carriage for forty miles over a hilly country that day. Unfortunately, just inside the gate there were two wide gutters cut in the ground to carry off the water from the road, and not covered over. Bump, bump, and I suppose something touched him, for in one moment in the darkness I saw two grey heels come through the dash-board, and I stood up and held hard, but in vain. Down the hill at the rate of twenty-miles an hour away he went. Once or twice he kicked, but soon the pace became too great, and he only galloped blindly, madly, on.

Then began such a kicking bout as I have not often seen. I could hear the splinters of the dog-cart fall around me as the frightened horse kicked, as a well-bred horse will kick, like a Nasmyth's steam hammer in full play. At last the destruction was complete, and feeling himself nearly free from the harness, he pulled me out from under the debris. I then let go the reins, fearing that he would kick my brains out if I held on. Then I arose, and in a lamentable voice enquired after my invisible niece.

'Where am I?' said she.

'Under the remains of a carriage kicked into smithereens upon Simonsbath Hill,' said I. 'Are you dead?'

Upon which I felt for her, and lugging her out found she could not stand. A great fear then took hold of me, because I dreaded that the horse had kicked her before we turned over, and I feared a comminuted fracture of a limb, so I pulled out a cushion, seated her upon it, and ran quickly down the hill to my house, where I found Mr Knight awaiting me. We took up a dining room chair, returned to the lady, and carried her down between us. Then Mr Knight, who was very skilful in the cure of bodily injuries, pronounced that no great harm was done to her ankle, so we applied six leeches, which I happened to have in the house, and sent for no doctor.

Then I went out with all the men I could muster, and we brought in the luggage and the chips of the broken carriage, with an occasional strap or two of harness. But what had become of the horse? I had given forty-seven pounds for him, he had done forty miles that day over hilly roads, the month was March and the weather cold, and Simonsbath is some 1,100 feet above sea-level.

It was necessary to find him, and we started in search. Strangely enough, the villagers declared that he had run like lightning past their doors, so we went on the South Molton road until it opened upon the Moor. As we did not find him we returned in despair, and presently rain began to fall. Towards midnight the waggon arrived from Tiverton, and the misery of the day was completed when I found that books, furniture and valuable prints were insufficiently protected, and dripping with wet. When morning came , after a night spent mostly in the endeavour to dry my damaged property, we found that the people in the village had been the victims of their fancy, for the horse was almost at my own door. He had never reached the houses, but had galloped wildly against the garden fence of Simonsbath House, had knocked a great gap in the mortared wall, and was standing shivering under the large rhododendrons, which are a feature of the place.

Never before, I should think, was a horse so cut about and damaged. It would hardly be too much to say that he was completely smashed, and as completely chilled, but I would have no farrier sent for. The events of the previous evening had gone far towards ruining me, and I did not think that the horse was worth anything, while the doctor's bill, if I had one, was sure to be enormous. So I doctored him myself, first with large poultices and afterwards with lunar caustic. Every morning for weeks I used to go to him and touch the lips of his gaping wounds with caustic, and the poor beast recovered rapidly.

In May my brother Reginald took his wife and children to Lynmouth, and they invited Miss Furnival to stay with them. Of course I rode over, and in the grounds belonging to Sir William Herries, by the banks of the West Lyn, I proposed to her and was accepted. Mr Furnival was very kind when I told him of our engagement. Moreover my dear father and the Miss Parrys promised to assist me considerably, so we were married about Midsummer from Larkbere, at Talaton Church.

We spent our honeymoon in the Lake District and at Liverpool with the Shands, but I had been put into damp sheets in a little inn on the night before the wedding, and I sickened with an influenza cold on my wedding day. I was horribly ill, but thought it to be my duty to hold on and to keep our engagements. I have never endured more misery, for I was fit only for bed and entire seclusion and nursing.

We went to the Manchester Exhibition, and to see a man tried for the murder of his wife – which, when I come to think of it, was a rather strange occupation of our time. After visiting the various lakes amid a crush of innumerable tourists – and I never elsewhere saw servants and horses so completely overdone – we returned to Simonsbath and began parochial work in earnest.

It was at this time that I engaged the services of Miss Emma Reed, as school mistress. She came from Chawleigh, and her father, I remember, upset her in the gig as he drove her over, so that her start was not of a cheering character. She remained with me, however, for twenty-two years and served in three parishes. My wife and I soon thought her life too lonely at the school, so we took her in to board and reside in the rectory, with the result that she is the oldest friend of all my elder children.

A strange gentleman, Mr Torr by name, at this time resided in a farm-house on the Exford Road. He had been sent from Wales by the Crayshaws to look after their men who were endeavouring to find iron on the Moor. He had a ladylike worn-looking wife and a family of children, among whom was a daughter named Joanna who was about seventeen, and consumptive. The father was a good sort of man, but mad as a hatter.

Well, the poor girl was dying, and I visited her constantly. One night, while the winds blew and the rain descended as it only descends on Exmoor, I received a summons, something very like a writ, calling upon me to repair at once to the farm-house where the parents resided, and there do my duty as a Christian priest, and in that way save the daughter's life.

I went down to Simonsbath House, knocked up Mr Torr, and together on foot we battled bravely over the Moors through the fury of that wild night. Mr Dash, on our arrival, insisted that I should perform the ceremony of extreme unction in order to save the life of his child, and he quoted the words of St James to that effect. I replied that rightly or wrongly the Church of England does not provide for the service, and that I could not do what he desired, but that if his daughter was conscious, I would gladly administer the Holy Communion. He showed me a bottle of perfumed oil, and protested that I was refusing to save her life.

Whilst I was in the middle of the Communion Service, he intervened, and advancing to the bed, anointed her, saying something to this effect: 'In the name of Jesus of Nazareth, rise up and walk.' That night she died, but not before the scene had made a strong impression on me, and I can now almost see again the dying, gentle girl, the weeping mother and sisters, and the wild and eager father, and the faces of the two drenched and troubled clergymen, as the dim light flickered in the sick room, and the wild storm raged noisily around. Verily we clergymen, even in country places, meet with strange experiences!

The people came to church very well, and my wife had a good choir and a Sunday school. I started a series of cottage lectures on week-day evenings, and held them here, there and everywhere, in order that I might better gain a footing in the place. A man named Kerslake was my devoted adherent and accompanied me on these occasions, wherever I went. He was the Exmoor carpenter, and a Wesleyan.

One day I preached against the use of bad language, and on going out of church Kerslake told the young black-smith, who was a most intelligent man and a great ally of mine, that the sermon was intended for him. On which the blacksmith declared that he would fetch some young fellows and duck him in the River Barle. Thereupon Kerslake came back to me to say that he was a martyr, suffering for conscience sake, and by way of comfort I told him that in my opinion he was a fool, suffering for folly's sake. But this candour only cemented our friendship the more, and I venture to say that, in my long clerical experience, I have never found that plain speaking does any harm.

One day I walked down to Simonsbath village and found a man on a tub, very hot, preaching! Mr and Mrs Kerslake and some noisy children formed his entire audience. As I went by he cast an angry look at me and declared that Exmoor was a place where the Gospel sound was never heard, and where all souls lay steeped in sin.

Presently I called on Kerslake and remonstrated with him for giving encouragement to such a spiteful, silly bigot. 'Does he know all our people here very intimately?' I enquired.

'Lord bless you, sir,' said Kerslake, 'he is not acquainted with one of them.'

'Then how does he know that they are all steeped in sin? And is it true that the Gospel sound is never heard in Simonsbath Church, Mr Kerslake?' asked I.

'No, it is not true, and he ought never to have said it; but, sir, I believe that the man is mad, and I should not have gone to hear him if he had not walked all the way from Lynmouth to preach the Gospel on a hot day, a very hot day, sir.'

'Humph,' said I, 'a queer reason, surely.'

'Yes,' was the stout rejoinder, 'and the day is so exceedingly warm that I really would have listened even if he had been a High Churchman.'

The stranger was one of the sect called Plymouth Brethren, and I have always found the members of this denomination more hard and censorious than any other religionists in the world.

It must, I think, have been in the September of 1858 that I received an invitation from my old friend Mr Stanley, a retired clergyman, to dine, shoot, dine again and remain for a second night. Mrs Thornton was poorly and had a friend with her, so I went alone.

Marley Lodge stands in the black fir-woods which run along the ridge of the Brendon Hills from Cutcombe towards Wiveliscombe. It is a good, substantial shooting box belonging to the Heathcote family, and at this period it was rented, together with great sporting rights, by Mr Stanley. The house already had a bad reputation, for some few months before my visit the cook had been found dead in it under circumstances peculiarly horrible. The coroner's jury decided that she had died by her own hand, but the country folk were not satisfied and talked of murder.

On my arrival I was shown into a large and handsome bedroom overlooking the front drive. I was told to dress quickly, as there was to be a dinner party. Many people presently arrived, among them Mr and Mrs Abraham, from Dunster. When the last of the guests was departing, I was left with Mrs Abraham in the drawing room, and she suddenly enquired if I was of a nervous temperament. On my saying that I was not, she quietly remarked that it was a good thing that I was bold, for all my courage would that night be required. She added that she supposed I was aware that I was to sleep in the room in which the tragedy had been enacted, and that no one had since been able to remain in it through the night.

I asked her what was the character of the ghostly manifestations which I had to expect, and heard, in reply, that a noise as of hands scrabbling upon the wall was usually succeeded by a sound as of the paper being stripped off, and that on one occasion a person had been terrified by hearing the curtains of the bed rustle as if they were being suddenly drawn aside.

I told her that I should be obliged to her if she would let all the household know that I was going to bed with the poker beside me, and that I was sufficiently alarmed to make me very savage if any tricks were played upon me.

Whereupon she laughed. Mr Stanley now returned, and I went with him to the kitchen to smoke a cigar before retiring for the night.

As soon as we were alone I told him what I had heard, and he said that he was vexed to think that I had been informed. Odd noises were frequently heard in the house, but not more often in that room than elsewhere. He and his man had sometimes remained in their clothes upon their beds, and when the noises commenced had by pre-concerted arrangement rushed, the one to the top and the other to the bottom of the house, but they had not been able to discover the cause of their alarm. The sounds were more like the movement of heavy furniture than anything else to which he could compare them. He added that the cook had certainly died in the room I was to occupy, but that it could not on that account be permanently left unoccupied.

I wished him goodnight and repeated my warning to the ghosts. On reaching the chamber, after locking the door and making sure of the fastenings, I made a most minute and careful inspection of the room, and placed the poker on the pillow by my side. It would have been a great relief to have kept the candle burning, but I had a feeling that any signs of timidity might be observed, and I therefore extinguished the light and lay down with an anxious heart. All my senses were strained and on the alert for some time. Then I became sleepy, and remained undisturbed until the servant called me in the morning.

When we met at breakfast I saw Mrs Abraham and Mrs Stanley looking inquiringly towards me, but I assured them that nothing had occurred, and that on a former memorable occasion I had laid a most notorious appari-tion with a stout stick; indeed, that such an appeal to his feelings was more than a modern ghost could endure.

That day we spent in shooting, and in the evening I once more made a careful inspection of cupboards, panels and recesses before I again went to bed in intimate alliance with the poker. Nothing happened, and after breakfast I drove away to Simonsbath.

That day, I think, or very shortly after, Mr Stanley rode out with the stag-hounds and made the acquaintance of a certain Captain Roper, son of the rector of Lower Sticking-ton. The young man was staying for the sake of the hunt-ing, in wretched quarters at the Rest and Be Thankful inn near Luxborough. Mr Stanley took him home and sent for his portmanteau. He was put into the room which I had vacated. Nothing was said to alarm him, and he knew nothing of the tragedy, ghosts or noises when he went to bed.

About two o'clock in the morning Mr and Mrs Stanley were awakened by a voice calling to them by name, and apparently from the outside of the house. On looking out of the window they saw something white and heard a voice saying feebly, 'Come down, Mr Stanley, I am hurt.'

On descending they found Captain Roper in his night-shirt on the gravel in front of the house, fearfully injured. He had fallen from the window of his room, the fatal room. One messenger was sent immediately to Dunster to fetch the doctor, who was Mr Abraham, and another across country to old Mr Roper at Lower Stickington. It was Sunday, and the old gentleman posted down as soon as he could leave after the conclusion of church service. He arrived just in time to see his son die.

A little later Mrs Abraham died suddenly. Mrs Stanley fell out of a window in that same house, and she and Mr Stanley finally gave up the tenancy because they were unable to procure servants who would face the strange noises and alleged apparitions – but then they did not have access to a poker, an instrument upon which I still pin my faith where ghosts and goblins are concerned. And have I not reason for the mistrust that is in me, when I remember that in 1847 I laid the Selworthy ghost with a bludgeon, and that at about the same time my friend Peter was equally successful with a shillalah, while in 1853 the most objectionable cook was kept in her proper place in the churchyard with the help of a poker.

Many years afterwards I had a guest at North Bovey who told me of noises still heard in Marley Lodge. What the meaning of the whole business was, I never knew, nor did Mr Stanley, but there was certainly in those days a kind of curious fatality connected with the place.

In the spring of 1858 my wife's aunt, Miss Elizabeth Shand, died, leaving a good legacy to each of her two nieces, viz. my wife and [her sister] Miss Furnival. The money was left to my wife and her children with remainder, but altogether excluding me. The testatrix, moreover, had done an unfortunate thing, annoying even to us who were very glad of the legacy. She had scribbled in pencil upon the margin of her will that she left two hundred pounds to this society and one hundred and fifty pounds to that one – to the extent in all of several hundred pounds. These entries were made after the will had been attested; they were not signed, and were only in pencil. The trustees would not and could not recognise them, but the ladies were generous, and, arguing that we were unexpectedly fortunate, determined to pay the societies out of income. This was done, keeping us for some years exceedingly poor.

In May 1858 our first child, a little girl, was born, only to live for a few short moments; she rests in Simonsbath churchyard. My wife went to her father at Larkbere to recover her strength, and began to fret at the extreme loneliness of our home, and to lament the distance (eleven miles) from a medical man, to whose absence she attributed the loss of her child. She urged me to find preferment in some more accessible part of the country.

One evening in June I was returning from a ride when I saw my clerk, a man named Vellacott, in animated conversation with William Court, the forester. I rode up smiling and enquired what they were so eager about, and was told that they suspected that William Burgess had murdered his little daughter Anna Maria. Upon hearing this, I pulled myself severely together and told them it was no light matter to make such allegations.

They said that Burgess had left the Gallon House Cot, where he lodged with his child, at six a.m. on the previous Sunday week, saying that he was going to take the little girl to lodge with her grandmother at Porlock Weir; that he had carried away with him a bundle containing the child's spare clothes, and had returned alone on the same Sunday afternoon. He, by himself, left Exmoor on the following

Thursday, saying that he was again going to Porlock. Since then he had not been heard of.

On Sunday a man had remarked to the landlady of the Gallon House Inn that somebody had been burning clothes in the Newtake at the back of her house. This statement excited curiosity, and one or two men, accompanied by Burgess's former landlady, Mrs Marley, went up to the place. They found little except ashes, but Mrs Marley declared that a piece of scorched calico looked as if it had belonged to Anna Maria's spare frock. On the strength of this evidence, the men were making free use of their tongues.

'Now look here, Will Court,' I said, 'you shall pay for your suspicions. Go up to my house, take my chestnut mare and ride down immediately to Porlock Weir, and when you get there, do not make a fool of yourself. Just look in, ask old Mrs Burgess how she is, and come back to me to say you have found the child alive and well. If by any chance the child is not there, say nothing about her, but enquire for William Burgess and return to me.'

I was an authority in the place in those days, so the man went off for his twenty-five miles ride over the Moors, and I went to dinner. Later in the evening he returned in a great state of excitement. He had seen Mrs Burgess, who told him that her son had arrived to breakfast on the Sunday week, and had left after dinner. He was alone. Since then she had neither seen him nor heard from him.

I made up my mind at once, and, taking Court with me, I went to one Fry, our local constable. I told him to start next morning to Lynmouth to make enquiries for Burgess, who had evidently *not* gone to Porlock, and I told Court to organise a party by daybreak to search the Moors for the child. Next morning I mounted Cochin China at three a.m. and rode to Curry Rival, near to but beyond Taunton, where the Chief Police Inspector of the country, Mr Superintendent Jeffs, resided. I was determined that no local men should bungle over the business, but that I would go to headquarters at once.

I rode up to the officer's door by eight a.m.. He was shaving, and put his head out of the window. In a few hurried words I told him my tale, and he said that he could

be with me as soon as he had eaten a mouthful of breakfast. I asked for a little more time to enable me to feed my
mare, and in half an hour we were riding back side by side.
I may here say in passing that I rode the old mare that day
quite seventy miles before noon, and she carried me, as
good horses always have carried me, game as a fighting-
cock.

On reaching the Gallon House we were met by a number
of people, who cried out that they had 'found the grave'.
We turned from our course and road eastwards over the
Moor. About a mile from the Gallon House, and in the
opposite direction to Porlock, there was a long line of that
the miners call 'deads'. This consisted of yellow earth
thrown out from a trench cut in order to discover the
direction of some vein of mineral. One of the party on
search had noticed that a portion of these deads had been
disturbed, and on moving the soil he had found in the turf
beneath a little grave as neatly cut as if by a sexton. The
sods were properly placed at the top, and these the search
party had removed, together with the soil to a depth of
three or four feet, but they had found *nothing*.

We turned our horses' heads and rode on to Simonsbath. There we met Fry, the constable, who had returned
from Lynmouth with the intelligence that Burgess had
crossed on Friday to Swansea in old Ned Groves's boat. On
hearing this the superintendent said that he also should
cross at once and take Fry with him, and he started in the
constable's cart for Lynmouth, leaving me to continue the
search.

I had no difficulty in finding volunteers for the work.
Gangs of men were soon poking, peeping, enquiring all
over Exmoor, and in this way the afternoon of Wednesday
was passed. On Thursday we searched again, and when
midnight came I was awakened by a shower of stones flung
against my bedroom window. Young Kingdom was below,
and he said to me, 'They have got him.'

I put on a pair of trousers and a dressing gown and ran to
Fry's house. All the people of the place were there, or
around, mostly in night-shirt and bedgown. I went straight
up to the prisoner and told him in eager tones that if ever a
man was in need of a friend, it was himself, and I added

that I was his clergyman, and would move heaven and earth in his behalf if he would only say where on the Sunday week he had parted company with his daughter, Anna Maria. He made no reply, and, my feelings being highly wrought, I turned to the crowd and told them that beyond doubt they saw before them, self-convicted, the very worst of murderers. I was afterwards much blamed for this by Jeffs, who said that I had interfered with the detection of the crime by thus letting the man know that the body had not been found. In his pocket were the boots which the child had worn when she went away from Marley's house on the fatal Sunday. Then Jeffs took the accused in Fry's cart to Dulverton, and we continued to search.

We searched all the rest of June, all July, all August, and then the Dulverton magistrates began to say that there was not sufficient evidence that a crime had been committed, and that they could not continue much longer to remand the accused. At this juncture a man came forward and asked whether, if he could throw any light upon the matter of the supposed murder, his own behaviour would be allowed to pass unchallenged. We eagerly replied in the affirmative, and he told us that on the night of the Tuesday after the disappearance of the child – the night during which, as Mrs Marley testified, Burgess did not come home – on that night, or in the darkness of the early morning, which succeeded it, he was on the hillside above Barle, near the Wheal Eliza deserted mine, between the mine and the child's empty grave among the deads.

He was, as he admitted, himself after no good, when he heard approaching footsteps. He crouched low, and some-one passed below him going in a direction from the grave to the mine, but he saw nothing in the darkness. That was all, positively all, but the Dulverton magistrates came out well when they heard the tale. They said they would have the mine emptied of water and searched, and if nothing came of it, they would pay the bill themselves.

Tenders were asked for, and, if I remember aright, the lowest was for about three hundred and fifty pounds, and this was accepted. The contractor had to pump the water out of a shaft more than sixty fathoms deep with long lateral galleries; the old machinery was rotten, and the leat out of order. When October arrived, the water was nearly exhausted, but the machinery broke down and the mine filled again.

At last, one morning in November, I was told that the shaft was clear. It was a bright, mild day, and I ran on to that lonely place, not deserted that day. I was in some sort of command, and I called for a volunteer. A young fellow stepped forward, we tied a strong rope under his armpits, and I told him to jerk it if the choke damp affected him.

There was an old ladder in an absolutely vertical position down the side of the pit, rotten, green and mouldy. By this he descended, while twenty of us held the rope to sustain his weight if the rotten wood gave way. Down, down, down for three hundred and sixty feet he slowly went, and we never felt the expected jerk. Then we became aware that he was at the bottom, and we slackened the rope to give him freedom below.

Presently we felt it pulled, and hand over hand we aided him as he climbed, or half-climbed, up the greasy ladder. I shall never forget the moment when his young, fair face, ghastly with bad air and distorted with toil, appeared on the surface of the shaft. And in his arms he carried a large parcel. A seaman's tarpaulin coat. I took this from him, and found it bound about with tarred cord. I cut the cord, and inside was a guano bag. I cut a slit in the guano bag, and inside was a second guano bag. I cut a slit inside the second guano bag, and inside was flesh!

There was an old cottage beside the abandoned mine, in which was one sound room secured by lock and key. I put the bundle into it, pocketed the key and sent a servant at full gallop into Dulverton with the news. Very soon, surprisingly soon, the coroner arrived, accompanied by three doctors, some policemen and a magistrate. The day was fine and bright when the ghastly bundle was placed on an old form and examined.

Tarpaulin coat, two guano bags and the body of a little girl were quickly laid side by side. Anna Maria Burgess had vanished in late June; this was the middle of November, therefore some twenty weeks had elapsed since death, but the body was very little decomposed. The face was gone, and that was all. Nothing but a little shift covered the poor remains, and two flat stones were pressed against the bosom.

The first question asked was as to whether anyone could identify the corpse, and Marley's wife declared that she could swear to the hair and to the shift. The doctors said that the body was that of a female of about seven years of age. The coroner requested me to stay beside the surgeons while they made a post-mortem examination of the corpse. He then swore in twelve men as a jury, and went off to Exford, four miles away, to hold the inquest. I had to witness a sickening spectacle, for the medical men did not examine superficially, but at last the mangled remains were handed over to me for Christian burial, and I treated them as reverently as was possible.

The verdict at Exford was one of 'wilful murder against William Burgess', and he was immediately afterwards sent off to Taunton Gaol, but not before he had made a determined attempt to commit suicide. At the assizes, I was subpoenaed, and then came the trial. I noticed that the prisoner had grown quite sleek and good-looking in prison. Presently the jurymen, actually, positively, weeping aloud, returned a verdict of 'guilty', and Burgess was condemned and removed from the dock.

I went to Mr Oakley, the Governor of the gaol, and requested an interview with the murderer. Mr Oakley replied that the Taunton authorities never compelled a condemned man to see anyone unless he so wished, and he added that Burgess was desperate, had nothing more to fear, and knew well that it was I who from the first had hunted him down. I persisted that I would risk an attack, and again requested an interview alone with the prisoner. So my card was sent up, and the answer was that Burgess would be glad to see me.

He was not fettered in any way, but a warder sat in his cell; at my request this man withdrew, but left the door ajar and paced the corridor outside. Burgess immediately acknowledged his guilt. He would not look me in the face, but stood with his back to me, leaning his arms on the wall and hiding his head. I asked him what made him kill a poor little girl of seven, his own child, and he replied that she cost him two shillings and sixpence a week, and that when he did not pay, Marley's wife pestered him for the money. 'The child was in her way, sir, and in my way, and in everybody else's way, and I thought she would be better out of the way.'

He declared that all he now wanted was to be allowed to kill himself, and all he feared was lest he should see the face of an old acquaintance when he came out to die (for those were the days of public executions). I remained with him for hours, and when I was about to leave, I asked him if I could do anything for him. Then he turned round and said that he would like to see his children, especially Emma, adding that he loved her best of all, almost as much as the one he had killed!

I told him I would do what I could to oblige him, but I said plainly that after killing one child he could hardly expect another young child to be very willing to visit him. Then he broke down, sobbing and saying that his own children were deserting him!

I drove away, drove my thirty miles that afternoon, got some dinner, and then mounted and cantered off to the farm occupied by Mr Hayers at North Molton, ten miles from Simonsbath, for Tom and Emma lived there as servants. As soon as I had told my errand to Mr and Mrs Hayes, I learned that the children knew nothing of the affair. The Hayes declined to assist me, so I sent first for Tom.

It is an awkward thing to have to tell a boy of twelve that his sister is murdered and that his father is going to be hanged, but this was what I had to do. I began by asking him whether he knew that his poor little sister Anna Maria was dead.

'Did father kill her?' was the startling rejoinder.

'Well, yes, Tom, he did,' said I.

'I always thought father would kill Anna Maria,' said he.

Upon this I grew quite desperate, and said that his father was going to be hanged and wanted to see him.

'I won't go. I don't care for he, he killed sister,' said he sobbing.

So I sent for Emma, and found her as little surprised as Tom had been. Both the children regarded their own murder by their father as a probable contingency. I promised them safety. I told them that I would send them to and bring them back from Taunton, and that in after years they would be sorry if they did not go. I obtained Mr Hayes's consent, galloped back to Simonsbath, and next morning sent my long-suffering coach-horse to North Molton, picked up the children and sent them with my man to Mr Oakley's care.

Burgess saw them, wept, and was hanged.

John Smith, the Lynmouth scoundrel, was at that time lodging with Joseph Steer in the village of Simonsbath, and had with him his little daughter Elizabeth. He not infrequently got drunk, and the Steers reported that when this was the case he was very rough with the child, quite cruel. My wife was naturally much excited over the Burgess affair, and often said that Lizzy Smith would follow Anna Maria Burgess to an early grave.

Somewhere about this time I heard that Smith had settled up with Steer and was about to leave the Moor for Williton, taking his daughter with him. He was to start the following day, and I only heard of his intention in the evening, Incautiously I told my wife, and in a moment she was in a fury of excitement. Murder would again be committed. I was responsible. The child should not go, etc. In vain I endeavoured to calm her and offered to go next day to bring the girl, to bribe the father to let me have her. This offer was met by the answer that next morning the child would be gone, and possibly murdered.

Finding that nothing less would do, I consented to take action that night, and off I went. On reaching the house, the family had, as I feared, all gone to bed, and as I dared not return home in a childless condition, I bellowed in the garden for Smith. It was a wild night, blowing hard, with some rain falling, but a window above opened, and the worthy father, in a night-shirt, put his head out.

I have done many strange things in my life, but never a stranger than when under these circumstances I proceeded to buy a six-year-old girl of her father. It was difficult to make myself heard, and more difficult to make myself understood, but at last we came to terms. Smith was to pay me two shillings and sixpence a week, and I was to clothe, board, educate and generally provide for the young woman until I could put her out respectably in the world.

When the bargain was concluded, I rattled old Joe Steer out of bed and made him a witness, and he promised that the child should not leave his custody until I took her away. By midnight I returned to Mrs Thornton, who consented to be satisfied with the arrangement. I had taken the precaution of asking Smith the name of the builder for whom he was to work at Williton, and I wrote at once to this man to request him, with Smith's consent, to stop two shillings and sixpence a week from the father's wages, and to pay me the money quarterly. This he promised to do, but at the end of a month he sent me ten shillings, with a letter to say that Smith had sold his tools and departed, whither nobody knew.

I think that quite seven years must have elapsed before I met with him again. Meanwhile I was saddled with the charge of a six-year-old child, full of bad blood and of worse education. She was timid, and when reassured she stole, and told lies with the utmost alacrity.

I have had to maintain several children of wretched parents, thrown upon my hands at an early age. I have done my best for them; I have given them very good chances, and the result has been uniformly most disappointing. If ever I have to adopt another child, I sincerely hope that she will be of what old Devonshire people used to call 'good havage'. Moreover, I do not see why the rogues, blacklegs and drunkards should have all the advantages, as is the case too frequently.

It must have been in the autumn of this year that I made the acquaintance of Mr Bisset, the master of the staghounds, who resided at Pixton Park. He was a good man, but he was very rough in his manners, and he rode quite twenty stone. I remember to have seen him find a deer on Tomshill, when we had a record run. He was riding Freemason, a horse for which he gave, as I have heard, six hundred pounds, and I was on a mare which I called Rebecca, a light-weight chestnut bought at Bideford. As soon as the hounds were laid on, I left him behind as a greyhound leaves a sheep dog, but two hours later, when I was crawling dead beaten up the hillside to County Gate, he joined me again, going gamely. Was it on this occasion that I asked Jack Babbage what was the best thing to breakfast on to carry one through a long hard day – for neither then, nor now, do I ever take out luncheon?

'Hard boiled eggs are good, sir,' he said, 'but chipped potatoes fried black will always stand by you until bed time.'

My wife now became most anxious to get away from Exmoor. So long as I was a bachelor, the place did very well, and so long as there was no baby, we could together move freely about. People were very hospitable, and we were always able to remain at their homes for the night after visiting them, but the baby was a tyrant; she could not be left, and her requirements were innumerable.

There was a difficulty, too, about inducing servants to live in so wild a place, and one, coming from Barnstaple, brought diphtheria with her, of which complaint she almost died. Our doctor, Mr Ley, lived at South Molton, eleven miles away. I turned our nurse and the baby out at once into a farm-house, while the rest of the household, viz, myself, my wife, the housemaid and of course the cook, were down with diphtheria all together.

Mr Ley brought a trained nurse from South Molton, and I kept four rammers, one for each patient, and I rammed myself first, and them afterwards, with sulphuric acid several times in the course of each day, That was our treatment. Sulphuric acid on rammers crammed down the throat, the burning effect being afterwards mitigated by copious libations of old port wine. All hail to the heroic treatment of those good old days! We eventually recovered, but a great hole was made in my cellar, and a baby died in the village. Poor little thing, it could not take the port, and succumbed in consequence.

One day I had a letter from Mr Pike of Parracombe, to say that he would be obliged to me if I would ride over by eleven a.m. and marry a couple of his parishioners. On the day in question I rode up to the old church, which occupied a position upon a hill, and began to look about for some place in which to stable my horse. There were two cottages by the church, and in the garden of one of them an old man was at work. I asked him if he could tell me where I could put my horse, and he replied that he had a shed full of tools and a wheelbarrow, with a grey goose abrood in it, but that we could turn out the tools, and the old goose would not mind. Only, he added, that the trouble was in vain, as there would be no wedding that day.

'But, my friend,' said I, 'I have ridden ten miles to officiate.'

'Never mind that,' he observed, 'this won't be the first young woman by many that Mr Jones will have played his tricks upon.'

Nevertheless, I trundled the wheelbarrow out, removed the tools, and putting the big blood mare into the little shed, I left her and the goose to converse with one another, while I took up my position in the churchyard. I could see all the church path down below to the village, and when my watch informed me that it was after half-past eleven, I went to the old man and told him that the law did not permit me to marry after noon, that there was no sign from below, and that I was going home; if the bridegroom should come, he was to present him with my compliments and recommend him in future to practise the virtue of punctuality.

While we were speaking, however, the wedding party emerged from the houses and came slowly up the hill. By the time they arrived at the church, it wanted only ten minutes to twelve, and the law was imperative. I went straight for the bridegroom and scolded him well, bidding him at the same time to be quick, and to get the church opened.

'Now see, sir, for yourself,' said he, 'what jealousy is capable of. The clerk of this parish wants to marry this young woman himself, and as she prefers me to him, he has gone away and taken the keys with him.'

I was desperate. I rushed at the iron gates of the church-yard, put my shoulder against one of them, heaved, and lifted it off its hinges. Down it went with a crash.

'Now then,' said I, 'for the church.'

The bridegroom made a back against the wall, the best man mounted upon him, and wrapping his pocket hand-kerchief round his hand smashed in a pane of glass; then he unfastened the window and disappeared head foremost into a pew. I can almost see his forked legs at this moment as he went down. The bride turned to me with a smile and said, 'This, sir, is what I do call a regular jolly lark.'

'Silence, you scandalous woman,' I cried, 'or I will see you at Jericho before I marry you.'

Then the bolt of the little belfry door was slidden back and we entered, the whole party in a titter of amusement. I hurried on my surplice, and entering the altar rails knelt down in order to steady them, but dared not remain upon my knees, as it was just upon twelve o'clock. When I reached the ring portion of the service, I bade Mr Jones put the ring upon the third finger of the woman's left hand, and say, etc. He seized the second finger and the ring would not pass.

'You stupid jackasss,' said she, 'what are you up to now?'

I hurried over the service, declined to take a fee, and 'discoursed' them, as the Irish say, in the churchyard as roundly as ever newly married couple were discoursed since the world began. I blew them up sky-high, and rode off, declaring that Parracombe people might in future marry each other with whatever horrid rites they thought proper, but that I would never again be party to 'burgling' a church to oblige the best of them.

About this time I bought a mare at the Exeter Bazaar for eighteen guineas. She was called Lady Godiva. I did not want her in the least, but she leaped like a deer and moved like a greyhound, so I fell in love with her, and men in love do foolish things. There were dark hints in the yard to the effect that she was of no use, that she would not hack and would not harness, but I scouted them, purchased and mounted. I rode her round Exeter and was delighted; so being on my way to my parents, I wrote to old Sanders to come up and fetch her.

Some time afterwards, when calling on Mr Knight at the Poor Law Office in Whitehall, I found that he had been down to Exmoor and ridden my new mare. Breeder of horses, steeple-chase rider, ex-master of hounds as he was, he gave me much pleasure by saying that for many years he had not ridden on anything that would swing across the open as could my new purchase. When I returned to

Simonsbath the mare had grown fat and was greatly improved. She was gentle as a lamb and a grand performer.

So matters went on for three months, until I displeased her by riding into the yard and then turning her to ride out again. This she resented; she considered that she had done one round, and had no mind for a second. Whereupon a battle ensued. The mare repeatedly rose so straight and so high that I thought she must come over backwards. I know well what it is to have a horse come back on me, and I do not like it; so I dismounted, led Lady Godiva out of my drive, and, shutting the gate, again mounted and gave her a five miles' gallop over the Moor. When I returned I told my man that she was underworked and overfed, and that he must for the future give her three feeds of corn instead of four.

Next day I again got on her back without a misgiving, but up she went straight as a line, and I felt the significant waver which tells that the balance is nearly true. After that she could only do one thing, and that was rear. She ceased altogether to walk upon four legs and preferred to go upon two. I determined to sell her again in Exeter, but Mr Torr came to me and offered to buy her at her original cost to me. I remonstrated on the ground that she would injure somebody; but when I found that my niece supported her husband in saying that the mare was a poor, quiet animal, overfed and irritated by mismanagement, I took the money.

Mr Torr immediately prepared to put her in harness. I said that when I bought her it was reported that she would not go in harness, but he put her in, and he and his wife smiled the smile of superiority as the mare walked away with the trap like a lamb.

'Wait a bit,' said I, 'she is a lunatic, and another day she will give you snakes.'

I do not know what work that mare did not do. I know that my friend drove her one day to Bridgwater and back, a distance, I think, of eighty-four miles. For about three months she went quietly, and then all of a sudden, without notice, rhyme or reason, she set to work kicking as seldom horse kicked before. She smashed the trap, she smashed herself, they could not take her harness off, nay, when I ventured to look in at the stable door she kicked so high that she kicked the ceiling.

No one could ride her, no one could drive her, she was intractable. Then old John Russell came over and bought her for fifteen pounds and never had any trouble. Afterwards I heard that she was well known in Somersetshire, that she was accounted to be magnificent for twenty minutes over any country at any pace, but that she was not good to stay, and that she would not do anything *certainly*, except with hounds – with them she was always quiet.

One day in December 1859, when a severe frost had given way to rain, I rode out to Sandy Way to see a parishioner named Blake, a widower, with two red-faced, good-looking daughters. They gave me some tea, and I sat chatting until I found that I had only a short time left in which to cover the seven miles to my house before dinner would be served. I was riding Cochin China, and the mare was in foal, but very lively, as was her wont.

The evening was foggy and dark, and my way lay over open commons, but I was altogether fearless and full of confidence in myself. So up I slipped through the two meadows above the farm-house to the gate which opened from the higher one on to the Moor. I could see nothing, but I knew that under this gate was a long, sharp stone, and that a clean-cut trench, deep but narrow, lay immediately outside, so I dismounted, closed the gate behind me and led my mare over the dangerous grip beyond. Then, remounting, I turned her head against fog and black darkness and sent her cantering into the open.

We were in a newtake of six hundred acres, bounded by the Sherdon Water on the south and the Barle River on the north, with the wall of Winter's head farm stretching away for a mile in front towards the west. I never doubted but what I could strike that wall within a short distance of the gate, and so get into the lane.

Suddenly, however, I conceived the idea that I was going on sounder ground than was right, for the mare was throwing up no water as she went, and there was an absence of the peculiar squelch which I wanted to hear. I stopped, and in one moment felt confused, so I buried my eyes in my hat and reflected. Where in the newtake was there any sound turf? I did not know.

Well, it was but six hundred acres in size, and if I only went straight on, I must come out somewhere. I did not know in which direction I was looking, so I faced the wind to avoid deviation, and rode on. Presently I heard water running far away below me and felt myself riding on sidling ground.

'Oh, here I am,' thought I, 'too far to the left, above the Sherdon Brook; if I only keep along the ridge I shall strike the wall to the left of the gate, and must ride along it until I come to the aperture.' Presently the mare stopped and snorted, and I told her that she was an old fool, that there was no bad ground thereabout, and she must go on. She hesitated, and I kicked her with my unarmed heel; upon this she plunged forward, fell upon her head, sent me out over in front, recovered herself, drew out her forelegs as if she was drawing two gigantic corks, and then, flinging herself across me, settled down in the bog with her chest upon my thighs and knees. I was on my face, and the icy water was coming up to my wrists as I supported myself above the mire.

It was foggy, quite dark, and no one knew where I was, nor did I know. So it was a case of life or of death, and I began to struggle in good earnest, but it is not easy to draw your legs our from under a heavy horse when they are deeply embedded in a bog, and I cricked my back and tore my clothes and barked my skin before I wriggled myself free. Then I walked round the mare, whose neck was above the mire. She had sunk up to the flaps of the saddle, and her tail lay straight out on the bog.

If I could only find firm ground I thought I would try to get her out, but I could not find firm ground, and presently I lost [sight of] the mare. She was close by me, I knew, but I could not find her. I lay down flat in the bog and looked along the horizon line in vain. I put my ear to the mire and listened for a chink of the bit, but in vain. Then I thought that my wife would be frightened, and that I could do no good by waiting. But how was I to get off the newtake? East, west, north and south I had lost all sense of reckoning, so I wet my left cheek with bog water and kept it turned against the wind to make sure that I did not circle.

Up to the waist I plunged in the honey-pot holes, and, extricating myself, struggled on. After a while the ground began to rise, the mire grew shallower, and there was no longer any fear of going round, so forward I went until I came to a stoned-up fence. But which? I did not know, so I clambered up and knotted my pocket-handkerchief into the thorns at the top to afford me a mark by which to find the mare, and went on under the fence until I walked right out over the head of a quarry pit. It was not very deep, some seven or eight feet perhaps, but there were stones at the bottom, and I fell heavily and bruised myself badly. Then I crawled out at the lower end and hardly dared to pursue my way lest some worse thing should befall me.

After a while, to my joy, I came upon a gate in the fence, and while endeavouring to open it I kicked my foot against something, and lo!, in one moment I understood everything. I was again in Farmer Blake's gateway, and was kicking against a sharp stone which I knew quite well. My mare lay helpless in the terrible mire above Sherdon Hutch. I had gone too far to the right, and not to the left, as I had supposed, and had been coming backward above the Barle River until I was immersed in the Sherdon bog.

I made my way down through the fields, threw open the door and astonished the girls and their old father, for I was black, torn, bruised and dripping. I begged for the loan of Mr Blake's black mare. I begged lanthorns and candles of the girls, and I promised two farm boys half a sovereign if they could get my mare out of the bog that night (it is only ten acres in extent), and away I rode into the gloom. Very careful was I over the Moor this time, and I struck the gate on the further side and reached home in dismal plight some three hours late for dinner.

The next morning I was up by five o'clock, and rode back to the Ferny Ball bog, above Sherdon Hutch, with old Sanders behind me on my carriage horse. We reached the gate above Farmer Blake's house, and turned up to the left under the wall until we came to where my handkerchief in the fence marked the point at which we were to turn off into the bog. However, we were too early to see much, for a thick white fog lay close on the surface of the mire. It was only a layer of mist, for we could see above it. Then presently, just after the sun had arisen, this fog began to curl upwards in spiral columns, very pretty to behold. After a while, as it lifted, it revealed a long, anxious face, a wiry neck and two uplifted ears.

Somehow or other the mare had managed to shift her position so as to stand a little higher out of, although still deeply immersed in, the deadly chill of the mire, and she whinnied when she heard us. Very quickly we saw where to lead her towards sounder ground, and set her free, Sanders remarking that 'her's cruel thirdle, surely', which means, I suppose, greatly tucked up.

It may be worth while to mention that she took no cold nor suffered apparent injury, but when in the May following she foaled, she had a colt with four curiously crooked legs, which, nevertheless, I sold to Mr Smith of Emmett's Grange for fifteen pounds as a sucker. He said that the legs would come straight, but they did not do so, and eventually I returned him five pounds of the purchase money. Since then I have been down in many mires, and I have seen many other people down also, but never again have I had to leave a horse immersed for the night.

Curiously enough, that same evening Mr Jekyll asked Mr John Carwithen of Challacombe to dine and stop the night with him at Hawkridge, but no Mr Carwithen arrived. At eleven p.m. some of the guests went away and some went to bed. About seven next morning Mr Jekyll was aroused by his rough little maid knocking at the door, when the following colloquy ensued:

'Please, maister, the gentleman is come to dinner.'

'Tell him we shall breakfast at nine, and light the dining room fire at once.'

'Oh, sir, do'ee please come down, the gentleman has gone a masquet, his beard and his hair be full of conker-bells, and he's most ago' – which, being interpreted, signified that he had lost his way, was covered with icicles, and was nearly dead. He had lost his way in the same darkness which had confounded me. He had lost his horse while trying to lead him over a fence, and he did not recover him for some days, and then, as he told me, with only the circlet round the ears to remind his owner of a vanished bridle and saddle.

CHAPTER EIGHT

Dunsford

THE YEAR 1860 was the wettest within my record, and many circumstances combined to make me desirous to leave Exmoor. So it was that we removed, seven miles to the south, down to the village of Dunsford. The vicarage, which had been built recently, was large and commodious, and the gardens were wonderful. We came, it should be remembered, straight from Exmoor, where the climate is so bad that an apple about as large as a walnut was preserved in spirits and exhibited for years on the chimneypiece of Honeymeade farm-house, as *the* apple which once grew on Exmoor.

When there, we thought ourselves fortunate if we could grow cabbages by July, or bring peas and beans to perfection before the sharp frosts set in very early in the autumn. In strange contrast to this highland sterility, we now had peas and ripe strawberries in May, and such a profusion of peaches, nectarines, apricots and grapes that we did not know how to consume them. But a heavy penalty had to be paid for these advantages. We both grew languid and depressed. My activity deserted me, and my wife also became unwell.

When I went to Dunsford the population was nearly one thousand, and was much disposed to church-going; but my expenses were many, and for the first time in my life I learned to my cost that people who subscribe liberally on paper may decline to pay up in cash. This I felt to be a great hardship, and I still consider the practice mean and very unhandsome. I have an idea that these sham subscribers think that they are aiding a cause by acting as decoy ducks, and that if they can thus induce others to give, they may well themselves be spared.

The living was nominally worth four hundred pounds a year, but the parochial expenses were so great that I received very little for myself. Our children, also, came on rapidly; the house was large, and for the first time in my life I began to feel very poor. My wife, moreover, was obliged to be frequently absent in lodgings at some place where the climate was more invigorating, and this also was expensive.

Is it the soil that affects character? I have often thought that it exercises a subtle influence. I never knew people who were so generally liable to depression of spirits as were my new parishioners. Strangers felt the climate at once. A governess came to Culver House to teach the children of Mr Lodwick, and she wept incessantly from the moment she arrived until the family mercifully sent her home to her friends. I myself became languid, and a victim to a malady which Mr De la Garde, the Exmoor surgeon, told me was generally confined to worn-out old men, or more often women. This greatly depressed me.

And the tone of the Dunsford people was peculiar. Calvinism, as a religion, is said to be most popular in the heavy lowlands, while the brighter Roman Catholicism flourishes best upon the hills. This may be fanciful, but some of the Dunsford people were peculiar; they were not like the Exmoor folk, nor yet like my present parishioners. They came to church much better, but worried me much more. They made me pay for everything – the school was most terribly expensive – and the rates and taxes were high.

Of course there were many good Christians among them, but some were very troublesome. They liked to decorate the church, and then they quarrelled over the decorations – one put up a text, and another said it was popish; that he would not come to church unless it was removed, and the other would not come if it were taken down.

In the summer of 1862 my eyesight failed me, and I had my first sharp attack of gout. I had, I believe, as a nursery child, lost the sight of the left eye in 1837, when I fell from a height of twenty feet upon my head; but no sensible inconvenience had resulted from the accident until the year 1862, when I strained my remaining eye by constantly reading the accounts of the American Civil War in very small print, at night. A London oculist ordered entire rest, and as the climate of Dunsford disagreed with my wife, I put an old clergyman in charge of the parish and took lodgings for the winter at Weymouth, close to my brother Reginald. I had with me a horse for which I gave twenty pounds, and upon which I saw one of the greatest runs that I have ever ridden to. We found at Yellum Wood, near Puddletown, and ran through Charminster to Cerne Abbas, up by the Giant's Head, almost to Sturminster Newton, and lost our fox in Lord Digby's park, from whence I rode back to Weymouth and my dinner.

In the early spring of 1863 we moved into lodging at Lynton, and here my daughter Kate was born. In June, my sight being better, we returned to Dunsford, to find that a locum tenens is not always a comfortable person to put in charge of a living. The gentleman in question was a Low Churchman, and he had altered and changed the customs of the parish without consultation with me. He had given up the practice, for instance, of baptising during service on special days, and he had taken other liberties of a similar description. Years before, on Exmoor, a clergyman similarly situated with respect to me had coolly lent my best books all over the parish, so that on my return I was confronted with the sight of a calf-bound copy of Macaulay's *Essays* in a labourer's cottage, the occupant being barely able to read!

It must have been soon after our return home that a very wonderful event occurred. I had come out of Dunsford Church on the morning of a Sunday, and was standing upon my lawn when I heard the report of heavy firing. It was quite possible to distinguish between the rattle of broadsides and the single reports of heavier guns. I wondered what could have induced the authorities at Plymouth to take to Sunday for gun practice; but on Tuesday I learned that I had been listening to the duel between the *Kearsage* and the *Alabama* off Brest, which ended in the sinking of the latter. I do not know the distance, but it cannot be less, I imagine, than sixty miles, and yet every shot sounded as if it were fired close by. Much in this matter depends upon the condition of the atmosphere. All sportsmen know, for instance, that you cannot well hear hounds in fog; and the wind, too, had a great deal to say to the result.

Mrs Thornton was frequently absent from home, seeking for bracing air, and I myself now fell a victim to the climate. All the steel and energy had immediately left me on leaving Exmoor, but I had not actually felt ill, until one day about this time when something seemed to go wrong internally. After consulting Mr Stephens, the Dunsford doctor, I went to old Mr De la Garde in Exeter, who said that he would like to call in Mr Kempe. These eminent gentlemen examined me, and came to the conclusion that I was suffering from a morbid malady, most uncommon, and never seen by them except, and that very rarely, in the case of completely exhausted people.

They ordered me to Exeter, and proceeded to cauterise me severely, using, first of all, simple caustic and going on with undiluted sulphuric acid. My agonies were intense, but I had the unutterable advantage of a most kind nurse, in the person of a middle-aged housemaid of my own. She pitied me, and went out and bought me some laudanum, and so, as soon as my tormentors were gone, I took a dessert spoonful of brandy and forty drops of laudanum, and dulled the pain.

After torturing me for a week, they said that it was useless any longer to defer a serious operation. This I underwent, and recovered completely, but the doctors never knew of the laudanum. After the operation I craved for the drug, but as I had no longer any pain, I resisted the temptation, and the desire for it soon disappeared.

I have mentioned in a former page how that, soon after the murder of the little daughter of Burgess, John Smith ran away, leaving me with Lizzy Smith upon my hands. I had now had the charge of this child for six years or more, and she was growing up to be a big girl. I had done my best for her. I had clothed, fed and educated her. I had quartered her with my good school-mistress, Miss Reed, and afterwards in my own house with my servants. But she had turned out badly. She had bad blood in her, and I had not secured her until she was seven or eight years old, by which time human character is greatly formed.

She was untruthful, thievish, dirty to a degree, and moreover at fourteen began to show promise of being in other ways most unsatisfactory. She was old enough to earn her living, and my system of treatment was evidently unsuccessful. Therefore I wrote to Lynmouth and enquired if any of her father's relatives had heard lately of his whereabouts. My informant replied that Smith, some months before, was working at Weston-super-Mare, at his trade, as a mason.

Next morning I left Exeter by an early train, taking the girl and her clothes with me. On reaching Weston I drove to the police station and enquired for John Smith, but I could get no information. After telling my story to the sergeant of police, I left Lizzy in his custody, and, promising to return for her, set forth upon my search.

When I was made a clergyman, a good detective officer, as I believe, was spoiled. I climbed the hill and looked down on the town for new buildings, and presently beheld a terrace of half-completed houses rising upon the hillside. As I walked wearily along in front of this terrace I came upon a house in which men were at work. There was an unfinished area ditch between the path and the first floor, and in a room on the latter two men were busy.

I paused, and then asked if either of them knew a mason named Smith. One of them glanced at the other, hesitated, and said that he did not; but I had noticed the look, and taking a spring I cleared the fissure and alighted in the room between them. Then running backward into the house, I came face to face with the man whom I wanted. He was listening behind a partition.

'Good morning, Mr Smith,' I said. 'I have been keeping your daughter for six years at my own expense, and now I am about to restore her to you. You deserted her, and you defrauded me, and now you must take her.'

He declared that he could not afford the expense, that he had a wife and a second family by her, to support, and required no elder olive branches to seat themselves round his table. However, he agreed to accompany me to see the girl, and to hear what further I had to say, so I led him, unsuspecting, to the police station and called for assistance. Then I cautioned the sergeant to keep his eye on the girl, and after telling Smith what I thought of him, I went to the clergyman of the parish and made him and his wife promise to do what they could for the child, as well as to take care that she was not maltreated – and then I went home.

Shortly afterwards I heard that she had been put out to service, and had robbed her mistress. The magistrates sent her to a reformatory, whence she proceeded to Australia and became lost to view. I hope that she has done better at the antipodes, but heredity is a powerful influence, and I have resolved that if ever I should again adopt or take up a child, it shall not be said of me that I continue to reward vice, and to turn my back upon destitute virtue. For why are the wicked to have all the advantages?

Tiring of Dunsford, I cast about for an exchange of livings. One day I was riding out towards the Moor when I came to the village of North Bovey, and entering into a conversation with an inhabitant I heard that the rector of the place was named Arden, and would be glad, if he could do so, to leave the parish. I rode into Exeter and told my lawyer to write to Mr Arden to know whether he would be willing to exchange his living for one nearer Exeter, and of about the same value as his own.

In due time we heard that he was quite willing to entertain such a proposal. Meanwhile I had ascertained that just as Bishop Fulford of Montreal was patron of Dunsford, so was the good Lord Devon patron of North Bovey. But was the change sufficient for our purpose?

There was a rather eccentric old doctor who practised at this time at Bovey Tracey, a clever man, and to him I went. He was busy, and could not see me for a moment, but his wife entertained me. Presently I heard him bawling out, 'Where is this man who wants to see me?'

'Gentleman,' remonstrated his wife.

'Is he ashamed, then, of the fact of his humanity?' said the doctor, advancing, to which I replied that I had not come to discuss the question of gentility but of climate, and that I would be obliged to him to sit down and tell me what he thought of the difference between the climate of

Dunsford and that of North Bovey, with both of which places he was well acquainted.

He sobered down at once and spoke most sensibly. He said that one hundred feet in altitude represents a geographical degree in latitude, and that North Bovey stands some four hundred and fifty feet above Dunsford. Therefore, he considered that the change would correspond to a movement of three hundred miles to the north, and he added that North Bovey stands on the granite and Dunsford on the clay formation. Soil, he said, was as important a consideration as altitude, and he bade me go and study the difference in vegetation between the one place and the other. In his opinion, we should feel the change greatly.

I thought that he had earned his guinea very well, and went off and took note of the vegetable kingdom. Roughly estimating, I discovered North Bovey to be three weeks behind Dunsford in the spring, and that many delicate plants thrive at Dunsford which will not grow well at North Bovey. So I called on Mr Arden and informed him that I was his anonymous correspondent through my lawyer. He was delighted at the thought of an exchange, and I told him that if he could obtain the consent of Lord Devon, I would write at once to Bishop Fulford.

Both patrons were very kind, but I owe most to Lord Devon, who made a considerable sacrifice, inasmuch as Mr Arden was fourteen years older than myself. Lord Devon, then as always, had but little thought save for the welfare of the people of the place, and he considered it desirable that Mr Arden should leave North Bovey, where he had been rendered thoroughly uncomfortable by reason of the unruly behaviour of some of his pupils.

Mr Arden had built a new rectory, but it was neither water-tight nor free from smoke, and he was glad to exchange it for the excellent rectory at Dunsford. The livings being of about equal value, there was no great difficulty in the way of exchange.

CHAPTER NINE

North Bovey

WE LEFT DUNSFORD in February, 1866, Mrs Thornton and myself, with our four daughters, leaving one little girl baby behind us in the churchyard, even as we had left another at Simonsbath five years before. The Dunsford parishioners were very kind and presented me with a silver salver and Mrs Thornton with a handsome Bible, but we were not sorry to leave, for the climate did not suit us.

On reaching North Bovey my spirits rose at once in response to the bracing climate, and really I had need of them, for the roof of the house leaked like a sieve and the chimneys smoked most horribly. My new parishioners were very turbulent people. The farmers, it is true, had recently given up the practice of fighting in which they had formerly indulged, more especially on Saturday evenings, but the women were awful. The whole village was greatly demoralised, and much addicted to scandalous gossip of the worst description, and some young men, who had lately left the parish, had given much occasion to the enemy to blaspheme.

Mr Woollcombe, my late neighbour at Christow, at once wrote to tell me how impossible I should find it to live at North Bovey, and he had been curate in charge of the place for more than ten years. Mr Nosworthy, the doctor, warned me against the parish churchwarden, with whom he said I was certain to fight, even as all my predecessors had fought with him.

Women, with blood streaming from their heads, would frequently run into my house, reminding me of the pictures of the Furies of old. They tore each other's hair out by handfuls, they flung crockery and stones at one another, and one actually leaned out of the window, pistol in hand, and threatened the life of a policeman.

But I did not mind this at all. I was in my element. Their ungoverned and ungovernable natures, which were as generous as they were fierce, suited me far better than did the cold, close respectability of the Dunsford folk, and yet the two places are only seven miles asunder, but the soil is different, the air is stronger, and many of the North Bovey people are descended from old, free residents upon Dartmoor, who were accustomed to follow their own inclinations, and maintained, as I imagine, small tribal wars with one another.

I set to work with a will. I engaged the services and the skill of an old working mason of the place, and he stopped the leaks in the roof and mitigated the nuisance of the smoky chimneys, while I waged battle with all the fighting women in turn and routed them one by one. They soon gave in when they found that they could not engage my sympathies by coming to me with their tales of woe, and they bore me no ill-will when I scolded them soundly all round and declared, as was my custom, that I did not believe in their version of their quarrels, but considered that they had behaved about as badly as women could behave, and that I felt inclined to get them all fined indiscriminately by the magistrates.

The Duke of Somerset, who was Lord Lieutenant, wrote to me at this time to ask me to be a magistrate myself, but I declined the honour on the ground that my parishioners were turbulent, and that it would be trying their patience a little too far if they were sent to prison by their own clergyman. They really much resembled the Exmoor people, and I felt quite happy and at home with them. The bellicose churchwarden was very amusing. He was an old man, and he would sit at a vestry meeting in the schoolroom with his hat on his head and a great stick in his hand. I was always voted to the chair on these occasions, and sometimes this is what would occur.

Someone would suggest something of which the choleric old gentleman disapproved, and then he would bring down his oaken stick with great force upon the table and exclaim, 'I won't have it. I won't have it, and it shall not be done.'

'But, my dear sir,' I would urge, 'the matter is not yet discussed, much less voted upon, and we must be guided by the voice of the majority.'

'Yes, yes, Mr Thornton, that is right, we must be guided by the majority, but I won't have it, I won't, and it shall not be done.' And then down would come the stick upon the schoolroom table. He and I never had an angry word with each other. He told me all his secrets, often sought my advice, and was glad to have me by him at the end when he passed away in his eighty-second year.

My neighbour, Mr Clack, the rector of Moretonhampstead, told me that this man on one occasion pursued him with a pitchfork until he rode his horse over a bank to get away from him; but on their meeting a few days later the old farmer came to him with outstretched arms, 'Shake hands, Mr Clack, do'ee. I ran after you with a fork the other day, but I be warm, sir, I know I be.'

There was nothing mean about these people as a rule. They would do me a good turn any day, lend me a horse, or fetch me a parcel, without expecting to be paid for such trifling services. It has ever been the same with the dear children of the place. Our intercourse has been kindly, and very free from mercenary taint, and I hope and believe that when I am gone they will say of me that what I had was also at their disposal, and that no sick person ever wanted for a carriage or a bottle of good port wine, if there was a horse in the rectory stables or any good stuff in the cellar.

And the same I say of the children. They have been very good. There has been no case of serious misbehaviour in the school, and the people have trusted to me and sought my aid freely for thirty years and more.

At this period of my life I was very active. My School Inspectorship took up much of my time, and the area over which I inspected was really large. It was not until 1870 that I became Dean Rural, but I added Sunday services at Vitifer, upon Dartmoor, to my own two at North Bovey; and soon, by invitation from the inhabitants, and with the consent of Dr Fletcher, the rector of Lydford, I often officiated at Postbridge, where sometimes I preached on a tub in the open air.

Then I set to work to collect money to build school-houses, to be used also for chapel purposes, at Huckaby and at Postbridge. Before long I had five hundred pounds, but Dr Fletcher resigning, and a new clergyman succeeding, I gave the money to him, and he carried on the work, after which I often did duty for him at Postbridge in the newly-built chapel.

Mr Bird was now appointed to the vicarage of Christow, and we resumed our acquaintance, for he had been curate-in-charge of the same parish during part of my Dunsford career. We became warm friends, for we were kindred spirits. He was great at schools, and also a keen sportsman, and as hard as nails. I was frequently at his house and he at mine. We thought nothing of the distance of some ten miles which intervenes between the places where we severally resided.

I was at this period often at Doddiscombsleigh, and it surprises me now to think of the journeys which I then accomplished. For not content with riding or driving, I would sometimes run over to Doddiscombsleigh and have tea, then go on to Christow to supper, and walk home to North Bovey after ten or eleven p.m.

Mr Bird was a wonderful man with dogs, and possessed a retriever called Fancy and a red setter named Nellie. These were two of the best dogs I have ever known. Fancy was marvellous. I shot with her for many seasons and came to know her well. She was almost human in intelligence. She could certainly reason. Sometimes she slept in my room, and would want to go out in the morning before I was awake. She would in that case stand up by the bed and poke her cold nose into mine. She would then go and pick up my socks and bring them to me to my bed, and fetch first one slipper, then another, and if I did not oblige her by rising she would take up a slipper and continue to thrust it against my face until she induced me to open the door.

I was shooting on one occasion with her on Sittaford Tor, where the heather grew long and high, when a brace of partridges rose together and fell, winged birds. Now Fancy was generally very dignified and slow in her movements, but she knew that two winged birds in long heather on a dry day in September would give her much trouble if she delayed, so forgetting her dignity, she dashed forward to the nearest bird, caught it, killed it with a crunch, and put it down upon the ground, and then went after the other and brought it to me without ruffling a feather.

So light-mouthed was she in general that in Caroline Mire she once picked up a snipe and brought it alive to Mr Bird from a long distance. I was by his side, and we agreed that it was a wounded bird left in the bog by some previous shooter, so he put his hand to her mouth which she opened, and away went the snipe like the wind. I fired two barrels, and Bird followed up with two more, but away went that snipe rejoicing. It had been for several minutes in a great dog's mouth, and had been fired at four times in vain.

Fancy had strong opinions of her own, and knew perfectly well whether an animal was wounded or not. She would not even put her nose to the ground in order to please an indifferent shot who declared that his bird was down on the other side of the hedge, but she hardly ever failed to recover game which was really crippled. Old Doctor Bird, Mr Bird's father, was a bad shot, but was fond of shooting. I have heard him ask Fancy to accompany him, and I have seen her retire sulkily into a corner, with a disgusted look upon her face. The old gentleman has then put sweet biscuits, of which she was very fond, into his pocket, and after giving her one has led her out on a string. After much coaxing and feeding I have seen him release her in a turnip field, and the old dog has followed him dejectedly until he fired, and missed, when she has instantly put her tail down and gone home, regardless alike of biscuits and commands; but with a good shot she would always go with alacrity.

I remember on one occasion to have seen her at her master's heels while two pointers were crossing and re-crossing a heavy field of turnip swedes. All of a sudden she stepped forward and pushed her nose against Mr Bird's hand. Then she turned round and pointed behind her steadily. Upon this we went back and found a partridge which the pointers had failed to find.

When we were shooting on Dartmoor we always knew by her action what sort of game was in our vicinity. For instance, she would spring up in the air and stare in a peculiar manner if wild duck of any description had been on the water or in a mire. In the house she was equally intelligent, and could do anything but speak, and most speech she understood. I have seen many clever dogs, and I have heard Mr Russell tell wonderful tales of canine sagacity, but I have never met old Fancy's equal.

Twenty-five years ago there were more game and fewer shooters on Dartmoor than at present, and Mr Bird and I worked very hard. We knew the Moor thoroughly, and also knew the habits of its visitors. Wild birds come to it and go again. In some conditions of temperature they frequent certain localities, such as deep bogs, and when the weather changes they shift their quarters.

On one occasion we were shooting when the snow was upon the ground and the snipe were in the mires. Late in the afternoon we found ourselves in Rota Marsh, with a fog rising all around us. My horse and gig were at New House, and after consultation we determined to walk rapidly to Teignhead before we gave up our sport.

On leaving Rota Mr Bird struck away, as I considered, too much to the right, and when I remonstrated he said that he had had enough of my short cuts and was going to take an easier route. I told him that he was wrong, but that I would not leave him in a fog, and bade him lead on. After walking hard for nearly an hour we actually crossed our own tracks close to Rota, and discovered that we had made a complete circle. After a good laugh at ourselves (for we thought ourselves first-rate moor-men), we decided to follow the brook to Powder Mills, as we were evidently not to be trusted to keep a straight course through the mist.

Mr Bird was very fond of his schools, and as I was the Diocesan Inspector, we had that interest also in common, and I was often with the children in his school. He was very keen also with hounds, and although a small man he insisted upon riding a horse seventeen hands high, which he rode at everything which came in his way.

On one occasion, after being up all night, he came to me before dawn, and I mounted him on a chestnut horse which I had bought at Cheltenham, and, on my famous mare Susan, I accompanied him to Morchard Bishop, twenty-four miles from North Bovey, where we met Lord Portsmouth. Finding a fox behind Mr Churchill's house, we ran to Tiverton, from whence we jogged quietly home. It was one of the longest days that I have ever known, but neither of our horses grew tired, and Mr Bird, notwithstanding his previous sleepless night, enjoyed his dinner and showed no signs of fatigue. He was at that time an iron man, and I think that we were both equally reckless of exposure and of toil.

And now, indeed, I met with a remarkable adventure. A trustee had proved fraudulent and had fled to Paris. I determined to go after him, and leaving North Bovey one Tuesday morning, I had an interview with a firm of solicitors in London and crossed to Boulogne by the night boat, reaching Paris at four a.m. on Wednesday. After making myself tidy and breakfasting at the great Hotel of the Louvre, I walked to the Place de la Concorde, and sitting down on a bench in that blood-stained spot, I meditated upon how to obtain an interview with my man.

Presently it occurred to me that I had heard that he often did monetary business through a little French *avocat* whose address I was acquainted with, so I made my way down two deep courts which lead one behind the other from the Rue Faubourg du St Honoré, and found the *avocat*'s name on a door. By much persuasion I induced him to send for his friend, and I allowed him to put me into an inner room. After waiting for a very long time I heard voices and, opening the door, revealed myself to the fugitive.

So great did my powers of persuasion prove that in the evening I left the office with securities for forty thousand pounds in my coat pocket. Truly I did not feel very easy or comfortable as I traversed Paris on foot to the hotel where I dined but, with the property still upon me, I caught the night boat, was with the solicitors next morning in the Old Jewry, and handed to them the rescued deeds, and I dined that night at home.

This must have occurred in 1867, and I doubt whether even now it would be easy to beat the record. I was absent from my home upon Dartmoor for only sixty hours, and yet I spent twelve of them in Paris and rescued a big property at some personal risk. If it had suited the *avocat* to make away with me, I should never have been traced, and Paris would have been the scene of one more undiscovered mystery.

It was at this time that I bought my famous mare Susan. I purchased her in Exeter of a man named Pedrick for forty-five pounds. When the bargain was concluded the vendor said that before I paid him he should like me to know that the mare had been condemned by five veterinary surgeons for spavin in both hocks.

'Let me have another look, Mr Pedrick,' said I, and I knelt down in approved fashion and looked between the forelegs at the hind ones carefully. 'I can see nothing, and I can feel nothing amiss,' I said, 'and the mare goes sound.'

'Of course you cannot,' he remarked, 'when there is nothing to see or to feel.'

'But what do all the vets mean by condemning her?'

'Mean? They mean that they are a set of blazing fools, that is what they mean,' said the angry horse-dealer.

So I paid my money and took home my mare, and rode her for eleven years without trouble from spavin. She was quite indomitable, and I tried her very hard. I have been upon her back for fifteen hours at a stretch, without feeding her or myself, and I never knew her to be tired. After carrying me for the best part of a hundred miles she would come home in the dark playing with her bit, dropping the end and catching it again, and at the close of the longest day, if I did but slacken the reins on her neck she would break into a gallop at once. There are plenty of people still alive who can testify to her extraordinary toughness.

She was as remarkable for wind as she was for endurance. It was well-nigh impossible to pump her out, but she was very rash, and dearly loved to play random pranks. If I put her at a gap in a stone wall, for instance, she would often swerve and top the whole wall out of sheer wilfulness, but she only gave me three falls in eleven years. They were, however, all bad ones.

I once rode her through the Dart River under Bengie Tor, in flood time, side by side with Colonel Morris, of Hatherleigh, and of light cavalry fame, and one Mr Charles Caning who is still, I am glad to say, like myself, with the minority. The Colonel and I got through, but our companion fell, and was parted from his horse, and swept down the roaring stream.

The other day, in company with three young ladies, and after a long drought, I walked through the river near where we crossed, and shuddered in recollection as I saw the character of its bed. There is something peculiar in the bottom of the Dart and its tributaries. The stones are rounder and more slippery, and the fissures in the large blocks are wider and deeper than is the case in the Teign.

Three times in my life have I ridden across the double Dart, taking my chance at random, and that is often enough. Indeed, it was only the other day that I saw Mr Coryton roll over, horse and all, while he was trying to ford the river just where the Webbern joins the Dart.

While on this subject I may narrate that on one occasion this same mare Susan, in crossing the Teign below Teignhead, got her forefoot hitched in a crevice. She fell with me, and then twitched as only a well-bred horse can twitch, until she tore away her shoe and with it much of the hoof. I was very fond of her and suffered miseries as I saw the blood running from the quick, and led her home staggering on three legs only.

I was a great walker as well as a hard rider, and it was now that with Mr Furnival I walked through Cornwall. The expedition was very enjoyable. We drove from North Bovey to Tavistock, and from thence walked through Callington and Menheniot to Looe. We passed Coldrenick late at night, and the valley looked very beautiful in the moonlight. Next day we reached Bodmin, and so on to Truro and Helston, and after a day at the Lizard we arrived at Penzance. My companion was a very High Churchman, and I proposed to him that we should spend our Sunday in the investigation of the working of Nonconformity in one of its strongholds. He replied that there was a very advanced church just outside the town, and that if I would rise early and communicate with him there, he would be at my disposal for the rest of the day.

We went to various chapels, and I was much impressed in various ways. They differed greatly from one another, and the attendances also varied very much. There is probably not as much stability in most chapels as there is in our parish churches. Their prosperity depends more upon the minister. One thing that struck me forcibly was the extreme civility shown to us by members of the various sects. When we went to the great Wesleyan Chapel, for instance, we were immediately accosted, and asked whether we preferred seats in the body of the building or would go into the gallery. We were provided with cushions and hymn-books, and were generally honoured and attended to.

What a contrast this was to a stranger's ordinary reception in church. *There,* as it seems to me, you are generally regarded either as the possible donor of small coins, or else as an objectionable intruder, and if you enter a sitting unsolicited it is more than probable that you will be rudely ejected.

I thought that the Wesleyan congregation at Penzance was much more elaborately dressed than is customary with church people. The sermon, which was able, carefully prepared, and to me doctrinally unobjectionable, was, nevertheless, highly sensational, and I wondered how it could be possible to keep any audience long at so high a pitch of tension. It is a mistake. It is like feeding people upon highly spiced viands and stimulants; reaction is the result. Great preachers, like Lidden, do not condescend to these practices, but are simpler and more natural.

We also went to the Bible Christians, and I punched two little Bible Christian heads for chattering and disturbing the preacher, who was a young seafaring man of strong convictions, and possessed of the charming simplicity so often to be found in men of his calling. There is a spirit, also, of patient endurance, frequently noticeable in those that 'go down to the sea in ships and occupy their business in great waters', which is exceedingly pathetic, and appeals to many of us very strongly.

Then we walked to the Land's End, and back by the north coast, visiting Newquay, Padstow, and Tintagel, on our way to Bude, from which latter place we struck across country to Holsworthy, Hatherleigh, and so to North Bovey. We were absent from home for ten days, and averaged about thirty miles a day, excluding the Sunday.

When we got back I was so seasoned that I felt fit for anything. The Cornish people appeared to me, so far as I could see in so short a time, to be generally very gentle, hospitable, and kindly; but in later days I have discovered that they have some of the faults as well as some of the virtues of the Celt.

Much of the coast scenery of Cornwall is remarkable, and the seas are magnificent. The quarter of a century, however, which has elapsed since Mr Furnival walked this round with me has, I fear, converted many a lonely fishing hamlet into a crowded watering-place, and I congratulate myself with the thought that I have had most of my innings in older and happier days.

Other people may feel differently, but to me my fellow creatures of all ranks are far more acceptable when they are engaged in their ordinary avocations than when they are massed together for a holiday. Moreover, as previously remarked, they generally do no good to the inhabitants of the places which, as holidaymakers, they frequent. These were the years of hot summers: 1868–69 and 1870 were very hot and dry, and went far to ruin the farmers. They were, also, years of great inflation of prices.

The Australian gold discoveries of 1851 had already raised prices. Mr Gladstone had informed the people of England that their prosperity was increasing by leaps and bounds; and as usual they had believed him. They therefore spent for the most part two years' income in one, and this created, of course, an artificial plethora of money, so that the warnings of these disastrous years of drought were too generally disregarded. Many a family with which I am well acquainted is regretting now in distressing poverty the foolish extravagance of that period.

In the year 1868 the well of my house gave out, and I sent a man down with a jumper. The well is only eleven feet deep, and he worked with the jumper until he had bored a hole two inches in diameter for another eleven feet, through the solid rock. Since that time the well has never become dry. It does not always answer, however, thus to deepen wells. You may, perhaps, knock the bottom out, and then all the water will run away. I have known such misfortunes, and other strange ones happen which are described in my paper upon 'Springs and Wells,' read before the Teign Valley Field Naturalists' Society.

The character of the society is, however, a good deal altered. When, for instance, I first joined, about the year 1862, we had no lady visitors. Our plan was to meet at some rendezvous with a sandwich or two in our pockets, and from thence we would start and search the neighbourhood, until we returned to our carriages, footsore and tired. If possible we contrived to induce some man of proved knowledge to accompany us, and we learned a good deal from him.

Now all this is changed. Ladies abound; the society is greatly enlarged; the picnic element prevails, large luncheons are deemed to be indispensable, and much exertion of either mind or body is deprecated; but we still maintain the paper. If *that* were permitted to drop, the whole affair would, I fear, degenerate into gossip, champagne and a drive in a carriage.

Out of this society grew a habit of making up walking tours: of these Mr Divett was the organiser, and with Lord Clifford and his son, Mr Hawker, Mr Anstice, Lord Coleridge, Mr Bentinck and others, I would often walk for three days at a time, visiting regions which lay quite beyond the sphere of the Naturalists' Society. In this way we became acquainted with all parts of the county and greatly enjoyed ourselves.

The Bishop worked me rather hard in those days. I was once serving him as Rural Dean for sixteen hours at a stretch, and I finished up the evening by getting kicked out of my trap on Langford Hill, and then being bitten by the horse. The maid who opened the door to me about one a.m. nearly fainted when she saw my bleeding condition. I often held services on Dartmoor after my own Sunday work was done, and clergymen at a great distance would, when ill, fall back upon my assistance, for I was very strong, very willing, and always well-mounted.

The parish of North Bovey is a large one, although the population was under five hundred. My church at this time was restored at a personal cost of about six hundred pounds, and I had a good deal of family business to attend to.

Many people, moreover, made a practice of consulting me upon their monetary affairs, and I have had in this way much trouble, especially with ladies, who would insist upon trusting to my honour and good judgment in a fashion that is perfectly reckless. Added to all this, I shot in the season, and sometimes rode out with hounds, most frequently upon the mare of famous memory and performance whom I named Susan.

Not contented with all these avocations, and some teaching at the school, I went down to Newton one evening and bought an estate called Potworthy and Bridge at auction. Together the two places contained one hundred and forty acres, and they are situated in the parish of North Bovey. A curious circumstance occurred when I purchased them. The sale was at the Globe Hotel at eight in the evening. I made up my mind to give one thousand six hundred pounds for the two farms, and I wrote down that figure on a paper before me to avoid being carried away by the bidding.

Somebody in the room offered one thousand six hundred and ten pounds, and I would not go on. Presently a red-faced man, who was seated opposite to me at the table, threw a little piece of dirty paper in my direction, upon which was written, *How much will you give me for my bargain?*

I wrote back that I would give one thousand six hundred and fifty pounds, and he came round to me and said that he wanted one thousand seven hundred pounds, and when I shook my head he exclaimed, 'What nonsense; if it is worth one thousand six hundred and fifty pounds to you, it is worth one thousand seven hundred pounds, so you may as well give in at once and save yourself and me all further trouble.'

Upon this I laughed, and told him that he was a queer kind of man, but must have, I supposed, what he wanted.

'You are a good sort,' he said, 'take that,' and so saying he put a ten-pound bank-note into my hand, and I drew a cheque for one thousand seven hundred pounds, or for the proportion of that amount which was required on the spot. The man turned out to be what is called, I believe, 'an auction shark,' and he made eighty pounds out of me that evening. He was reported to have acted on this occasion for an old farmer of Temperleigh, who went by the name of 'King Law,' of whom the story is told that when a clergyman came down to officiate at Temperleigh, with a view to inspecting the small benefice, Mr Law invited him to dinner between the services.

As they were going from the church the clergyman asked him how he had liked his sermon, and received the reply, 'I liked it well enough the first time I heard it, but I am most tired of it now.'

In the evening at tea the preacher said, in an aggrieved tone of voice, 'Well, Mr Law, I hoped you liked the evening discourse better than that of the morning. I am sure you have never heard *it* before.'

'No, I never didn't, and I hope I never may more.'

Two old brothers named Kerslake had rented the farm, and they gave it up to me. Thinking to improve it and at the same time to amuse myself, I took the place in hand and set to work with vigour. Already I had the glebe of twenty-two acres in my own occupation; the two farms contained one hundred and forty acres, and I went down to Harberton Ford and took ten acres of fat land at nearly ten pounds an acre, for change for the cattle. Then I engaged two labouring men under my own old hind, and I bought three farm horses.

Carthorses were very dear in 1871, and the people about North Bovey asked me seventy pounds for a good one, so one morning I put on a black tie and a grey coat and, accompanied by my little daughter Florence, started very early for Crediton. I left the child with an old servant who was married to a painter in the town, and started on foot to Stockleigh English, where there was a sale of farm stock, with many horses included.

I gave a couple of shillings to an old labourer, and after asking particularly about the cows, said casually, 'Are any of the horses good for anything?' and he told me that a bay and a grey were excellent farm horses, so I bought them both for fifty-eight pounds, and told my North Bovey friends on my return that I could buy better horses abroad than at home.

My conscience was a little uneasy, for I was farming one hundred and seventy acres, as well as carrying out improvements. I feared that I was outside the four corners of the law, but I laid the flattering unction to my soul that the Act forbids 'taking,' and I did not 'take' but 'owned,' and that I only intended to farm until I had improved my estate. Moreover I had read somewhere or another that no man dies with his duty done who has not become the father of a child, written a book, and planted a tree. I had to a certain extent accomplished the first requirements, and now I planted vigorously.

I cut down a plantation of about four acres and sold the trees for five hundred and twenty pounds. I blew up rocks and drained bogs. I began with very young cattle, and did not expect to make any money for the first year, or until my stock had matured. It was all expenditure, no return, and I succeeded famously.

My stock prospered, my land began to smile, my crops were excellent, but one day I met old Kerslake, the late tenant of the farm, and he began:

'A nice little place that of yours was before you took and spoiled it.'

'Why, my dear man,' said I, 'I have only drained the bogs and blown up the rocks, and improved the buildings, besides manuring the ground; the place is now worth a lot more than it was when you left it.'

'I would not give thee so much for it by twenty pounds,' said he. 'They moors were nice cow ground before you took and drained 'em. Now they ain't worth nought,' and I began to wonder whether it was wise to go on. Then soon there was produce to sell, and at once my troubles began. I could grow crops with anyone, but I could not face the markets. My man somehow or other could not sell, and when I myself went to market my good friends would gather around me and say, 'Here you come, you are a gentleman, and we mean to pull a pound or two out of you today,' and they pulled it.

So I had an auction and sold everything, realising about one thousand three hundred pounds, which repaid me very well for my outlay. Then I let the farm for seventy pounds, but my tenant always wanted to have the rent laid out again in repairs and improvements, so I began to grow as weary of landowning as I was of farming. I offered to let him spend at my cost anything he liked in improvements if he would pay me five per cent on the outlay. He, however, replied that he wanted the outlay, but did not want to pay the five per cent. So I determined to sell the place, and soon found a purchaser in a Mr Palmer, who in 1878 gave me what I had given, and also paid me again for what I had laid out in improvements. Then I fell back upon the glebe, which I still farm to advantage, as I myself consume the produce.

The fact is that a sensible gentleman can farm as well as anyone else so long as he consumes his own produce, but when he buys and sells each operation costs him ten per cent more or less than it costs his professional neighbour who knows the markets, and will not take less than fair value, or pay more than market price.

In 1878 Mr Lodwick proposed for my daughter Florence, who was many years younger than himself. His offer took me altogether by surprise, and I was in great perplexity. She was but seventeen years of age, and he was considerably older. I told him that I was flattered by his proposal, but that I should take the girl to Italy for three months, and must request him to remain at home and not further press his attentions until after our return to England. She required time, and change of scene, before she could make up her mind to a step so important.

He acquiesced, and to Italy we went. My eldest daughter also went with us. Mr Lodwick was neither to write nor to follow, and I vainly thought that I had done a good stroke of business and given my daughter some time to make up her mind. But really in these matters a man is practically helpless, as the event soon proved.

On the evening before our departure Mr Palmer called upon me with a request that I would relieve him of two thousand pounds, the price of the farm. 'But, my dear sir,' said I, 'I have no title deeds to give you, they are with my lawyer, unsigned, and I do not even know that your solicitor is satisfied with them.'

'Never mind, sir,' said he, 'I am oppressed with this burdensome money, and take it you really must.'

So I accepted his cheque and gave him nothing in return; but, stopping next day in Exeter, I signed my name to the necessary papers, and directed my lawyer to forward the documents to the purchaser at once.

We went to Marseilles, and from thence by steamer to Naples, and put up at a new hotel. There we remained for a week, driving about and visiting the city and the neighbourhood. Afterwards we went on to Sorrento. The two girls rode donkeys about the hills by day, and danced by night in the big chamber below the ground in the Tramontano Hotel. Then we went to Capri, where I met with the native-born Lady Grantly, and little thought that I should soon be connected with her family by means of a daughter's marriage.

At Capri I thought that my daughter Florence seemed to be poorly, so I took her in an open rowing-boat across the bay to Ischia, and we were for a whole day on the water. When we reached the landing stage at Casamicciola she was very ill, and I could hardly get her to the hotel called the Piccola Sentimella. On entering, I was terribly alarmed lest the landlord should refuse to admit her, but was much relieved when the landlady, one Madame Dombré received us with every kindness. The sick girl, whose face was already pinched and drawn, while her eyes appeared to be abnormally brilliant, was put to bed.

I asked about a doctor, and Madame Dombré told me that she had great confidence in her own medical man, who of course, was only an Italian country practitioner. There was no English doctor nearer than Naples, where Dr Strange had lived for many years. Naples is twenty miles away. I sent for the Italian, who said at once that my poor child had contracted typhoid fever at Naples, and the disease had been incubating at Sorrento and at Capri. I suggested that we should call in Dr Strange for consultation, but the Italian replied that if Dr Strange came he would not further attend the case, adding, 'I have a great respect for your English doctors in England, but not here. They never can remember that they are practising at a distance of six hundred miles to the south of their native land. They make insufficient allowances for climate. If Dr Strange comes he will order milk and brandy. I will not allow her one drop either of one or the other. She shall have clear beef-tea and good claret only.'

What could I do? I gave in. He did not separate the sisters, but allowed them to occupy the same bedroom. The landlady was kindness itself, and the many inmates of the house behaved nobly. They did not remonstrate, nor leave the hotel. In a few days Mr Lodwick heard of the illness and declared that his arrangement with me was ended by circumstances. He wrote impassioned letters, but directed them wrongly. There were Thorntons in Southern Italy besides ourselves, and into their hands this correspondence fell.

Just at the crisis of the complaint, when life was trembling on the balance, the poor child was inadvertently told of this contretemps by Madame Dombré, and in her excitement she burst a blood-vessel in her head. I could not stay the bleeding from the nose, but the doctor came and applied cold bandages and put her into a particular position; nevertheless next day her condition was desperate. I was in an agony, for besides my natural distress I knew that if she died I should be blamed for not having called in Dr Strange; and I knew also what troubles people have with their Protestant dead in Italy. Madame Dombré was with her patient constantly, and I engaged the services of a peasant woman of the place as nurse. She slept on the floor with a string round her wrist, and her patience, piety, and moderation in charges again raised the Roman Catholic religion in its practical aspect very much in my estimation.

That good woman never once came in the evening without having first gone to service in church, and after each weary night (she held on for fifteen or sixteen consecutive nights,) she always attended church again before she went to bed for the day. She was never tired, never cross, and expected exceedingly little reward.

There was a large family party of the name of Mangles in the house, with whom, when her sister began to improve, my daughter Mary and I made many expeditions. Robert Mangles had been Mr Lodwick's intimate friend and companion at Haileybury and in India, where both had been employed in the finance departments. He little suspected what was occurring, and spoke unreservedly of his friend.

On one occasion we went all round the island, the ladies mounted, Mr Mangles and myself on foot. It was strange to have to leap over the streams, which flowed full of boiling water down from the mountain to the sea. The people generally were very good and gentle. I was told that there was no lock upon the one prison door in the island, and that on a memorable occasion, when they had actually put a prisoner in the gaol, he was so supremely unhappy that the authorities, almost weeping, went themselves to take him out, with earnest entreaties that he would never offend again or transgress the law in any way.

While my daughter was ill, I nearly wore off the sole of one of my boots by climbing about the rough sides of Mount Epomeo. Loitering in this condition through the main street of Casamicciola, I saw a shoemaker at work in an open shop, outside of which was an awning with a bench below. Mustering all the Italian I knew, I asked the shoemaker whether he would resole the boot while I waited outside, and as he nodded affirmatively I drew off the boot, lighted a cigar, and sat down upon the bench. I was wearing white cotton socks, and my appearance must have been peculiar in the extreme, and so thought a troop of Italian girls, who came running home from school down some steep steps.

There is something peculiarly attractive in young Italian girls; I thought so then, as with shy, sweet smiles they turned away from the steps to go to their dwellings on the slope. But my appearance was so very funny that one little maiden of about eight years of age could not resist the temptation to turn back and have another look at me before she ran off to rejoin her companions.

I was tired of waiting, the demon of mischief was in me, and the child's second look stirred him up, so as soon as her back was turned I jumped up from the seat and with one shoe off and the other on, dashed up the stairs, rounded the corner, and pounced upon my prey. She was terrified, but I caught her up in my arms and ran with her down to the bench. Then seating her on my knee I said she was very naughty to laugh at a half-shod Englishman, and that for a punishment she must say her lessons to me. She was quite reassured to find herself so close to the old cobbler, and opening her book began very prettily to repeat what I thought were rather unsuitable lessons for so young a child. Her companions meanwhile had come down, and were now standing around looking on. After a time I searched my pockets and found half a dozen copper coins, which I gave to little Amelie, who slipped away with them into the town.

The shoemaker was slow over his work, and before he had finished I was surprised by the child, who returned laden with flowers, begged as I suppose from neighbours who had gardens: she jumped into my lap, and insisted upon decorating me . She put flowers into every available buttonhole and about my hat, so that I returned to the hotel most gaily decked out, to the horror of a very nice Free Kirk young Scotch lady, who was one of the most attentive of my Sunday congregation.

On the following day, while passing through the town, I met little Amelie again, and the child came at once with outstretched arms, holding up her face to be kissed. Then she informed the other children of the place, and soon I was regularly mobbed. It was impossible to leave the hotel without being beset by ever-increasing swarms of children who gave me flowers, instructed me in Italian, and conducted me about the country to show me whatever they thought was pretty or interesting.

My friends at Casamicciola were children, but in Capri a few weeks earlier I had been quite captivated by the older Italian girls, who carry baggage up the mountainside. I had a conversation with a band of them on the landing-place, and the principal spokeswoman informed me that they were not handsome – they did not call themselves handsome – but they were good, and one of them was *sposi* (engaged) to an Englishman, some artist probably. They were tall and slight, active as cats, and as graceful as gazelles. Signor Scoppa of the shop told me that some of them could carry on their slight necks and pretty heads as much as one hundred and fifty pounds weight, and that, too, for a mile uphill. I once begged of a party of these girls, saying that I was dying of famine, and they all entered into the joke and offered me halfpence.

The mountain Epomeo occupies the centre of the island of Ischia, and the ground gave forth an ominous hollow sound in response to the foot. When a stone was kicked up, a jet of steam would rise into the air; and often (as I lay awake during the night full of anxious forebodings for my daughter) I felt uneasy as I thought of the volcanic nature of the entire locality. But I little dreamed at the time how near, terrible, and destructive was the danger. Less than one short year later, Madame Dombré was walking home to her hotel in the warm moonlight of an autumn evening, together with her daughter, Madame Menella, and her two grandchildren. All was serene and peaceful. In the saloon, where for six Sundays I had conducted divine service, a gentleman was playing 'The Dead March in Saul' to a large company of visitors.

Suddenly the walking party were flung to the ground, and overwhelmed by the stones which fell from the neighbouring vineyard walls. There, unable to move or to speak to each other, they remained until the morning, when they were dug out. Madame Dombré was uninjured, Madame Menella crippled for life, and both the dear children were dead. When Madame Dombré reached her house she found it level with the ground, and she was told that more than forty corpses lay buried beneath its ruins.

The hotel had been largely built with borrowed money, and her husband was completely undone. The havoc wrought was, however, very general, and a European collection was made for the sufferers. I dislike wide corporate action if it can be avoided, so I wrote to my daughter and to Mr Rudgett, and forwarded thirty-five pounds to Madame Dombré through the Wesleyan chaplain at Naples.

As my second daughter recovered, I left her in the charge of Mrs Rudgett, and took the elder one to Rome. We went first to the Hotel d'Allemagne, but not being comfortable there we migrated to the Hotel de France, where we found some old Devonshire friends.

After a fortnight in Rome and its environs, during all which time my daughter, regardless of malaria, slept with her window open (such risks do fond parents run), we returned to Casamicciola. There picking up the convalescent, we took passage in a French steamer from the Levant to Marseilles: this vessel had broken down in her machinery. We were the only passengers on board and, my daughters becoming seasick, I had to dine alone with Frenchmen, who could only talk their native French. So we set up a dictionary at mealtimes, and when I broke down we would refer to it, to the amusement of all the party. They were always most kind and polite, as I think sailors generally are.

On reaching Paris Mr Lodwick met us and we went to the great hotel, at which I have often resided, but which now, for some unexplained reason, is much contracted. It used to make up eight hundred beds. My daughter finally accepted Mr Lodwick's proposals, and he insisted upon showing her the sights of the gay city. The result was that she had a relapse, and fever laid hold upon her again. Then we found out what it is to be ill in a foreign land under ordinary circumstances, and we remembered with gratitude the Piccola Sentinella and the kindness of Madame Dombré.

Soon after our return my daughter Florence was married at North Bovey, and left me to reside in a nice house in Surrey, which my son-in-law had bought when he returned from India. It was the first breach in the family circle, soon to be followed by the marriages in succession of Mary, Kate, Agnes, and Ethel. During my absence in July, the clergy made up their minds to substitute Mr Taylor for myself as Rural Dean. I had held the office for nine consecutive years, and it was somewhat expensive under Bishop Temple's Diocesan management, for in those days there was no fund from which to pay even out-of-pocket expenses.

I felt a little aggrieved, even as I felt aggrieved over the summary dismissal of the voluntary inspectors of schools. It is not wise, however, to permit oneself to take these things to heart. Life is full both of kind, unexpected acknowledgments of small services, and of somewhat ungrateful neglects; and a sensible man who, having a competency can afford to do so, had better proceed on his way unconcernedly, regardless of all human attention or neglect, contented to do his duty.

It was about this period of my life that I first began to feel the effects of advancing age. Until I was fifty I knew no difference, but now I began to think that a comfortable bed suited me better than a deal board, and that I felt happier if I had taken a good breakfast before I started for a long day's run on foot with the otter hounds.

Old Sir Fairfax Moresby told me that it was at the age of about fifty that he also first began to find that he had a body which required consideration. So frail and feeble is man! Ever since 1862 I had been liable to occasional fits of gout, and these gradually became more frequent and severe; so after fifty I began to go to Bath or Wiesbaden once a year, as Dr Budd, of North Tawton, recommended. My plan was to drink the waters, starve myself, reduce my allowance of alcohol to a minimum, walk and boat a good deal, and sit down every other day for twenty minutes immersed to the neck in water at one hundred degrees Fahrenheit.

My dear old friend George Collyns, of Moretonhampstead, used to warn me that I was running risks by so lowering my constitution, and prognosticated that some day or other I should not be able to recover myself, but would go out like a candle, exhausted. He was my doctor, and a sensible man, but so far his predictions have not been verified, and I have managed by this system to keep back the attacks of my enemy for three or four years at a time on an average.

No medicine has ever done me any good, and the advice of medical men as to gout treatment has in my experience varied with the practitioner. I therefore eat and drink whatever I like, take a good deal of exercise, expose myself to all weathers for long hours without food, and on the whole fare better than other gouty men of my acquaintance, who live by rule. Dear old Sir Thomas Acland and Admiral Moresby adopted similar tactics, and one lived to be eighty-four and the other ninety-one, with only occasional attacks of gout, while some of my friends who were careful have suffered more continuously and severely.

On one occasion Dr Jones, of Bath, bade me leave off my beer and drink claret instead . I went to Dr Budd at North Tawton, who said, 'Never mind Jones, and stick to your beer; it is better than his cheap washy claret at any time. Jones forgets that our thin, pale ales bear but little resemblance to the strong stingo once drunk by our ancestors.'

I drove back that day by Moretonhampstead and saw Dr Utting in the street. 'What, Dr Utting,' said I, 'is a patient to do when his doctors disagree? Here is Jones of Bath forbidding, and Budd of North Tawton recommending, me to drink beer.'

'How much beer do you take?' he enquired.

When I told him a pint daily he laughed, and said that so small a quantity could not affect me at all. 'I am going now,' he added, 'to visit a patient who has the gout. He drinks about two gallons of strong beer daily, and I think it affects *him.*'

Gout is, however, a nasty complaint, and has in turn affected my eyes, my knees, and my feet, besides producing lumbago and, worst of all, sciatica, which once held me in its horrid grip for nearly six months. I am, however, inclined to believe that a man who has gout suffers seldom from other complaints; and as I get off with an average month of pain at intervals of about four years I have not much to complain of.

In 1881 I took my daughters Constance and Kate to the Channel Islands, and through Brittany to Paris, where we greatly enjoyed ourselves. While we were in Jersey, we drove round the island in a very long char-a-banc, and the driving was marvellous. The roads in this island are often curiously tortuous, and the manner in which our driver negotiated the short zigzags with his long team and longer vehicle excited my admiration. Twice I have been nearly cast away on the shores of the Channel Islands in foggy weather, but I never fully realized the dangers of the coast until on this occasion when we saw the reefs between Jersey and St Malo. It is scarcely possible to pass between them, and my nephew Mr John Thornton very nearly lost his life in a French fishing-boat while attempting an unusual passage.

We were much charmed with Dinan, the quaintest of all old French towns. While we were there, we became very friendly with four young American architects, who were taking sketches of the strange medieval buildings with a view to reproducing old-world peculiarities in brand new American houses. The effect must be remarkable.

We stopped at Chartres to see the cathedral which, with the exceptions of Notre Dame and the cathedral at Rheims, impressed me more than any in France. French religious sentiment has, I fear, fallen very low, although it is said, and I hope truly, that now there is a revival. At Chartres we felt sorry for a grand old priest of the ancient order, as we noticed the coarse features of the rest of his clergy, ignorant men who ministered with him in that noble edifice. What can you expect in a country where, I believe, the pay of a priest is only a thousand francs yearly, and where the masses of the people have ceased to believe.

The cathedral was out of repair and untidily kept, and yet it is a noble national monument, reared in those days when France was truly called the eldest daughter of the Church of Christendom. My daughters enjoyed themselves greatly in Paris. We went everywhere and saw everything, for I know the gay city well and am an excellent guide.

In 1885 my daughter Kate married Mr Billinghurst, and I began once more to take an interest in shooting, A year or two before this time I had given my gun away to a young Mr Radford of Down St. Mary, who was found dead in the road some time afterwards, but not, I am glad to say, through the instrumentality of my gun.

The fact was, I had discovered that a growing-up family, increasing business transactions, the charge of a parish and poor law, and other work, occupied my time pretty fully. I was, moreover, fond of hunting, and if I did anything in the way of sport I liked to go to hounds. A great change also was creeping gradually over the country. All wild sport was coming to an end, and preserved sport was taking its place. I was used to the freer system; age, too, was beginning to tell upon me, and I was no longer able to boast that distances were of no consequence; but with this new son-in-law I again tramped the moors almost as vigorously as ten years before I had tramped them with that prince of sportsmen, Mr Bird of Christow.

Now, however, for the first time I carried no gun, but Mr Billinghurst is a capital shot, and we have had many a good day together. Moreover he fishes, and I occasionally wander with him still by many a brook, and, while I carry his basket, think of the days long since gone by when I was able to bring home two fish to his one. This, however, reflects no discredit upon him. He is an excellent fisherman, but the rivers are not now what they were when in the fifties I filled my creel so copiously.

I am sixty-six, and I can still walk twenty miles or ride one hundred, but I am apt to feel tired when I walk with the boys. They are too quick for me, and my feet grow weary before the day is over. Little of this infirmity came upon me, however, until I was fifty-five or more, so I must not too greatly complain.

CHAPTER EIGHT

Changing Times

DURING THE FIFTY years in which I have known the West Country and its inhabitants, many changes have occurred in both places and people. Towns have grown larger, and the country has everywhere been pierced and interpenetrated by railways. Education has become general, and wealth has greatly increased and multiplied. Above all, people from other counties have come in among us, and have altered our habits, as they have built or occupied our houses.

In my young days almost all the gentlemen who resided outside the towns were clergymen, and as Mr Baring Gould has remarked, clergymen are in some respects unfortunately situated. You rarely hear, I mean, of the good ones. It is a necessity with a country clergyman that he should be obscure unless, indeed, he betakes himself to literature, and that is in itself a snare. I well remember how my dear old father expressed his disapproval when I consulted him upon the question of becoming curate to a vicar who was compiling a county history. He thought that the man would be buried in his books, and being absorbed by his researches, would neglect his parochial duties the better to attend to his literary work, and he feared lest I should learn from him to take a low view of my duties towards my parishioners. But of the ordinary country clergyman who attends to his schools and his classes, who visits the sick and helps the needy, and maintains the public worship of the church in its various departments efficiently, why, what is there to be said about him?

He goes on for forty or fifty years doing his duty quietly; he makes his friends and oft-times outlives them: indeed, people grow rather tired of his protracted old age, and when he dies he is decently buried and forgotten. There has probably been nothing very remarkable about him, and the little acts of good service which he has done, here to a soul, and there to a body, are not matters to be chronicled, remembered, or even so much as talked about. But let him be bad, or very eccentric, and then his memory flourishes for generations, and it is generally supposed by a credulous public that such as he was, so in his day all clergymen were.

If I were to tell tales of the good men whom I have known, you would not care to read them. So perforce I shall be driven to narrate histories of very queer people indeed, and in my early days there were several of that description to be found in the northern division of the County of Devon.

The state of society itself was in that district then exceedingly strange. Perhaps it will be enough to say that the moral tone was decidedly low, and that it was customary to bandy in a jocular tone soft impeachments of a description which would not now be alluded to. Nobody minded. I can remember when many gentlemen did their best to cheat one another in the matter of most things, and of horses in particular, and if they were successful they gloried in their rascality.

Mr Blackmore has written of a clergyman who was well known to me. He calls him Parson Chowne. I knew a great deal about him, and he was a bold bad man, as well as a clever one.

It so happened that Parson Chowne wanted a horse, and he asked his dear friend, who was the novelist's Mr Jack, if he knew where he could find one that was suitable.

'Would my brown horse do?' said Mr Jack. ' I want to sell him, because the hunting season is over, and I have too many horses. Come into town on Saturday and dine with me in the middle of the day, and see the horse. If you like him, you can have him, and if you do not, no harm will be done.'

On Saturday, into East Dolton came Parson Chowne, and stabled his horse at the lower end. He was by nature suspicious, so instead of going to the house, he went to Mr

Jack's stable and found the door locked. This circumstance made him more suspicious than ever, and looking
round he saw a man on a ladder from which he was
thatching. He called to him for assistance, shifted the
ladder to the stable, ascended, and went by the 'tallet'
door into the loft. He got down the steps inside, opened
the windows, and began carefully to examine the horse,
which he found to be suffering in both eyes from incipient
cataract. He climbed back, got down the ladder, and
shutting the windows, went to a shop to have his coat
brushed before he rang at his friend's doorbell. The door
was opened by Mr Jack, who said, 'You are early, Chowne.
Come across to the bank with me for a moment, if you do
not mind.'

In the street there was standing a Combe Martin cart
loaded with early vegetables, and in the cart was an old
pony, stone blind, with glassy white eyeballs. Chowne
paused, lifted the pony's head, turned its face to the light,
looked at the white eyeballs and remarked, 'How blessed
plenty blind horses are in this town just now, Jack.'

Not another word was said. The dinner was eaten, the
bottle of port wine was consumed, and Chowne, delighted,
rode home without have been asked to see the horse. The
other knew that the game was up, and that his little plan
for making his friend view the horse *after* he had dined,
and not before, had lamentably failed. But that was the
way, and I am not quite sure that one or two of the old
school do not yet remain in the county. I am sure that
there is one left still in South Devon, a most notorious
rascal.

In those days, men told of these transactions over their
wine, and were applauded rather than blamed for their
acuteness. All the ridicule fell upon the unfortunate dupe,
who very possibly had only erred by trusting to the honour
of a so-called gentleman.

Indeed, it was only last week that I met in Plymouth with
an acquaintance who had recently returned from Australia. In the course of conversation he said, with reference
to one of the greatest and most famous of the North Devon
celebrities, whose name I had accidentally mentioned,

'Yes, I know him. My father sold him a pack of harriers; he had the hounds, but he never paid the money.'

These men would condescend to the smallest tricks. They would trick you into letting them just *try* your horse, as they called it, and then would ride away and hunt him for the whole day, and return him to you with their compliments at night. When next you met them they would roar with immoderate laughter, and exclaim, 'Here comes the man who walked about in his boots all day while I rode his horse. Does he not look like the kind of beauty who *could* be so green? Never mind, old fellow, once bit, twice shy; we will help you to cut your wisdom teeth presently.' And then the ill-used man would blush, and vow inwardly that he, too, would cheat some one of other before very long, and so recover his tarnished reputation. I have seen a great deal of this kind of thing done in old North Devon.

There was a certain well-known clergyman, afterwards a Prebendary of Exeter Cathedral, whom Chowne hated. The prebendary was a very active man, rector of two little parishes, a scholar, a tutor of pupils, an active magistrate, chairman of Quarter Sessions, great at all public meetings, a big farmer, a good shot, and a hard rider to hounds. He was also very friendly with Mr Newton Fellowes, and was often his guest at Eggesford.

Chowne hated Mr Newton Fellowes because he was a road maker, and opened the country which Chowne desired to keep to himself; and he hated the clergyman because he was active, and because he went to Eggesford. He, therefore, said spiteful, witty, caustic things about him, which were remembered and often repeated for fifty years and more.

Chowne always had around him a tribe of vagabonds, whom he harboured. They beat the coverts when he shot, they found hares for his hounds to hunt, they ran on his errands, they were the terror of the countryside and were reputed to commit crimes at their master's instigation. He never paid them anything, or spared or sheltered them

from punishment. Sometimes they were in gaol, and sometimes out. They could always have as much bacon, potatoes, bread and cheese and cider at his house as they
pleased, as well as a fire to sit by, or a rough bed to lie down
on.

Plantations were burned, horses mutilated, chimneys
choked, and Chowne's men had the credit of these mis-
deeds, which were generally committed to the injury of
some person with whom Chowne had quarrelled. I have
known him say to a young farmer, 'John , I like that colt of
yours. I will give you twenty-five pounds for him.'

The owner has replied that it was not money enough,
and Chowne has retorted, 'You had better let me have
him, Jack. I have noticed that when a man refuses an offer
for a horse from me something goes wrong with the
animal. It is very curious really that it should be so, but so it
is.' And the horse would be sent to him for twenty-five
pounds.

One day a nice little girl in Chowne's parish went out for
a walk and did not return. Search was made for her, and lo,
on the grass by the wayside her bonnet was found stained
with blood, and near it was one little shoe. The excitement, of course, was intense in the neighbourhood, and
the active clerical magistrate who lived very near to
Chowne was in the saddle from morning to night. When
the local police failed to discover the body, he want by
coach to London, and brought back a detective with him,
but in vain. After a week or so, and when the magistrate
was in the court-house at East Dalton, Chowne entered
with a nice little girl by his side.

'Mr Dash,' said he with a smile, 'I hear that you have
been looking for a little maid for some time past. I wonder
whether this is the one you want.' The parents of the child
were Chowne's tenants, and the little thing had been all
the time at the rectory. This was what he called 'getting a
rise out of Dash.'

He was frequently engaged in litigation, and one day Mr
Cockburn (afterwards Lord Chief Justice of England, but
then a wild young fellow enough,) was engaged against
him, and Chowne lost his case. Cockburn then, or so it is
said, left the court in the Castle of Exeter in order to have

some luncheon. In the Castle Yard he saw an old country-man in yellow leggings and a long blue coat, who had an ash sapling in his hand. As the great lawyer passed him, *whack!* Down came the stick across the silk gown upon his shoulders.

'Be you the young rascal who spoke up against me in court just now?'

'I suppose that you are Parson Chowne,' said Cockburn. 'I was against you, and I am very glad that I succeeded, and now I am inclined to have you up for striking me.'

'No, you won't,' was the reply, 'you will come and have luncheon with me instead. You are a deuced clever young chap, and I am hanged if I ever have a case on again without employing you. So come along, you little beggar, and I will stand you a bottle of port.'

Cockburn went, and frequently afterwards he would stay with Chowne; and I have been told on most excellent authority that to the end you could not please the great lawyer better than by telling him some anecdote of his notorious acquaintance which he did not already know.

I could tell many more of these stories, and if my narrative is doubted, I can only reply that those were the days (not long gone by,) when the straw hat, with its blue ribbons, was exhibited on the western gallery of Countesbury church, together with the silver spoons, prizes for the wrestling match on the morrow. Those were the days when here at Moretonhampstead, when confirmations for the neighbourhood were being held, every public-house was open, and the young people, unrestrained, danced and revelled until late in the following day. Those were the days when old Parson Dash, whom I knew so well, gave out the meets of the stag-hounds in church.

Days when, before the commencement of the stag-hunting season, Parson Jones is said to have preached to the assembled sportsmen, who had just sung with gusto *As pants the hart for cooling streams*, a sermon long remembered, from the text, 'Lo, we heard of it at Ephratah, and we found it in the wood.' They were a wild set then in old North Devon, as wild as had been their Irish neighbours in County Clare half a century earlier. And some in South Devon were not far behind. But things are better now.

Some of the men resembled their masters, and I have a lively recollection of the peculiarities of Jack Babbage, of Limpety; of Whyte Melville's Red Rube, whose real name was Blackmore; and of many queer old smugglers, poachers, and sheep-stealers, who were well known to me in my younger days. Indeed, I have gone so far as to consort with the gipsies, at a time when gipsies – real dark Spanish gipsies – were still to be found in the land. I have in my youth been patronised by gipsy girls, and have been taken by them into their tents, and told of their ways and lawless habits, but I believe that those gipsy girls were, nevertheless, very careful of their reputation, and I never saw them exhibit the slightest indication of impropriety of behaviour.

Some of the clergy were exceedingly shy, and unused to society. Dr Richard Budd, who was until recently with us, told me that on one occasion he was sent for by Parson Griffith of Trentishoe, who was suffering from varicose veins in the leg. So he rode from Barnstaple to Trentishoe, and by a gate in a harvest field he saw a man of whom he enquired the way to the rectory. On reaching the house he found the door open, and a fire in full blaze, but no inmate. After waiting for some time, and shouting, he rode away, and on again reaching the harvest field he asked a labourer how he could find Mr Griffith, and was surprised to be told that the man who had directed him to the house was the rector himself, who had been too shy to receive him and who, after sending for him and misleading him, was actually hiding out of sight.

Even the bishops of those days were different from the present ones. There were learned bishops, and courtly bishops, and grand bishops, and friendly bishops, who really very little resembled the present race of what I will call parochial bishops, in manners, habits, or mind. I have known well in my day the grand, courtly Sumner, in all his magnificence; and Henry Philpotts, with his keen, bright, legal mind; as well as the captivating Samuel Wilberforce, with his ornate oratory and winning ways. Good Lord Auckland also who, when I was with him, was often like an old Eton schoolboy, hearty and kind. 'I say, William Henry,' he has said to me, 'you must now go to my secretary and pay no end of fees. It is a horrid shame, I know, but I can't help it. Go and talk to Marianne there about it. I would sooner have her opinion than that of the whole bench of bishops; yes, I would.'

He would lend me his horses, and laugh at me if I could not hold them. They do not make bishops like that nowadays – more's the pity!

The other church dignitaries are also greatly altered, as I think. They were bigger men in those days, and heartier. They would give you a good dinner, and they knew a great deal of Latin and Greek and Theology; but they were not so frequently mixing with all classes of people as do our present ones. We have gained in some ways, I suppose, and lost in others, as is usual in human life.

The squires of the past are gone, clean gone from my acquaintance, or rather, I should say only two or three very old ones remain. They were once the backbone of England, and were the men who saw us through the last great war. When the next war comes we shall miss them, for I doubt the staying powers of the new democracy. They are better in many ways than were their ancestors, these latter-day men, women, and children; but I question the stern grip of their tenacity. We have wheat now at twenty shillings, the old-fashioned squires are all dead, the farmers are half ruined, the labourers gone from our fields; when wheat goes up with a bound to one hundred and twenty shillings, what will our improved multitudinous town masters say and do? Will they disregard their famishing families, grip their rifles, and die hard with empty stomachs, as the old men would have done? I knew plenty of that sort in my youth, fellows who would fight cocks and dogs, swear hard, drink hard, fight hard, and die hard. We have improved them away, and I can only hope that we shall not again require such services as they rendered, at least in my time.

No change, however, strikes me so much as the change that has taken place in the matter of providence. The old men and women were exceedingly provident; in great matters as in small they were provident. Now all classes, politicians more particularly, live from hand to mouth.

The old people lived hard and saved for their children; the modern ones frequently spend all, and the children may take care of themselves.

The other day I was talking to a man who owns the coal under two thousand acres of Staffordshire land. 'How long will it last at the present rate of output?' said I in my old-world way.

'Thirty-five years,' he replied.

'And the coal of the country?' I enquired.

'They say for one hundred and fifty years, if we do not increase the consumption; but never mind, there is a lot in China,' said he.

They did not talk in that way when I was young, nor yet sacrifice the great future for the sake of a little present popularity; but they do so now. The women, also, are wonderfully altered. They used to be carefully looked after, and were apt to be rather prudish and precise. They would not go about without protection; they only read books that were approved of.

Last June I stood on Shillingford Bridge at night, one hundred miles above London by water, and *whirr, whirr,* with a twinkle and a flash, bicycle after bicycle ran past me in the darkness, with a girl astride upon each. Oh, shade of my grandmother! Oh, scruples of the past!

Not but what there were some dashing girls in the olden time, but then they were few and were not in favour. I remember how forty-five years ago, in Hampshire, I roughly thrust aside the head of a chestnut horse in order to jump up from a road into a field, and how next moment a young lady came up beside me as I galloped over the furrows. I lifted my hat and begged her pardon, saying that I did not know at the time that I was jamming up against a lady. 'Never mind me, young man,' she replied, 'you have plenty to do to take care of yourself,' and with that she put her horse at a gate on the swing, and marvel of marvels, it closed beneath her, and she cleared it without a fall. But ladies of her type were exceptions; now I think they are more common.

The old Devonshire lady was very precise and particular; she had great ideas of duty and of tidiness, and she did much work at home. The young ladies were generally shy and diffident, but they suited me well enough.

I have elsewhere written of the old professional men. They formed a class by themselves; they were very provincial, and often very witty. I remember how one in Exeter wrote the following lines whilst old Mr Newton Fellowes was, during an election, thundering that, 'For his part he would never consent to be priest-ridden, nor for that matter bishop-ridden, let his Lordship say what he would.'

The old lawyer below him wrote on a scrap of paper which he threw to a friend:-

Thou ridden! That thou'll never be

By bishop nor by priest;

Balaam is dead, and none but he

Would ride on such a beast!

But they are all gone now, manners, habits, dress, and turn of mind; all gone.

The old stage coachman is gone, and too often the old sportsman. I know masters of foxhounds now who do not know the names of their hounds, much less their ways, gifts, and peculiarities. The old sailors are gone, but not so completely, somehow, the old soldiers. The old servants are gone, although I still always manage to secure and retain very good ones. I really believe that I am about the last man left of whom his servants, male and female, always speak as 'master.' I never tell them to do so, but I smile as I hear them, for the word sounds to me like a sort of tribute to a consciousness of the fact that I am one of a bygone sort. I would do anything for them, and somehow they not only for the most part stay with me until they marry, but they generally marry from my house and not from their own.

When I went to Countisbury in 1853, the people used always to sing as they brought a corpse to the churchyard. There was a blind man with a blind sister in the choir; he had a high, cracked voice, and these two always came with the flute and the bass-viol up to the gate. As they approached, they sang, *'The meek companions of my grief shall find my table spread,'* and with that noble sentiment they concluded, and allowed me to commence my part of the service.

That blind man was a marvel. He was the regular letter-carrier of the district, and he used to traverse the narrowest and most dangerous tracks which run along the cliffs. One day he had rheumatic fever and was racked with pain, but he declared to me that he could not account for his illness, and that nothing particular had occurred. The fact was that he had become tipsy on sour cider and had fallen into a water-course, where he had remained for several hours.

Many of the old farmers were very remarkable. I once went to visit an old man aged one hundred years, and I asked him if he could remember the battle of the Nile.[3] He said that he could, and that he was a big boy when that event occurred. He also said that he was in his shirtsleeves hoeing turnips when the Scots Greys went by to Waterloo. 'But, lord a' massy, sir, I was an old man then.'

I told him that I was afraid that he had been a rough old fellow in his time, and had sworn harder and tippled more than he ought.

'Now, look here, meister,' said he, 'don't you go telling up such trade to me. I will never believe that God Almighty will be hard on a man who has grown such crops of oats as I have.'

He fully thought that he was born to be a Dartmoor farmer, and that he had fulfilled his vocation in life. I saw him out shooting a fortnight before he died of bronchitis, at the age of a hundred. I once asked him whether he ever said his prayers, and he answered with great satisfaction that when he heard the wind blowing hard on the moors he often thought of the sailors out at sea, and said, 'May the Lord have mercy on all poor souls,' This he considered a sufficient prayer for all occasions, and at least it was better than the Winsford farmer's petition, offered up when I was on Exmoor, 'God bless me and my wife, and nobody else.'

---

[3] Fought at Aboukir Bay near Alexandria in 1798.

I knew one old 'wrecker.' He never told me that he had committed any crimes in his calling, but he told me many smuggling tales. I have personally no great opinion of total abstinence from intoxicants, as I have met with a great deal of insincerity among total abstainers, and I fear that pledge-taking sometimes breeds deceitfulness; but I rejoice to think how much more temperate the people of the county now are than they were in my early days. I have more than once seen two bottles of port consumed by each man at a dinner party, and I have been in the company of yeoman farmers who drank a bottle of spirits and such during the evening. At the present time I only know of one or two such seasoned topers, but then on the other hand some of our young men nip wine or spirits all day long, which is, in my opinion, a worse habit than was ever known to their forefathers.

Since writing the last page, tidings have reached me of the death of one whose life and character have ever been peculiarly connected in my mind with the district and the times to which I have mainly been referring. I refer to Mr George Owen, a remarkable man, well known to many in Devonshire.

Born in 1810, he had a slight recollection of the Peace rejoicings of 1815, and a lively recollection of seeing Napoleon the First on board ship at Plymouth; of Newman playing the fiddle at Trinity, considered rather effeminate by the subject of these reminiscences, who was stroke of the college eight; of Lord Waterford and Hillsborough killing his friend in Christ Church quadrangle; of the Continent, including Metternich at Vienna, and of playing a rubber with King Ludwig at Munich; of a winter at Hamburg; then of a voyage up the Baltic on a timber ship, and down the Danube on a log raft. A man never without a gun or a fishing-rod in hand, and with the keen eye of a naturalist to keep in tune with them; with a taste for music, and an eye for a good painting.

Leading in youth the very life of life, he was a thorough Bohemian nevertheless at heart. Speaking French and German fluently and never, until yesterday in death, forgetting the classics. Whyte Melville knew him well and has vividly portrayed him in *Katerfelto*. It is strange that he should have lived to the age of eighty-six, an age to which his old friend John Russell said he never would attain. It was Russell's own age. Now he has followed his ancient friend, and 'our George,' as the people of East Devon would affectionately call him, has passed away from the hills and the valleys which he knew and loved so long and so well.

Almost as I heard of his death it was my fortune to meet with the lady to whom I dedicate these reminiscences, and she has reminded me that forty years ago I knew one Parson John (I will not give his surname) in North Devon. He was of yeoman type and extraction, and in my curate days I had heard that he was a great necromancer. People used to send for him to lay ghosts and to pronounce spells. Well, my lady friend was quite recently staying with her god-daughter, who is a great-niece to old Parson John. This niece told her that she is still in possession of the old man's books, but had looked in vain among them to find his book of charms. The lady begged to be allowed to go up into a loft in which rubbish was kept, and her search was rewarded, for she found the tattered remains of the formidable book. Her god-daughter begged her to take it away, as she dreaded to have the uncanny thing any longer in the house, and my friend has written about it to the authorities at the British Museum.

Strange to say, Parson John had a farmer brother who went to Germany and, returning, built for himself a little tower, which is still called by the people of North Devon the Wizard's Tower. So a love for the black art seems to have run in the family.

People were formerly very superstitious in the county, but I do not think much of that, because educated people are even now superstitious. I know an Oxford master of arts who lately took his sick child, who was very ill, to be touched by a seventh son. And any number of educated ladies and gentlemen believe that warts can be charmed away, or dangers foreseen by magic.

Nevertheless, I may as well write down some stories of superstitions that were current in parishes where I have been serving. A man at Slattenshade, near Lynton, when I was curate, thought, for example, that his wife was possessed by a devil, and he cut her arm badly to expel the demon. Moreover, his poor wife, I believe, was willing to be so treated.

One of my present parishioners told me the following story, which she vowed to be in every particular correct, and which she could personally verify, as it had come under her own observation. Forty years ago, all the farmers' wives at Manaton simultaneously found that their cream would not rise on the milk. They heated their pans and they waited, but no cream came. Then they met together in consultation, and soon found that one of their number had given grievous offence to a noted witch who lived in Chagford. So they sent two of their number to call upon her. These emissaries found the old woman seated on a settle in a deep chimney-nook, muttering.

They took the key from the house-door and flung it into the embers on the hearth, for they knew well that no witch on earth could stir from her place if this were done. Then they heaped up the fire until the chimney roared. 'If you are too warm, mother, you had better come out into the chamber,' they said, but the old witch did nothing but mutter. After they had roasted her properly through and through, they drew the key from the fire, and then the old woman rose and stumbled away to her bed, on which that night she died, for her liver and lungs were clean roasted within her; and lo! the next day all the cream rose sweetly on the milk in all the Manaton farmhouses.

The same woman told me that she was once well acquainted with a seventh son who could cure anybody of anything. He was a clergyman, she said, and did not like to refuse poor sufferers; but it took so much out of his own system to cure his neighbours, that his strength soon went away from him, and countless hordes of black flies beset him, and tormented him, until at last one night he fled, leaving no trace behind, to begin life anew where his secret was unknown.

My own servant, to my knowledge, has risen up early every morning to carry his baby down to a certain brook, to cross it and recross it, to cure the child of obstinate whooping-cough. But after all, kings and princesses, prime ministers and bishops, if they have the natural turn that way, are just as absurd about these things as are the Devonshire labourers. Who, that is of my age, but remembers how forty years ago London society was convulsed by a rascal who, for heavy payment, allowed his dupes to discern the future by gazing into a drop of ink in a glass bowl in the dark? Table-rapping, table-strapping, table-kicking, why – I have seen the best men in England and in Germany deluded by these things. Indeed, it was only the other day that I had a letter from a well-known London clergyman in which the writer said that, in the interests of the Psychological Society, he wished I would give him an account of all such weird things as I had known to occur in the West, for that 'no one could do it better.'

I replied by return of post as follows:

Dear Sir,

I can supply you with any number of well authenticated cases, all lies.

Yours truly, W.H.Thornton

After that, I did not hear from him again; nevertheless, I do not doubt for a moment but that, in fresh fields and pastures new, he is still pursuing his interesting researches into the obscure. He is a very good man , very capable, but credulous, and he recently asserted confidently in my presence that a feat which years ago I had doubted is now accomplished easily by every tyro who aspires to distinction in what I suppose is no longer considered to be the black art. I allude to the reading of the number upon a bank-note concealed in a box. I responded at once, and offered to risk one hundred pounds against five pounds, to be given to a charity, but somehow my challenge remains unaccepted.

It is remarkable that the most sceptical people with reference to religion are often the most superstitious. Human nature is allied to the unseen universe, and if legitimate belief in the supernatural is denied to it, it takes refuge, as I suppose, in the illegitimate.

For my own part, I have no belief at all in modern ghosts, goblins, dreams, presentiments, or miraculous healings, or prophesies. It is not that I disbelieve in the reality or even the nearness of the spirit world. It is that, as a matter of fact, all cases of alleged supernatural revelation in which I have been interested have so far broken down under my investigation.

I believe in spirits, but I do not think we can see them, and I doubt their power of speech. These manifestations serve no useful purpose. If some inspired little rogue can really tell me where I have to look to find a hidden pocket-handkerchief, why does he not tell the detectives of the place where Mrs Langtry's stolen jewels are deposited? He ought to make himself useful, and not confine his miraculous gifts to the mystification of simple folk in drawing-rooms.

There was great force, also, in an objection raised some time ago in one of the reviews, in an article entitled *Where are the letters?* Somehow or other, the recipients of letters which say that the writers have dreamed that their sons have been eaten by boa constrictors, or that their daughters have been kidnapped by cannibals, immediately burn these interesting documents.

It would assist to convert us sceptics vastly if we could see the original letter, with its date, in its envelope, with its stamp, and then compare this with the registrar's certificate, or some other authentic document; but, as the reader of these pages knows, a man who has several times routed bad ghosts with a broomstick or a poker is not likely to entertain much respect for the shadowy confraternity.

That there are about us spiritual forms I do not doubt, but I do not think that we can see them, and I do not believe that, bound to silence as they are upon great and most solemn subjects, they are occasionally permitted to break that silence on behalf of some special individual, to whom they generally communicate intelligence remarkable for its useless absurdity. If, moreover, all the wonders foretold were recorded, we should find ourselves overwhelmed by the mass of discredited politicians; but no notice is taken of these, and the ordinary process followed is to hear first of some tragedy, then to say that we mysteriously knew of it when it occurred, and wrote to a friend to tell him at the time, but unfortunately he burned the letter, as friends somehow always do.

My own wife has told me for five-and-thirty years, with surprising regularity, that she knows there will be a bad accident with a certain horse, and that I have no right to trust a lady upon him, who will undoubtedly be killed. For five-and-thirty years, poor dear lady, she has happily prophesied in vain. Some day, in the ordinary course of events, something will occur, to the great confirmation of the beliefs of the credulous.

CHAPTER NINE

On Sport

FIELD SPORTS ARE said to be cruel, and so, I suppose, they are, but they are not so bad as at first sight they appear to be. The prick of the hook is, without doubt, unpleasant to the fish, but the pain cannot be very bad or the fish would not continue to feed with a fish-hook in its mouth, as I have known one to do. A hunted fox has a bad quarter-of-an-hour at the end, but until the end comes he rather enjoys the sport. This assertion may seem to be absurd, but I have seen some curious confirmatory occurrences which my old sporting friends, I am sure, will gladly back.

Some fifteen years ago, when my dear old friend Mr Clarke kept hounds at Great Fulford, he found a fox in the park. The animal made for the deep Dunsford Woods, and running through a farmyard picked up a fowl, and carried it off. I remember the clatter of the women's tongues as the riders passed in pursuit, but the fox ran for nearly a mile with the hounds close behind him before he would drop the bird.

I was sitting on my horse beside old Mr George Luxton, of Winkleigh, one day. We were in the hollow between Ashridge Moor and Ashridge House, when a fox broke cover, and coming down the steep bank, made fun of us. I never saw anything more ridiculous. He threw his hind legs into the air, twisted his brush round his head, and frolicked exceedingly before he would run away, although Lord Portsmouth's crack pack of hounds were speaking to him not fifty yards behind. I remember the occurrence well, for at the moment Colonel Holley, of the Artillery, came crashing over the bank and, seeing the steep descent, laid hold of a mountain ash with both hands, and hung, swinging like Absalom, in the air, as his horse slid down, to be caught by us below.

I was riding with Mr Clarke one day near Dennis Down, and we heard a shout from Spreyton Woods below. Mr Clarke had an old worn-out hound and a couple of puppies at his heels, when out over the bank close to us tumbled the fattest fox imaginable. The old hound and the puppies jumped at him, but he curled himself into a semi-circle and hissed at them, so they hung back. Then we cracked our whips, and the fox ran away. I rode down into covert to tell the huntsman, and when I came back with him and the hounds, we found the fox sitting up on his hinder end like a judge in the middle of an open field, into which he had gone when we cracked our whips at him. He would not start until he had given the pack a good view.

Then he ran down to Bow Railway Station, where there is an embankment with gutters running through its width; into one of these this old joker ran and out on the other side, and up on to the railway line and so into a hole again. Mr Clarke and the huntsman were in terrible alarm for fear of the trains, and they got the hounds away as soon as they were able to do so, while this audacious animal, who had just run for half a dozen miles before the pack, was waving his brush, and playing bo-peep on the line.

It is not long ago that, near Sampford Courtenay, I said to Charles Littleworth, Lord Portsmouth's old huntsman, 'Charlie, look at yonder fox in the fallow, he is in a gin or is crippled; see, he keeps falling down again and again.'

'Nonsense,' said Littleworth, 'he is only *itemising*. They will do it at this time of the year. Tally ho!' and he blew his horn. Away went that fox like lightning, and saved his brush at Brushford.

It is only a year ago, that while the South Devon hounds were running hard over Hamildon, I saw a fox in full pursuit of the hounds. The little beast ran for a mile or more almost up to the sterns of the tail hounds, for fun. I cannot, therefore, believe that a fox feels frightened until he begins to feel exhausted. He has escaped similar perils ever since he was a little cub, and he thinks he will escape them again. No doubt the ending is bad, but he is saved sickness, and starvation, and want in old age, and as Mr William Collier says, 'Which of us would not gladly compound with destiny for a bad quarter of an hour at the end?' Besides, the beast owes his existence and long toleration to the chase. If there were no hounds there would be no foxes, and those which at present exist would perish much more miserably in gins and by poison.

Shooting is undoubtedly much more cruel, because of the wounded which escape; but then I do not shoot. Neither need the ordinary public complain until they have abolished trapping, which is a thousand times more cruel than shooting. Really I do not know of a more pitiable sound than that which comes from a hillside at night when a trapper is about; and a trapped cat's complaining is something too heartrending and horrible to hear. Why, again, are people allowed to bring sheep from abroad in layers one above another, until the lower ones are quite drenched and foul with abomination, and are slaughtered in this horrible condition, to the prejudice, one would think, of the national health?

Truly, we are a wonderful people. We strain at a gnat and we swallow a camel. Nevertheless, shooting, in my judgment, is the most cruel of the sports. A fish that escapes is never seriously injured; a hunted fox is generally only fatigued; but wild animals, and especially birds, are sensitive creatures, and must suffer when wounded. Therefore my advice to the merciful sportsman is to shoot straight.

Of course, there is in some quarters a great deal of feeling with regard to a clergyman's hunting, but I do not think that the measure which is commonly dealt out is altogether fair and equal. In the first place Christianity is very old; no new revelation has been given, and bishops and abbots in ancient days followed the chase and even kept hounds. In my own time I have known three canons, all of whom were of more than ordinary repute, who have ridden straight and hard. There is one living whom, when he has been mounted on his brown horse Anchor, I have found it quite impossible to catch. He is the hardest of the hard, and the boldest of the bold.

Prebendaries in numbers have in my time occasionally shouted, 'Tally ho!' and one of them at one time kept hounds. I do not see why a different measure should be dealt out to one man than to another. They are not all aristocrats, these clerical sportsmen, or popular preachers, or great authors, like the late Canon Kingsley.

If it were so, one could better understand why one man should be allowed to do that which is denied to another. Besides, what is the real moral difference between shooting and hunting? And if the former is objectionable as the latter, then goodbye to the reputation of some of our leaders, indeed.

I once heard a bishop speak hardly of hunting, but I remembered that he was himself a famous player at whist, and I reflected that the Puritan party would consider that his pastime was by far the more objectionable of the two. I have myself played a great many games of billiards with the famous Samuel Wilberforce. Yet my first squire and his wife thought no scorn either of whist or of hunting, but if I had attempted to play billiards their hair would have bristled upon their heads. As a general rule, you will find that most people

> Take part in sports they are inclined to,
> And damn the ones they have no mind to.

The only logical position is, I think, to be found in one or other of two alternatives: either life is too solemn a thing to allow of any amusements, in which case the bishop's whist and billiards are as bad as the curate's croquet, or the canon's warm corner at the bottom of the wood; or else that which is lawful for a layman is not wicked for a clergyman. And then it all becomes a question of degree and of moderation.

From this it would seem to follow, further, that a mild ritualistic curate, who plays lawn tennis five times a week, is a greater sinner than an old-fashioned rector who hunts on a Monday. But sometimes it is said that the language and general behaviour of men in the hunting field is particularly bad. I deny the assertion. I do not understand either why those who raise the objection, so often delight to honour the hunting men as soon as they have taken off their red coats. Is it supposed that sportsmen change their nature and their habits with their breeches? And if not, is it right to consort with them in the evening when you have been obliged to avoid them throughout the day?

For my part, off and on, I have ridden to hounds for fifty-five years, and I deliberately assert that very many of the best men that I have known throughout that long period, both lay and clerical, have ridden by my side. For nearly forty years, I was acquainted with John Russell, and he, as I thought, gave too much time to hunting, and made his pastime too much his business; but that is another matter.

I will finish these remarks by stating that what troubles me now in clerical life, as in other departments of our national life, is not occasional sporting but the growing unreality which saps the foundations of belief.

Men sometimes run churches as they run coaches, in order to fill them; or bury notorious free-thinkers with Christian rites and ceremonies, pronouncing over their remains the most touching expressions of confidence in the salvation by faith of the unbeliever below. These things, which are now only too common, trouble me greatly, but the men of whom I have been writing are not the ones who practise them.

Peersonally, I must own that ever since, as a schoolboy, I caught perch, or shot rabbits over the lonely wastes on which Clapham Junction Railway Station now stands, with its thousand daily passing trains, I have been something of a sportsman. Nothing has come much amiss to me, from sniggling loach in the Avon with a noose of wire, or catching eels with a clot of worms during a dark wet night in a thunderstorm, to landing salmon at Ballina, or hauling in heavy congers from the depths of the Irish Channel.

At one time I caught quantities of pike in the Thames, in days when house boats were unknown; but my principal scaly victims have been trout, and of these I have taken thousands, but chiefly of small size, from our Devon streams. The best river that I am acquainted with is the Test, in Hampshire, but I have had excellent trout fishing in Ireland and in Scotland, and good sport in Dorsetshire.

The old days are gone by, however, and no one will again rise (as I have done often at Selworthy, and at Lynmouth) early in the morning, gallop to Badgworthy or Cornham, put up his horse for twelve hours, and return without having seen a second rod upon the water. In those days we asked no permission, we required no licence, and we caught many trout. It is a curious fact, also, that then, when anybody could do anything, and each farmer had a spurt-net in his house, trout seemed to be thicker in the streams than at present. I do not know how to account for this deterioration, unless it be that more big fish are now left in the pools to eat the little ones.

Of course there are many more fishermen than there used to be, but nine out of ten of these catch nothing worth mentioning, and the scarcity is not owing to them. They make fish shy, perhaps, but they do not catch them.

I have known trout killed with a rifle, and it is a curious thing that they rarely appear to have been wounded, as they come to the surface upside down, without any mark upon their bodies. They are stunned, I suppose, by the passage of the bullet very near them. It is hard to hit a fish even when he is close to the surface of the water, and it is not a good thing to shoot at trout, as nothing that you can do will make them more shy. The best plan, as I have been told, is to fire at the ring which they make at the moment when they rise to take a fly.

The great art in fishing is to conceal your person. It does not much matter whether your tackle is fine or coarse. I have caught big trout upon ordinary whipcord, when it has been left all night in a river; and I do not think that they greatly mind a splash, but the smallest shadow, even that of the line upon the water, will frighten them away.

Of late years there have been more salmon in the Teign than formerly, or rather I should say that there was a period of scarcity, for the old labouring men have told me that in their youth, and when working for Dunsford farmers, they have been surfeited with salmon. The mines at Canonteign, when they were working, poisoned the fish, but now many of my friends catch a great many peel and salmon from Newton all the way up to above Chagford. .

Strange to say, I have never seen an otter in the water except when hounds were about; but I heard a shout once from a companion, who told me that he had seen one sitting upon the bank. My first day's otter hunting was with

Sir Robert Hill, in Shropshire, when I was ten years old; and since then there are few streams in Devonshire up which I have not scrambled in pursuit of this watery beast. The sport is not very good as a rule, for otters are scarce and shy, but it is pleasant to range with one's friends along the pretty brooks in the early morning, and to smell the bog-myrtle and peppermint as you crush them underfoot.

It is marvellous to see what ladies will sometimes do with otter-hounds. Some years ago I rode out with a friend from North Bovey to Teign House by about four a.m. It was just dawn when we arrived and put up our horses. In the road was a carriage containing an elderly lady, a young one, and a little girl. They had come from Torquay, a distance of eighteen miles. The hounds, on being taken to the water, gave tongue at once, and we all raced downstream, over hedges and ditches, past Ashton Bridge to the next below, then up a little brook to the summit of Haldon, to the bog by Kiddens. There we discovered that we had been running 'back-heels,' and the otter had gone the other way. The huntsman, good Mr Budgett, blew his horn, and we turned to retrace our steps.

Already, and at the best pace, we had covered nearly eight miles. I looked paternally at the child, and feeling a little exhausted myself, I went to the young lady and said boldly, 'Madam, you will kill that child. She cannot stand it; she has not been to bed all night, and the sun is now blazing hot.'

'What am I to do?' said the other, 'I am very sorry.'

'Give her to me,' said I. 'I don't know the people here from Adam, but I know the sort, I will make it all right.'

So I took the child and ran with her to a neighbouring white farmhouse, told my story to the farmer's wife, begged her to take charge of the child until I could send for her, turned round and raced down until I caught the hounds. Back we went by the way we came, and we never left off until we reached Chagford. So that we must have traversed some twenty-five miles over boulder, and fence, and watercourse.

Then I turned to the young lady and said that she must send a carriage from Chagford, past Ashton to Kiddens, and ask for such and such a farmhouse. This was done, and at about five o'clock in the evening that child was found sitting by the fire shelling peas. She had had her breakfast, been put to bed, given her dinner and tea, and is now, I believe, a distinguished ornament of polite society; but she owes really her health, if not her existence, to my timely intervention that day.

The scent of the otter is very strong. When the animal is out of the water, it does not emit much odour, but let it put even one toe down and the hounds will roar to the smell. They will sometimes hunt the water which has flowed over an otter's back for a long distance. The otter may have stopped in a hole, but the hounds will hunt the water and will have to be brought back to the place.

A male otter is generally much bolder than a female, and shows more sport. He will go downstream and away, while she sits in a stronghold dug deep under the bank of the river. Of all scents that of the otter is strongest, then comes that of the stag, then the fox, and then the hare. Scent is, however, an inscrutable thing, a thing which no man understands.

Otters breed at all seasons of the year, have two or three cubs at a birth, and generally, I think, bring up their young in the cliffs by the seaside. Later on they make their way to our rivers, often cross at the top over dry country, and descend by another watery route . Many an otter, I imagine, leaves Teignmouth, and arrives in this way at Barnstaple or, perhaps at Dartmouth. They bite very hard, and have skins so tough that the hounds are unable to tear them. I have seen many an otter with its bones all fractured by the teeth of the hounds, and the skin unbroken.

Although they are not numerous, they are very self-conservative animals; and my idea is that there will still be otter-hounds kept when our masters of the democracy have destroyed all other packs.

I was never a good shot. For years I kept a book, and my average was thirty head of game for every one hundred shots. I thought this bad shooting, and it reads like bad shooting, but for all that I have seen scores of men who were accounted to be good with the gun who have done no better. I did not shoot when on Exmoor, but while living at Dunsford I took up my gun again, and I have enjoyed the wild Dartmoor sport with Mr Bird more than any shooting I have had elsewhere, although the bags were small and the days exceedingly hard.

It was with Mr Bird that I once shot a jack snipe, which went to ground in a rat hole and had to be dug out like a fox. It was from him, also, that I once received some shot in the face. It was in Caroline Mire, and I shouted to him on the further side, 'Bird, you have shot me!'

'I ought not,' said my cool friend, 'for I have killed my bird right over you.'

I was then rural dean, rector of a parish, father of a family, much sought after by other people to do their business, and fond of hounds. I had little time for shooting, but was unwilling to annoy my friends by refusing their kind invitations to shoot, so fifteen years ago I gave away my gun, and have hardly discharged one since that time. But I still sometimes walk with the shooters, and mark for them. Their shooting is certainly better than ours was in former days, just as men's proficiency in all games becomes more marked as time goes on.

I can almost remember when percussion caps first came into use, and I quite remember when old flint and steel guns existed, and were used. It was in my father's time that a country newspaper inserted a notice to the effect that a certain colonel was coming into the neighbourhood, and added the information, 'We believe he shoots flying.'

But hunting has been my more favourite amusement ever since I rode in 1840 with the Brighton harriers. I have ridden most things with four legs, and have been very variously mounted, but if hereafter people should speak of me in this connection, it will be together with my indomitable mare, old Susan. It is impossible to chronicle all the memorable gallops of one's life, but on her I have seen some very noticeable runs with the staghounds on Exmoor, and with foxhounds in Dorsetshire and in Devonshire.

On several occasions I have seen a hunted animal hold on for quite twenty-five miles, which was the estimated distance covered in Mr Coryton's famous run, to which I have already alluded. A friend of mine got five falls during that gallop.

My day is nearly done, but for half a century I have liked the sport. I have liked the master and liked the men. I have been fond of the horse, and admired the hound. It has been a pleasure to me to wander through the nooks and corners of our dear old country, side by side with many a genial companion perhaps, only too probably, no longer to be met with.

But great changes have taken place. The old squires, the natural masters of hounds, are mostly gone. The new masters are good fellows, but they are not of the same sort as the old, and they do not go down so well with the people. Think of old Mr Farquharson, who hunted in Dorsetshire for half a century; or old Squire Trelawny, or the late Lord Portsmouth, or the Dukes of Beaufort today. What influence these men have had.

It is unfair to name them with the gentlemen who write M.F.H after their names, and disappear at the end of a season or two. Not that I find fault with the new men. We are exceedingly glad of their services. Some of them ride hard and are very keen, besides being pleasant and courteous enough in the field, but they were not born to their business, and they do not stick to it. They are, moreover, sometimes scarcely aware at first that there is a great deal in foxhunting, as in other pursuits, which is known only to those who have been long initiated.

Let me draw a slight sketch of a day's proceedings to show, perhaps, that I am myself not altogether uninitiated; to show that sport is one thing to a sporting man, anothing to the ordinary amateur, who only comes out occasionally.

Until quite lately, it has ever been my habit to disregard the field and to adhere to the hunt servants. This is a little irregular, perhaps, but the old masters have known that I am keen, and have allowed me to take liberties.

So it has been my delight to slip away with the whipper-in, ride fast down the cover side and out over the fence into the meadow at the bottom of the wood.

Then there is silence, while the man and I cling tightly to the corner of the cover, and wait. The holly bushes glisten with the rain as the sun shines brightly upon their glossy leaves. Presently there is a rustle inside, and Rockwood comes into view among the brambles. The old hound is quite unconscious of our existence. Every muscle is standing out, clear and distinct on his perfect figure. We can see him turn over the dry leaves with his eager, sensitive, expectant nose. Then a hound challenges deep down in the recesses of the wood, and up goes the noble head to listen.

I can see the look of disgust which comes over his expressive features as in dog language, quite comprehensible to me, he mutters to himself, 'Only that wretched puppy again, just rioting as usual, I suppose,' and down goes his head among the leaves. Then comes another note, and he seems to say, 'That is Dudley. By Jove, that is right, anyhow,' and he is gone in a moment to join his friend.

We sit still on our horses, and soon with a quick, active jump, a fox springs over the fence into the meadow, and smells the ground. There is no taint of hound outside, and away he steals, crouching his back down low, and making himself look small. We let him reach the bottom of the field and then we holloa. Up go our horses on their hindlegs, and turn round and round in their excitement. Then we hear the huntsman's horn with the note which says, 'broken covert, gone away,' as he comes galloping down the ride in the middle of the wood and out over the fence where the fox broke, with half the pack at his heels; the other half are already skimming over the meadow grass or breaking the fence beyond.

We have a fair start in advance of the field, and I look at the huntsman and resolve (for one short hour at least) to keep only unto him until death us to part. With a swishing sound from behind up come one or two lightweight men on fast horses, indulging in the immoral enjoyment of the scurry, for you should never scurry. Then we settle down in our places, and with eyes well forward, to note possible gaps and rideable fences, allow our horses to go as fast as we think they can go to last.

Then perhaps assistance needs to be rendered to a comrade in distress. 'My mare is down in this horrid bog, do come and help me to get her out.' The other day two friends of mine in this dilemma took off their red coats and placed them under the animal's hoofs. With a grunt and a struggle up came the mare, and down went the coats. They did not look very red when they came out of the black peat bog. As the night was frosty and one of the riders had far to go, he felt rather chilly, but he is not any the worse, nor yet is his coat; both are only a little better seasoned.

And then the conversation with the farmer, who tells you that he cannot grow any more wheat. It only entails loss. He has twenty ewes cored also, owing to the wetness of the season; they must be fattened as soon as possible and made the most of. Will you come in and have anything? And then the long ride home, at almost walking pace, with this or that companion, who leaves you in the darkness as he turns away to his home. It is a curious fact, but it is true, that tired horses freshen as they go on. The exhaustion consequent on the excitement and exertion of the gallop passes off, and at the end of sixty miles they are gamer than at fifty.

Thus, I have attempted to describe shortly a sample of the pleasures which I have found in foxhunting, but they are the pleasures of a sportsman, and the men who can enjoy them are, I fear, growing fewer: they are, generally, of the old-world sort.

Many foxhunters of these days know nothing about the fox, where he was bred, and by whom preserved from the many enemies of his playful infancy, whether he is dog or vixen, cub or old fox.

They know nothing about the farmer and do not care to talk to him. They do not know one hound from another, and make no enquiries after his ancestry. They have no fellowship with their horse, which is to them but a machine. They do not know their companions, with whom the sport has created no sense of kindly brotherhood. They hunt to ride and perhaps to grumble, and they do not obtain many of the gratifications which old sportsmen experience. Perhaps they come down by train from a distance – and never come again.

The old order changes, and England and English have altered more in my fifty years than in any previous half-century. I remember that I heard Mr Trelawny, when he was eighty years old, say that the greatest trial of old age is

caused by the loss of friends. I do not know how long he
hunted over Dartmoor, but the famous men of the Waterloo period, who once rode by his side, were all gone when
he spoke. So in a smaller way with myself. I ride still over
the old graceful valleys and climb the same steep hills. My
horse is as good as ever, and so is the sport, but where now
is John Russell, and George Luxton, and Lord Portsmouth, and Christian Budd?

It has never been my habit to carry luncheon, or a flask,
and in this I resemble the elders. The last time that I saw
Russell was in August, 1881. I had ridden down to Eggesford the night before in order to hunt an outlying stag,
and in the morning Lord Ebrington came with the pack,
and Russell came with him . We found the deer close to the
station, and ran by King's Nympton Park to George Nympton and Castle Hill, killing under South Molton at about
eight p.m.

My daughter's horse, which I was riding as my own was
not in condition so early in the year, was inadequate to my
weight, and was tired as I turned my head for Eggesford
and dinner. Presently there was a clatter behind me, and a
nice boy said, 'O, sir, your horse *is* tired. Come home with
me. My father is always glad to see a sportsman, and I
promise you faithfully that your horse shall be thoroughly
well done by.'

I told him that he was a good chap, who would come to
nothing but good, I was sure, and that I should like to
know his name, although I would not accept his offer. He
proved to be one of the younger sons of Mr Connop of
King's Nympton Park, and he rode on. Then a voice said,
'Hulloa, old friend, come home with me,' and old Mr
Luxton came alongside on a horse which looked quite
fresh.

He declared that he would not leave me until our ways
parted at Newnham, and I said, 'Do you still go without
luncheon, Mr Luxton? You are eighty years old and it is
now after eight p.m. *You* ought to trot on. *I* cannot.'

He said that he had breakfasted at seven a.m. and had
not eaten since. He should get his dinner at Winkleigh by
eleven p.m. and that would do very well; he would not
leave me. I asked him whether such abstinence did not at

eighty make him feel faint, and he said, 'No. When I was a young fellow of fifty I used to get hungry sometimes, but now I don't care; that is all.'

Russell that day was eighty-six or thereabouts, and he told me that he had ridden up to the meet from Porlock Weir, a distance of nearly forty miles. I never saw him again. Trelawny, Russell, and Luxton were perhaps the three hardest octogenarians I have known.

I remember the Squire, as they called him, when about eighty years old, cantering away from Lord Portsmouth's house at Eggesford for Plymouth, after having hunted at the opening meet. This, although he had a change of horses on the road, seemed to me to be a marvellous feat. Russell was simply not capable of feeling fatigue, and I have known Luxton hack down in the early morning from Winkleigh to Lynton (forty miles), drag young Newton Fellowes (the late Lord Portsmouth) out of bed, hunt with the staghounds all day, and ride back to dinner on the same horse which had carried him in the morning. He dined on this occasion after midnight.

I said to him, when he told me of the performance, 'But did you not find your horse very stiff and stale? It must have been bad work over Mole's Chamber and Chittleham holt in the dark, on a hack that had done forty miles in the morning.'

'I generally keep an old hunter that is good for nothing else, for that kind of work,' he said with great simplicity.

But it is time for me to have done with my tales of these iron men. There are a few of the old sort still left; not many. Mr Calmady has recently left us, but Mr Coryton will, I am sure, forgive me if I number him with the mighty dead. I did not know many of the companions of these ancients, who had mostly passed away before I came into the County, but I have heard of a Valhalla of granite chambers in which Tom Philips, Paul Treby, John Russell, Colonel Coryton, and Morth Woollcombe still stable their ghostly steeds.

Many of the successors of these men, and some of the men themselves I have known, and their spirits often appear to be very near to me as I revisit the old familiar haunts where I have so often accompanied them in the flesh. Mr Westlake taught me much of what little wood-craft I know. He was a funny old fellow of the yeoman class, but I was very fond of him, for he was a sterling, honest, good man. Full well do I remember his astonishment when Mr Dash (a man much higher in social position than himself, and with whom at the time he was staying) asked him to play at whist on a Sunday evening.

'Good Lord, sir. What would my old father say if he heard you? No, I am going to church, sir; and then I am going home. I will not stay in a house with such goings on. I hope you will all lose your money and have a bad headache besides. Goodbye.'

He was rather deaf, and would often make me listen for him, but his keenness of sight was wonderful. I have seen him ball a fox on a dry and dusty turnpike road as he went down it at a canter. The feat seems an impossible one, but I saw him perform it near to Goodstone Gate, on the road which leads to Halshanger. He could see at a distance of fifty paces where a single hound had passed through a covert. 'Look at the leaves, sir, look at the leaves; where are your eyes? Now, you listen for me. Can you hear 'em?'

'Good morning, Mr Westlake,' I said to him one day, 'I hope you are well.'

'Not so well as I could wish, sir. I feel pluffy, very pluffy indeed, and not fit. I gave a little party last night, sir, and Mr William and Mr George both came to it. I am very partial myself to a veal kidney, and I gave 'em one; and they drank my sherry wine, sir, and they drank my port wine, and when I wanted to play at whist, sir, they said no, they would play at vingt-un, and they played a sovereign out of my pocket, sir, before ever I stopped; but they will never set me dancing to that tune (vingt-un) again, I can assure you, and this morning, sir, I feel pluffy, sir; I assure you, sir, quite pluffy.'

The professional huntsmen whom I have known have been men as remarkable as their masters. I have a dim recollection of Limpity with the Dartmoor, as well as a clear one of his successor Boxall. No bolder rider than the former ever crossed a horse, and the latter was famous for his kennel management. I knew Jack Babbage with the staghounds, and Arthur Heale, and Huxtable. These three have hunted the Exmoor red deer, with the exception of short intervals, as long as I can remember. Beale, who was with Sir Walter Carew, I have seen, but not until after he had relinquished his horn.

The Eggesford pack will always be connected in my mind with Charles Littleworth, by whose side for forty years I have occasionally galloped. He was always cheery, and had a melodious voice, besides a separate note of the horn for each changing vicissitude of the chase. He knows, I verily believe, as much about the manners and customs of a fox as does the animal himself. Chubb was a good man with the Stevenstone, and Sam Gilmore, still with Mr Tremlett, is a character. These are the veterans, but more recently Yeo was a grand man with the Mid-Devon, a wonder over a country, and Brely goes with them still like a bird. Collings is equally good with the South Devon, and Yelverton's fame is widespread.

These are all good men, as good as their predecessors of old time, but they must forgive me if I say that, in my poor judgment, Philip Back is the finest horseman of them all. He is the quietest and boldest man on a horse imaginable, perhaps the very finest rider I ever saw cross a country in my life. It does not seem to matter in the least how he is mounted. It may be on an ancient thoroughbred stallion with marvellously crooked legs, or an old brood mare, or a pony. No matter the country, no matter the horse, no matter the fences, I will back Philip Back to be well forward, very quiet, very civil, always cool and smiling, and at the end of the day he will have taken the least exertion possible out of his horse.

Yeo is a marvellous man to get over a difficult country. He has an instinct which serves him in good stead. I well remember how, on one occasion, a farmer said, 'This is my land, and you cannot get out at the end of yonder wood. The fences are impracticable, and the ground so deep that a horse will be swallowed up immediately.' The fox, however, broke that way, and to our amazement we saw Yeo skim somewhere over the bog, jump the impracticable fence, and sail away up the hillside beyond with his hounds; but no one ventured to follow. He has a natural eye for country, and is a bold, determined man, but I used to think that he sometimes took, when with us, a good deal out of his horse.

As for myself, in a strange country I never could lead. If ever I make the attempt I find myself hopelessly blocked by some deep gully or morass, or other impediment. But as a compensation, my memory is excellent, and if I have not been in a valley more than once, and that twenty years before, still I know exactly how I got out, and can go at once to the weak places which then were pointed out to me. I do not think that I often forget any field into which I have ever been introduced.

One word on the subject of hunting-ladies. Some of them ride very straight and hard. I saw a lady in North Devon, some years ago, ride in a way that quite frightened me. She charged a bank, on which ran a narrow footpath, against which was another bank, quite perpendicular, with a strong growth atop, and the gap on the summit of this second bank contained the greasy stool of a great elm tree. At this horrible place she sent a well-bred horse at speed, and she got over. Chubb was there, and neither he nor anyone else attempted to follow her. I have see other women ride in like wild fashion, but very seldom with judgment, and not often for long.

My daughter, Mrs Frank Gotto, and a well-known lady with the South Devon, are exceptions to this rule. They can take care of their horses as well as of themselves, and know what is practicable, and what is not to be attempted. Most ladies make me nervous in the hunting-field. They seem to expect their horses to take care of them instead of taking charge of their horses, and before now I have seen them knocked off by boughs under which they were carelessly riding. They are, however, generally lightweights, and their male relatives mount them upon clever horses, so that they get off pretty well on the whole.

And now it is time to conclude. The old Rugby boy, the Trinity graduate, have had their say; the rector of North Bovey has spoken. This last chapter has been written with reference to sport – sport which still lingers in our land, the increase of population notwithstanding. How much longer it will last I know not, but this I know, that at sixty-seven years of age I begin for the first time to feel that I cannot go as well as formerly, and that with all kindly wishes for their welfare, it is necessary for an old man to give place to a younger generation of sportsmen.

Russell, however, rode to the end, and in the year 1876, when he was eighty-one years of age, he rode – if I am not mistaken – from Swynbridge to Mr Williams' house at Scorrier, in Cornwall, seventy-six miles on one horse in one day, in order to judge some puppies. He was poorly at the time, but mounted and rode back again in one day towards the end of the same week.

Let me conclude this chapter with a story of the veteran which is quite true, but is not told by Mr Davies in his *Life of Russell* and is not generally known. Russell was living at Dennington, and Mrs Russell kept turkeys, while her husband favoured foxes. On two successive mornings, the good lady missed a turkey and complained.

'My dear,' said Russell, 'you are a lighter sleeper than I am. Wake me if you hear the hens cackling in the night.'

About two in the morning of the following day she woke him, and after listening for a moment, he rose, slipped a coat over his nightshirt, and stealthily crept downstairs. He quickly saddled his horse and then, opening the kennel door, called out his hounds and cast them round the house. The dew was falling on the grass and the moon shone brightly as the hounds struck the line of the marauder.

'Ya-a-at him!' shouted Russell in his nightshirt, and away they went with a blazing scent. About four a.m. Russell came back to his wife. 'I am coming to bed, my dear,' said he, 'don't trouble about the turkeys, there's the brush of him.'

CHAPTER TWELVE

On Horses

THE GREAT CHANGES which have taken place in the course of the last half century have altered the horses in the West Country almost as much as they have altered the people. When I went down to Selworthy in 1847, the pack-horse was the animal most frequently to be found. He was a light cart-horse, with active habits. At the present time I have at least two of the same class in my stable, and I am never without them, but they are not exactly like the old pack-horse.

They are bred between a cart-horse and a light hackney mare, and chance has given to them the necessary shape, whereas the old-fashioned pack-horse, instead of being the result of compromise, was bred from a pack-mare by a pack-horse. He was, therefore, in some sort a thorough-bred unless, indeed, he had a strain of pony blood in him, which would make him more valuable if something smaller. He was a very useful animal. Generally about fifteen hands one inch in height, he could do anything. People were much poorer then than now, and their horses had to be useful.

I can well remember the time when I could always select for about twenty pounds, from the Coombe Martin lime-carts, a horse, tough as hemp, which could carry me hunting or hacking, a thing which he generally did very safely; carry a lady, go in double or single harness, and plough or draw coals if required to do so.

If anyone thinks this picture overdrawn, let him come to me, and I will now show him two or three horses which will do all this and do it fairly well, but, inasmuch as they have a strain of the heavy cart-horse in them, they are not quite so tough as were their predecessors. They will, however, draw or carry me for fifty miles very willingly, so I need not find much fault with them.

What made the farmers get rid of the old pack-horses I do not know, for they were quite invaluable, and some of them could trot very fast. They have, however, been so completely crossed up with the thoroughbreds that they are fairly extinct.

People, I suppose, do not require them now. The age has grown luxurious, economy is a lost art, and a hunter must be a flyer, a hack must do nothing but carry a man upon the road, a carriage-horse must be sixteen hands two inches high, and a trapper must show blood; a lady's horse must be all elegance, and a cart-horse take a ton. Everyone says that he is ruined by reason of the badness of the times, and yet nobody but myself will condescend to the old cut and contriving methods of fifty years ago.

They were good animals, these old pack-horses. In a banking country they were hard to beat, and for many a long year of my life I thought them good enough. I have one in my stable now, twenty years of age, and still active. Before I had him he had carried a man who weighed more than sixteen stones to hounds for years. No banking fence that is practicable would, can, or will stop him, or cause him to tumble down. He is a perfect model of the old-fashioned pack-horse, but he is not pure bred. People, I suppose, do not want now to go the long distances by road which their fathers went, and they fancy that better bred horses will accomplish the shorter journeys more quickly than will those of the pack-breed, but my old horse has done some quick things, and will do them again.

Better even than the packhorse for some purposes is the cross between a thoroughbred and a pony. An animal of this description rarely rises beyond fourteen hands two inches in height, and he must not be asked to carry much weight, but with ten or eleven stones on his back he is apt to be indomitable, if not invincible. Why more of these galloways are not bred I do not know, but if I had to mount a ten-stone man in Devonshire to perfection, I should try to obtain one.

I have heard Sir Frederic Knight say that in old days Mr
Edward Sandford, Rector of Combe Florey, had one of
them which, over Exmoor with the staghounds, was unap-
proachable. The three Knights, with Charles on Commodore, and Frederic on his famous steeplechaser Tory,
would race after this reverend gentlemen on his pony, and
if he had a fair start, would race in vain.

The best harness-horse that ever I owned was bred out of
a mare half cart-horse, half-pony, by a thoroughbred. He
cost twenty-three pounds one night at the George Inn,
South Molton. He was then out of mark, and he lasted me
for fourteen years. He was barely fifteen hands in height,
and he had a mouth like iron. He was enormously powerful and exceedingly fast, and did not know what it was to be
fatigued.

The journeys which this old horse accomplished would
seem to be incredible. I remember on one occasion driving him down to Tor Cross from North Bovey without
stopping, and I am quite sure that he could have run the
forty miles back in the evening if I had asked him to do so.
He was very cunning, and knew who was driving him. With
Mrs Thornton he would go at the rate of five miles an
hour, and for a lady he would stand at shop doors for ever,
but if I took up the reins he would start away at the rate of
sixteen miles an hour, and, pulling my arms nearly off,
pass everything on the road. This horse never did any
serious harm, but he could not bear to be hurt, and if he
had a trifling injury he was difficult to approach. If his
back was at all sore he would throw anyone who insisted
upon mounting him.

I was so fond of him that in later years I bought a mare,
half pony, half cart-horse, and put her to a thoroughbred.
My son-in-law, Mr Billingshurst, now has the colt, which is
only fourteen hands three inches high, too small for me,
but no better looking or better animal of his inches is
running in the County of Sussex today.

Some people believe only in thoroughbred horses, and I
have had very good ones in my time; notably a famous
mare called Susan, in connection with whom I may perhaps be remembered, if in these days of swift oblivion I am
remembered at all. I rode her for eleven seasons, and

during that long period she only gave me three falls. She
was absolutely invincible. No man could tire her in one day
if she was only fairly ridden. I have hacked her for sixty
miles and ridden her for a long day's hunting, all between
dawn and night, and she has not been tired in the least.

It is needless to say that I did not mean to give her so
severe a day when I started in the morning, but it is a fact
that she carried me that day from North Bovey to Dolton
by North Tawton and Wembworthy, and after a memorable run for two-and-a-half hours she came back with me
from Chawley without being fed. In this last respect rider
and horse of course fared alike. And on other days she has
done as long or longer a journey.

Some will say that her great performances were entirely
to be attributed to her blood, but not so, for I once bought
a horse of equal merit with herself which was reputed
indeed to be thoroughbred – but thoroughbred cart-horse
only. He belonged to a certain captain in the army who
resided in North Devon. No one could ride and no one
could drive him, so I bought him for twenty-five pounds.
This horse had been up, over, and into a gig, displacing the
occupants thereof. He also readily stood on his hind legs
in saddle and pawed like a chestnut bear. He would go out
of town by one road only, resolutely refusing to travel on
others.

The truth is that he had originally belonged to a farmer
living in the neighbourhood who, when the colt was two
years old, used to put his children upon him and thus sent
them daily to school. The poor beast was shut up in a shed
and starved all day, so when some good Samaritan had
hoisted the children on him in the afternoon, he would
graze his way home and the children would not mind, or if
they minded and kicked their heels against him, he did
not mind but only munched the more. But he grew fatally
attached to that particular road, and being a horse of one
idea he believed in no other.

Lamentable differences of opinion therefore arose
between him and the captain, who had to ride in various
directions, and when a sharp bit was forced into his mouth
to coerce him, his motto became 'Excelsior.' I reasoned

that if I purchased him he would be away from his favourite road, and also I thought that I could find a snaffle. So I bought him with the reputation of being a sort of man-eater, and at once I put my little girls upon his back and sometimes I drove him.

He had funny eccentric ways of his own, but he never injured or frightened me or mine. People who knew him from a suckling colt have assured me that he was a cart-horse and nothing else. Well! I chanced to be on his back at Hindabarrow Cross one memorable day when Mr Coryton drove his fox to Blackadon, beyond Lidford, and killed in the open. About one hundred and twenty horsemen and horsewomen started in the morning, and about eighteen were left at the end. I saw the hounds catch the fox, and the horse gave me no fall all day. Mr Melhuish, of Clawton, and Colonel Holley asserted that it was the finest run that they had seen over Broadbury for quite a quarter of a century, and I was well carried throughout.

Next day the newspapers were full of its praises, and one writer amused me much by declaring that it had proved for ever that only high breeding can last through so long a gallop. Certainly I was on a very hairy-legged animal, reputed indeed to be thorough-bred, but only thorough-bred cart.

My daughter, now Mrs Gotto, rode that horse for five seasons; nothing could stop him, no pace was too hot for him, and he could stay for hours. One the day in question, with nearly fourteen stone upon his back, he lasted from near Hallwell to far beyond Lidford, when all men were racing for their lives.

For myself, I do not believe in any general cut and dried theories about the breed of horses. You may have a cur of a thoroughbred, and a lion of an under-bred horse. But heredity is apt to show itself, and my chestnut, notwithstanding what was said of him, must have had some excellent relative, perchance, in the far by-gone past, and he inherited from him. I have known good horses bred in all sorts of ways. Mr Holley had a very good one, half pony, half cart-horse. I have seen the Colonel go on this horse like a bird. Some of the secret of going is in the man, however, and it is not all in the lower animal.

I never had a horse fail me nor completely stop in all my life. I have never injured one by over-exertion, and I have tried them hardly enough. People say that modern horses will not work like the old ones, but those I have now in my stable are just as tough as were my favourite mounts in the olden times.

The owner's treatment has much to do with the result. I love my horse, understand him thoroughly, and if he begins to tire or to run short of wind, I know it as soon as he does, and ease him. The result is that all my horses, well-bred and common, go for ever, and never come to any harm. And so it is with my friends. Their horses are in good condition and they are treated with consideration. In return they will last through almost any gallop, and ten or twenty miles, more or less, is to them a matter of no consideration at all.

I once drove a mare eighty miles in twenty-four hours, and she went to play at the end of the journey. She was cross-bred between a roadster and a pony. She cost eight guineas at the Exeter Bazaar, and after six years of my service an old general officer bought her to ride. I have turned my head homeward after a long day and returned to North Bovey from near Tiverton, on a four-year-old; from Burrington also; and from Germanswick. It cannot be said that these distances are trifling, or that my weight, which is thirteen stone seven pounds, with the saddle, is light.

Some time ago in the House of Lords, a nobleman said, during a debate upon horse-breeding, that he had a horse which had once carried him for thirty miles, thus showing that the breed had not degenerated. Bless the man! Our horses, well bred and common, old and young, have done and now sometimes do, as much as that after their day's work is over, and they never seem to me to wear out. One is in my stable now, as fresh as a colt, although he is nearly twenty-one years old. And yet many dealers declare that it hardly pays them to let horses out for ten guineas a month, so terrible is the wear and tear.

I write for those who will come after me, and the secret is soon told. Your horse *must* be adequate, up to your weight; he ought to be in good condition, well fed and cared for;

he should only be called upon when he is wanted, never forced beyond his natural pace, and spared on the hard high-road. Given these conditions, together with a good understanding between man and beast, and a horse will go well-nigh anywhere, and do anything without suffering or wearing out.

It is not blood which does it, nor yet altogether condition. You require blood if the work is *continuously* severe, and condition is requisite if you want frequent exertions, but it is astonishing what a horse out of condition will do for a single day.

There is not much faith to be placed in fancies, such as that a chestnut is always soft, and a rat-tailed horse tough. But I do think that bad-tempered horses are often good ones. The same thing indeed may be said of people. Life is lived on a principle of compensations, and easy good nature is seldom energetic.

I remember well when Mr Luxton, of Brushwood Barton, rode a black mare with a vile temper. He never carried whip or spur, for she would throw any man who touched her with either. She bit other horses, kicked at hounds, and went with her ears back, showing the whites of her eyes, but she would gallop all day and jump to distraction.

Horses sometimes have very odd tempers. There was one at Ashhampton until a year or two ago, a mare, which belonged to a farmer of somewhat intemperate habits. He was afraid to go near her when he was sober, and he was hardly able to mount her. But when he was the worse for liquor he would tumble up against her or scrabble awkwardly on to her back, and she would neither bite him nor kick him until he was sober again.

I have a horse now with funny ways. Sometimes he will not turn, and if I pull him round he rears. Then I pat him on the neck and pull him the other way, and lo! he is immediately quite anxious to be obliging.

I am sure that some horses are lunatics. I have myself owned one or two. I had a bay mare once called Lady Godiva, which I sold to John Russell. How he managed I hardly know, but when I owned her she would be gentle for months, and would then without provocation rear and kick as no sane horse ever behaved. The people of whom I bought her said that she never went wrong while with hounds, but that she could not be depended upon apart from their company.

I have never been a high feeder. As a rule my horses are large, sixteen hands (if I can get them,) for riding purposes. They only have a peck of oats, and a pint of beans daily. This is low feeding for a big horse, which may be asked to carry a heavy man for very long distances, but people say that my horses always look well; certainly they never fail me, and my stable is free from that fearful scourge, fever in the feet.

A change of food is very good for a horse. All mine will eat anything, oats, maize, beans, bran, linseed, oilcake, clover hay, land hay, mangolds, swede turnips, carrots, salt and sugar. But beware of wheat and barley, and above all things of dusty hay.

When I was young I used to trouble about my horses. People who know nothing take delight in teasing a young man who knows less. They will tell him that his horse is going blind, or has a ring bone, or spavin. It used to make me miserable, and now I say: 'Spavin? O, yes, certainly, that gives him more bone in his hocks; that is what he jumps with, you will see presently,' And then my candid friend ceases, and I ride away. These people hardly know a horse's head from his heels.

It is time enough to doctor a horse when he becomes lame, and then the best treatment is to turn him out in a soft meadow and let him run for three months. I hate all strong measures. When I was a boy the veterinary people were in favour of firing horses, now they are ceasing to believe in the efficacy of this remedy, and my heart sinks as I reflect upon the cruel sufferings which have in the meanwhile been needlessly inflicted on gentle and generous animals.

Only six months ago my neighbours were urging me to have my cart mare fired for side bone. I told my servants to leave her alone, and to take no notice until she went lame. The side bone is now set, the mare is practically sound for life, and has escaped intolerable torture.

I often buy horses with spavin or ring bones, or something or other, with my eyes wide open. The fact is that most horses have something or other the matter with them, and if they stand work it does not matter. Flat feet are apt to get bruised, and then they take a long time to grow sound. They are a nuisance. And yet the very best horse I ever saw in Devonshire had feet like great pudding plates. He was called Merlin, and at one time belonged to Mr Rolle who, it is said, refused two hundred pounds for him when sixteen years old. He was not, I imagine, fit to travel the roads, but no one ever knew how fast that horse could go, and he would put all four feet on the top of a mortared wall and jump off it with the certainty and agility of a cat.

I have a horror of hereditary disease, and people really ought to be fined if they breed from unsound animals. In my belief most complaints are hereditary, and you can easily have a horse which is not exactly unsound but is full of the germs of unsoundess, only waiting to be developed. Thus I have seen young colts go hopelessly lame with navicular disease.

I do not believe in long prices. The price of a horse depends very much on the reputation of the owner. If some men have a horse to sell they will make four times as much of him as I could, and yet the animal be the same. All the great performers which I have known have been low-priced horses. I have seen a Master of Foxhounds carried magnificently for three pounds ten shillings, and I have seen a great judge of horses quite unable to go well for a mile on four hundred pounds.

This, no doubt, is partly owing to the fact that the man upon the four hundred pounds horse is afraid to ride him, and the other lets his horse go. Moreover, the expensive horse has been coddled up, and the other is in better condition. Much also depends upon the rider, and I know men now who will go well upon anything, and others who cannot go at all.

Horses' mouths are very deceptive. I have owned several horses whose age could not be rightly ascertained by looking at their teeth. It has been an amusement to me to puzzle the veterinary surgeons by showing their mouths to them. The show yards have, I think, done harm to our horses. They have stimulated the production of good-looking brutes. On one occasion I went round a show yard with Mr Elliot (a well-known judge) and he pointed out to me several constant prize-winners which were, as he said, quite useless.

The jumping competitions are most mischievous. If you want to train a young horse to jump, you should put him at a stiff fence. He must get over or fall. But the fences in the show yards are so constructed as to give way. They are excellent contrivances, therefore, for rendering horses dangerous over a country.

If I may venture to advise a young man in search of a horse, I would recommend him never to buy a young one, never to give much money, and always endeavour to secure an animal with whose performances he is already acquainted. So shall he not go wrong. When he has his horse, let him talk to him, make a friend of him, never over-drive or hurry him, and the horse will do his best, he may be sure.

Nearly all my horses are quiet in the stable, and out of it. They will generally run about over the country after me, jumping the fences exactly like dogs. I talk to them if anything goes wrong, and say, 'The strap has broken, Billy, don't kick.' They know, and if you are kind to them they are not nervous.

If a horse is sick, give him rest and a bran mash. If he is lame, turn him out; otherwise do not look at him too critically. If once you begin to examine you will find, or fancy you have found, something to disturb your peace of mind. All horses at times get out of order, and expensive ones rarely appear to be in. Blood means wind if it means anything, and long horses go wrong more easily than short ones.

Swelled legs imply debility, and the remedy is beans. These must be given judiciously, but they are useful when a horse is changing his coat. It is a great strain upon an animal's constitution to have to produce a thick jacket from out of the depths of his inner consciousness. Deer feel very unwell when they are changing their horns.

A horse which has been out of condition will tell you himself when he is fit to go. I always rejoice when one of mine, up to then steady going, suddenly takes hold of the bit, and starts away and flashes. He does it to throw off a newly acquired feeling of superfluous energy.

Rich men generally have stables full of useless horses. To bring about this result is the special function of some stud grooms. The man with one horse can generally go faster and better than the man with three, two of which are perhaps being poisoned with physic. I myself rarely give physic to man or beast, most rarely of all to myself. I do not like it. For a horse I prefer a pint of linseed oil, which answers every purpose.

Therefore, my dear young reader, if you want to ride fast and cheaply, buy some old horse which you have seen go well for a score of times. Be considerate, make a friend of him, never call upon him until you want him. Disregard all suggestions of evil concerning him. Do not look at him too narrowly, frequently change his diet, feed him well, give him no drugs, and keep him exercised. So doing, he will probably carry you faster, further, and longer, than any two horses will carry your more wealthy friend.

Never, except at water, ride him fast at a fence, for nine falls out of ten occur because the hurried horse has miscalculated his distance, and the falls thus caused are heavier than those which follow a mishap at a slower pace. Never pull at a horse when he is jumping. One of the finest riders in the county told me that when he is banking he likes to take hold of the mane and drop the reins.

I have known excitable horses which were very dangerous when down, and I have had others that it was almost a pleasure to fall with. My own practice is to stand off my horse when nothing is doing, and to walk down hill on my homeward way. These little indulgences do not hurt the rider, they only soil his boots, but they help the horse to perform those marvellous journeys which mine have so often accomplished; they are the old-fashioned ways of an old-world man, who cannot expect much longer to repeat the performances of his youth.

CHAPTER THIRTEEN

Parish Matters

I WAS CHRISTENED in the parish church on Clapham Common, and once over five I was taken to church twice every Sunday – and I survived! It was a tremendous ordeal to which to subject a young child. The very weight of the respectability of the surroundings was appalling. The church maintained a beadle, a heavy pompous man, attired in a uniform of semi-regal magnificence. There were black-gowned vergers also, with white wands, very terrible to behold. I have been in that church for three hours at a stretch, from 11 am until 2 pm, and the sermon would frequently last for an hour.

The Church of England, fifty years ago, was, I think, very much the church of the upper and middle classes in the towns, and was dependent upon the squierarchy in the country. I am writing of a period just before the mania for Restoration of churches set in, and my youthful recollection is for the most part of heavy services, conducted by heavy clergymen, for heavy citizens, in unrestored churches, in which every family sat serenely entrenched in its family fortress. I am no great innovator, but if any clergyman had done in Clapham Church, in 1840, what I now do weekly in mine, I am disposed to think that its eminently respectable congregation of bankers, lawyers and merchants would have had a fit, a general, universal, simultaneous fit.

And then I passed on to Selworthy. It was like passing at the present time into Texas, only the contrast was more marked. Urged on by my piscatory instincts I soon made acquaintance with Withypool, and there was John Milton as parish clerk. One day a strange clergyman came to officiate, and John addressed him thus: 'Do'ee preach from the steps, sir, for the old goose is abrood in the pulpit. Her's come cruel hard on hatching, and must not nohow be disturbed.'

In the 1840s my stipend was £20 a year. A curate at Brendon walked to a sale at South Molton, bought a chest of drawers and carried them home on his back across the moors. There were no resident gentry then in that neighbourhood. Old Sir Thomas Acland came occasionally, and he was of much the same type as my own father; they were both good old-fashioned Evangelicals, a little bit toned down and modified. The farmers were very moral and well-behaved as a rule, although they drank a good deal of gin as well as of cider. They were very Evangelical. They did not at all like innovations, but I only wish their grandsons would read their Bibles, say their prayers, and come to church as conscientiously as they did.

The poor people were for the most part very ignorant, and Church of England services must have been what I used to hear called 'heathen Greek' to them. They came to church, however, even as the school children came, because they were told to come, and they always had come. And they sat up solemnly, thinking probably for the most part of nothing at all.

Boys must begin farming by about twelve if they are to learn and like their work. As it is, there is a sad decline in the value of our younger labouring men; they do not understand all work as the old men understood it. It is the old men still who can do any odd job that has to be done: who can thatch a rick, or kill a pig, or shear a sheep. The younger ones are not so handy. There is always a danger also that machinery should increasingly displace skilled labour. How do the Brussels or Honiton lace-manufacturers contend against the machines? I do not know. How will it be with us in the next naval war? We used to depend upon our superior seamanship. But steam and machinery tend to level all such distinctions, and a Frenchman working a handle inside an iron box is likely to be as good as an Englishman. The turn of the tide is not here in our favour.

Dull country parson as I am, I must have galloped about the country for nearly a week before I could bring to the bedside of an injured man his wife and grown-up daughter. He was an officer in the Royal Navy, who had once possessed nearly £2,000 a year in land, but he was for the period penniless, and no one would own or befriend him. He had lunched, on the day when I found him, upon a bottle of champagne, a quart of bitter beer, and a biscuit. He was bruised all over and quite mad with delirium tremens, and suffering from the effects of a heavy fall. I hired two men to keep him in bed, and as he altogether refused to take any nourishment, under medical advice I drenched him frequently with beef tea, mixed with brandy, using a cowhorn for the purpose, which I borrowed from a farrier.

The family, very grateful for the trouble which I had taken, and the unrepaid outlay which I had incurred on their behalf, to say nothing of the risks which I had run in drenching a mad sea-captain with a second-hand cowhorn – risks not to be lightly enterprised – deemed it necessary at parting to make me a present by way of acknowledgement of their many obligations, and they considered a *crab* to be an appropriate offering! It was certainly a large one, but it was not very fresh.

One summer afternoon at about four o'clock I thought that I would visit those of my parishioners who reside on the western, or Dartmoor, side of the parish of North Bovey. My walking powers not being what they were, I told my man to saddle my horse. He is a compact animal, not much more than sixteen hands in height, and possessed of a fine fiery spirit. As I rode down the hill there was, and very much in my way, a little girl with a baby in a perambulator. She had posted herself in the centre of the crooked and narrow bridge at Black Aller, and was amusing herself and the baby by blowing the heads off numerous dandelions.

I skirted the baby and nodded to the nurse. The steep Yarde hill in front of me was covered with school children, all looking, as is the way with school children nowadays, exceedingly small. They were doing everything that children can do otherwise than making the best of their way to their homes. Some were scrambling about the banks seeking for wild strawberries and stringing them when found upon pieces of long grass, and others were at play. With a word of kindly recognition from me, and an answering series of bows and scrapes, the big horse threaded his way through the little crowd, and I passed on.

Half-a-mile further I fell, not from the horse, but into temptation, for, turning from the road I passed beneath an ancient ash tree which has a hole in its fork some fourteen feet above the ground. There was nobody to observe me, and I knew that before now that hole had contained a nest. Is the old owl at home, and, if so, has she hatched out or not, and what is the number of her family this year? Thus meditating, I got off my horse and tied his double bridle to the lowest branch of the tree. Then I began to climb, not now, alas, with the alacrity of youth, but still I hope respectably.

Just as I put my fingers into the mouth of the hole to obtain a purchase for the final ascent, the wicked old owl took flight. She had an unexpected bolt-hole on the further side of the tree, and out she went. She is no doubt one hundred years old, and she looks it. She was that day a fluffy, untidy old materfamilias in a nervous and irritable frame of mind, induced by sedentary occupation persisted in too long. But, alas, she went like a cannon ball right over my horse's head.

It was too much! There was a jerk of the long snaky neck, a toss of the small, clean-cut head, and he was free. I, on the contrary, was up a tree, indeed, very much so.

Neglecting the interesting young occupants of the hole, I turned to the horse and said, 'Whoa! Steady, old man. I am coming down.' In vain. The brute made himself look as big as an elephant. He threw his head into the air, snorted loud and long, trotted two strides with extravagant action and then, breaking into a gallop, disappeared into the lane, going homewards at the rate of some thirty miles an hour.

The lane is only about ten feet wide, and was full that day of little, dawdling school children. I thought sadly of Rachel and Ramah, and of what incredibly long tongues some of my Rachels are possessed, and where I should disconsolately pass the blighted and remorseful remainder of my days. Then the recollection of the perambulator appalled me, posted as it was in the centre of the crabbed little bridge.

There was, however, clearly but one thing to be done, so taking the broken bridle in my hand I turned towards home. How many corpses, I wondered, bestrewed the narrow way? As I advanced I came upon little lots of scared children in detachments, hugging the hedges most affectionately. They were too frightened to speak, so I asked a man on a hedge with reference to the horse.

'Had he any pace on, John, when he passed you?'

'Forty miles an hour, Sir, and right down Yarde Hill,' said the man.

But when I reached the bottom my apprehensions were relieved. Horses will not injure except by accident, so he had (presumably) topped the perambulator, taken the nursemaid in his stride, and provided much innocent amusement for the baby.

In my yard stood my man, who said, 'Thought you was coming, Sir; had word home.'

'Put another bridle on him, George,' said I. 'I have been birds-nesting this afternoon, but it is hardly a sport to ride to; I won't attempt it again on horseback.'

My horses are always a nuisance to me when I am on my parochial errands. There is seldom anyone at the houses which I visit to hold them, and if I put them into a stable they tie themselves up into knots, or roll on their saddles or harness. When I was again mounted I rode away and stopped at an old farm house in which resided a labourer and his wife of the bygone, excellent sort. I managed to dispose of my horse, and entered the cottage. The man was away at work, but his wife was at home.

As soon as the ordinary salutations had passed between us, I asked after the welfare of the family, and the old woman replied to the following effect: 'Thank you, Sir, they are all quite nicely, except poor George.'

'And what is the matter with him?' I enquired.

'Well, you see, Sir, he went up to Heatree on Thursday, and Mr Kitson has a nasty old bull. George thought he would walk across the fields by the shorter way, and there was thicky old bull. Times and times my boy has a-passed him, but something had put him out of temper that morning, I suppose, for he up and made for poor George, and knocked him right down into the ditch. Yes, he did so. George, he scrambled and scrawled until he drawed himself out at last through the gutter hole. You never saw such a mess! Poor dear, the breath was knocked right out of him, and he comed back straight home and could eat no dinner.

'Now, Mr Thornton, if he had been took with a fever, or the measles, or even the whooping cough, I should never have complained, no, nor his father neither. We know better than to complain of what Providence sends us, Sir. We must submit (so father always says), and us do; but to be picked off like that by an old bull is different, of course. Why, there ain't no Providence in it, Sir, none at all, and that *you* very well know.'

I do not quite see the force of her distinction, but she is a good old soul, so I will not combat her peculiar theology, but ride on.

At another house I dismount to condole with a mother who has just lost a daughter suddenly, in service at Torquay. 'Yes, Sir,' she said. 'It was very sad. The other maid called her at 6.30 am, but her never answered, only sighed, and when the other came to her again, her was dead. Now if that maid had only shaked her well she would have come to, all right – of course her would – and the doctor said so; but the silly thing was that scared, her never shaked her, nor nothing. Some folks are like that, Sir, there's no sense in them.'

As I return I call at a farm-house. The farmer comes in and I say, 'The rooks are pulling up my wheat as fast as it shows itself, in order I suppose to get at the grain; how can I hinder them?'

'There now, Mr Thornton, I always do say that they jackdaw rooks be the worstest crows of all; shoot to mun, Sir, shoot to mun.'

'Have you broken the chestnut colt yet, farmer, and how does he shape?'

'I don't know no more about 'orses, Mr Thornton, than 'orses know about gnats, and I never didn't; but that colt is by the shivering door, Sir; he is for sale, and he seems to be quiet like.'

'Shivering door?' I say in perplexity. 'I have heard of a horse shivering timber, but a shivering door! He must have caught cold in the wood, I should think, and even that is unusual.'

Then a light streams in upon my mind, and I remember that Mr Calmady has a colt by Chevron d'Or.

'Oh, yes, I beg your pardon, I had forgotten. I know Shivering Door, a thundering good horse. I congratulate you. Good night.'

I look in at a cottage where there is an anaemic girl (a modern improvement in girls), and I say to her mother, 'Polly is just killing herself with tight lacing, Mrs Brown, that is what is the matter with her.'

'Well, Sir, she do like to be a little thereafter, an, of course 'tis natural, but I said to her yesterday that she was bracing too tight. My dear, says I, it must go somewhere, either up or down for certain, says I, if you don't let it bide where it is.'

'Yes, Mrs Brown,' I remark, 'you are perfectly right. She squeezes her waist quite up into her throat, and that naturally spoils her appetite' – and then I tell her dear old Admiral Moresby's tale, how when he was dining with Queen of Honolulu, her Majesty endeavoured to gratify a large appetite in a French-made gown, and became so embarrassed in consequence, that the English sailor, kindly seizing the carving knife, slit it down from the nape of her neck to her waist. After which operation Her Majesty felt much relieved, and was enabled comfortably to go on with her dinner. 'You may depend upon it, Mrs Brown, that we shall have to serve Polly the same,' I continue very gravely, 'and then we will measure the gap.'

I will now leave my record of a round of parochial visitations, with the humble confession that I am so inferior as to take considerable interest therein. Such life as I have been describing is rapidly passing away, together with the men who have lived it. The coming clergyman will not climb a tree, for there will be no trees to climb, or look for a bird's nest when birds are extinct, or ride on a horse when all men travel by electricity.

The inducement to poach is not so great as formerly, although there are still professionals left, but I am inclined to think that a good deal of modern poaching is the outcome of drink. Half-a-dozen rough fellows meet at a public house and leave at midnight well primed with liquor, and one of them suddenly says, 'Come on, mates, let's have a crack at old somebody's pheasants.' Guns are then found, and one of the party is sent to a cover in a wrong direction with instruction to fire two shots at random and then to run away. The rest go to a good cover in another direction, and looking up at the roosting pheasants shoot for five minutes and make off. The impromptu adventure is undertaken more for the pleasure of boasting and the love excitement than for the sake of profit. In big preserves the keepers put dummy birds into the trees to take in these poachers.

But there are many still more *unprofessional* people than these who poach. Their name is legion. We are, all of us who reside on Dartmoor, fond of the black game, and we find them very scarce, and they are hard to rear. I believe that before the season commences a good many poults are caught in a curious way.

It is the habit of these birds when young to sit very close, and I have taken in my hand half-grown poults out of the heather on several occasions. Now it is the case that when these birds are young, the Moor is much traversed by mounted sheep owners, who are often accompanied by great, long, galloping sheep dogs. Many a brood of black game is, I am certain, ridden up, and ridden down, and caught by these dogs before the poults can well fly. These birds do not find their way to market, but go to make the inside of a savoury pudding in some lonely farmhouse kitchen. A good many fox cubs, also, are in this way coursed and killed. Some of the Scotch dogs kept on the Moor are very quick and ready at this sort of work.

At certain seasons of the year our professional tramps and beggars take to egg stealing.. Pheasants' eggs are worth about a shilling each, so the business is lucrative. The plan generally adopted is to walk over commons and public places near preserves, to note the nests and put down a mark. Then at night the poachers go to the marks and empty the nests. Some time ago I was much amused to find an old Sussex game-keeper up in an oak tree with a telescope. He was watching a party of markers, and when they were gone he went to their marks and removed all the eggs. The markers, so he said, had saved him a great deal.

The Ground Game Act is a perfect nuisance. It has multiplied ground game by a hundredfold. It has led to a very cruel system of professional trapping, and it has induced many labourers to become poachers in a small way. The whole country now swarms with rabbits. The farmers, who under the Act have only a joint right to these rabbits, have claimed a sole one, and encourage them to breed.

I believe that the most dangerous professional poachers of the present time are the river poachers, who catch salmon even during the close season of the year. In North Devon they call these salmon 'red hake', and dispose of them in a manner half open, half secret.

We often hear of ingenious devices for catching game, such as boiling beans and then running pig's bristles through their soft substance in order to choke the pheasants which pick them up; and attracting birds from neighbouring coverts either with raisins or with fresh 'cheese' from cider presses, and then catching them in wires or gins, or shooting them. But I believe these tricks are much more talked about than practised.

In the Dartmoor district gins are the curse of the game preserver, They are the product of an Act of Parliament which was framed in order to annoy preservers, and by killing vermin they foster the animals which they are supposed to keep down. They catch everything that runs, and most things that fly, and I am continually meeting with poor gin-mailed creatures – rabbits with three legs and birds with only one.

There is an organised crusade against vivisection, with which one is in some sort compelled to sympathise, but after the queer fashion of our English people the trapper is left unrebuked to pursue a trade which causes far more suffering than vivisection, and which cannot be said to be necessary. In this respect as in others, many others, we English strain at a gnat while we swallow a camel. The truth, I think, is that most of us are heedless of cruelty until some person of influence thinks fit to make an outcry, and then we all follow like sheep. It is not very rational or dignified behaviour, but it is our way, and it arises, in all probability, not from callousness, but from a national, Saxon-bred want of imagination. We require to be told.

Some very cruel things are done to wild animals, although few, perhaps, exceed those that are done by the ordinary trapper. The pole trap is the worst of all traps, and I see it everywhere in use. Birds of prey like to perch upon bare poles in upland situations. So a pole is constructed with steps at intervals, and a gin or steel trap secured by a chain is set on the top. Then a poor hawk or owl settles down upon the plate, and both legs are broken by the teeth of the trap, and the bird, after flapping wildly for a few minutes, falls forward and hangs suspended by its broken legs until it dies or is taken down, more commonly the former.

It is not a humane contrivance, and personally, as a lover of nature and of wild life, I am sorry to see one species after another of the most beautiful of created things exterminated. I can remember the peregrine falcon on the Countesbury cliffs and the swallow-tailed kite on the Sussex downs. I know that, practically speaking, both species have ceased to exist, as have, also, the delicate merlin and the hen harrier of rapid flight. It used to be a great pleasure to me on dewy evenings to watch the mousing white owl, as, bent on his useful errand, he quartered the fields like a setter after game. He was a beautiful, harmless, and useful bird, but I rarely see him now. The raven's nest is for the most part deserted, and country life is losing much of its charm.

My own opinion is that moderation should be observed in all things, and that some of even the worst of these birds might be permitted to live, and that others should not be interfered with at all. But man is by far the most deadly of all the animals.

The clergy with whom I was brought up, and with whom I have mostly lived, were some of them rather curious old fellows; but at least there was no wide gap between them and the laity. We were, clergy and laity, all in one boat, and we pulled together, and we understood one another.

My rector, Mr Mundy, belonged, I should say, to the old-fashioned High Church school. He was a scholar, a moderate man in all things, a very good man of business and fond of society, but he was not particularly well versed in outdoor pursuits. He owned, when I was his curate, a stout, mealy-nosed cob, half bred between a cart horse and an Exmoor pony, a very quiet animal, but not particularly good-hearted.

Twenty miles away, at South Molton, a Mr Maitland was vicar. He was a decided Evangelical, with a strong Calvinistic bias, but theological differences of opinion were not then, as between clergymen, so pronounced as at present, and he requested Mr Mundy to come over to South Molton on a certain summer Sunday to preach twice for the Church Missionary Society. Mr Mundy, in his turn, induced some clergyman visitor at Lynton, to assist me in taking the Lynton and Countesbury services.

He started on the cob for South Molton by way of Cheriton Ridge, Hoar Oak, the Chains, Mole's Chamber and High Bray. He reached the George Inn a little before eleven o'clock. There was at that time a beer-befuzzled old ostler at the hotel, a relic of still older coaching days, and Mr Mundy, knowing no more about horses and their comforts than horses know about gnats, merely told this ostler to loosen the girths and feed the cob.

After that he went to church, and asked very earnestly for more missionaries. Then he dined between services, had some tea, preached again, and went off to the George for his horse. Knowing as little about saddles and bridles as he did about horses, he never looked to his girths, which the tipsy ostler had forgotten to tighten, and so rode off on his homeward way.

As he mounted the track to Mole's Chamber he encountered a fog, as well as the darkness of a summer's night. The path was broken, narrow and rugged, and in order to keep it in sight he peered about as he descended the hill. Over-stretching his balance, the saddle turned round, and in falling he broke his collar-bone.

The wind howled and whistled, the fog got into his eyes, the darkness deepened, and his shoulder became very painful. Any decent horse would, under the circumstances, have kicked to distraction, but the old bay cob was quite patient with the girths over his backbone and a clumsy saddle between his legs.

Poor Mr Mundy was unable to put it right, or to take it off and leave it behind. Then he lost the track, and still the wind howled and the fog got into his eyes, and his collar-bone hurt him as he wandered on, now into a bog, and now brought up by a stonewall. Towards midnight he saw a light in a cottage window, somewhere, I suppose, on the Challacombe road, and with infinite pains he reached the garden gate which led to it. A woman in a bedgown, with a candle in her hand, heard him and opened the window.

'Who is there?' said she, and the wind howled and whined and the fog put out the candle.

'I am Mr Mundy,' he shouted.

'Get out, you drunken dog,' said she, 'it's Sunday.' And she went to bed.

There she would not long have remained if the poor man had been represented by his curate, for I would assuredly have kicked out the panels of the door, or perished in the attempt; but he was meeker, and he wandered away until he was found in the morning by a moor-man, who put his saddle downside up and mounted him.

When he reached Lynton and had had some breakfast, Mrs Mundy sent for a post-chaise and rattled him off to Exeter, fifty miles away, where old Mr Barnes set his collar-bone. In after days he always said that what with one thing and another he had had a rather bad time of it until his arm was attended to. He was not a young man, either; but we were harder then than those of the new division are now. Afterwards he used to look to his girths. Thus good comes forth from evil!

We were all harder. I remember a man whom we used to call 'The Long Captain'. He had been out with the Spanish Legion in the War of Succession and had come back very impecunious. He had a boy with him who had been brought up abroad and was consequently soft. Being a cousin of Mr Knight's, he was staying at Simonsbath House, and Captain Moresby was also there. We went for a ride, mounted the boy on a pony, and Mr Knight made him ride at a gap in a stone wall. He fell off his pony and lay on the grass and howled.

'Are you not ashamed of yourself, Jack?' said Captain Moresby, 'a great boy like you?' (the poor little chap was about ten years old). 'How often, Jack, have I seen your uncle Fred there, with his thigh-bone sticking up out of his waistcoat pocket, and not crying at all? Get up, Sir. Get on your pony and ride.'

Sailors are sometimes remarkable for a certain redundancy of expression, but Frederic Knight was a hard man, and had experienced much heavy falling in his day. The Long Captain lodged over an eating-house when in London, and used to look around before he ventured out, as he was afraid of the bailiffs. Thackeray knew him, and said that he would write a story, and call it 'The Siege of the Tripe Shop: or the Knight of the Nineteenth Century.' But it never came out.

They are all gone. Moresby, Knight, the Long Captain, and, I think, the boy. I only remain, and have had my tumbles. You should kick your feet out of the stirrups and fall clear of your horse, and then falls do not much matter until you are seventy. After that age it is as well to be careful, although my old friend, Mr Crockford, at eighty, still refuses to turn his head, and tumbles about over big fences with a smile of contentment on his face. He cannot see, or hear, or talk very well, but he rides as straight as anyone.

Some years ago the late Lord Clifford told me that he had been out shooting with a very well-connected, well-known Cornish clergyman. They were fellow guests at the same house, and the parson on a previous occasion had not tipped the head gamekeeper sufficiently to satisfy the aspirations of that rather exorbitant functionary. Indeed, some gamekeepers do expect an amount in tips rather trying to the pockets of poor gentlemen.

The keeper, therefore, on this account, wanted to score off the clergyman in the presence of an influential man of a religious persuasion other than his own. So as they were walking homewards he touched his hat respectfully to the parson, and said, 'I beg your pardon, Sir, but I wish you could relieve my mind on a matter which is perplexing me. The truth is that I cannot find in the New Testament any passage which would seem to give encouragement to shoot to a gentleman of your profession. I do not find any mention of the gun, for instance, when I read of the doings of the Apostles, Sir, and I thought that perhaps you would now be kind enough to explain to me how the difference between gentlemen like yourself and them can be accounted for.'

'You are an intelligent and thoughtful man, Mr Stokes,' said the clergyman, 'and I will endeavour to satisfy your mind. The truth is, Stokes, that in the days to which you refer, there was a great deal of poaching done in Palestine, and the keepers were not very attentive to their duties, as when I go out shooting I find to be the case also in England not infrequently, Mr Stokes, at the present day. There really was very little game to shoot, so they took to fishing instead. I hope that you are satisfied, Mr Stokes' – and the keeper shook his head and walked on.

I think that one reason why I like primitive man is that with him one is still an individuality, not merely number so-and-so in forty millions of equally unloved and uncared-for, monotonously similar uninteresting units, none of them necessary, or even agreeable, to the others. And yet this is what our educational and other reformers are working day and night to bring about, just as if England did not owe everything to her spontaneous eccentricity. We shall soon be as bad as the French.

Let us take a look at Devonshire as it was in the closing days of the last century, and nearly continued to be until fifty years ago, and then let us look at it as it is today. Almost within the lifetime of living men there was no conveyance of a public character between Barnstaple and Exeter. Then in 1796 the first coach, called 'The Flying Stage', was started to run, 'all the way in one day' if weather permitted. In the same year a coach was put on at Taunton to run twice a week to Exeter.

People were evidently beginning to grow restless, and would not any longer stay quietly at home as had been their habit formerly, but gradually and without making great progress, or altering lives and manners much, until my own times, when the railway system was introduced, and the great leap forward for good or evil was made throughout the country – say in 1840.

The roads were in a very bad condition. The old Roman ways, long neglected, were nearly gone. The Devonshire devious ways had originally been formed by the feet of pack-horses, who wandered right and left to avoid soft places until a track was made,, against which banks were gradually thrown up to keep the cattle from straying from adjacent fields (thus stereotyping for ever the wanderings of the horses). These trackways were deeply water-worn, and often shelved to a point in the centre, where large, loose stones lay roughly scattered.

In 1808 Mr Vancouver, who was employed to make a report by the then Board of Agriculture, writes from experiences of the horrors of a charge of a string of pack-horses in one of these defiles. On they came, without bridles or conductors, with their burdens brushing both sides of the deep-cut lane. There was nothing to be done except to turn and fly to a wider place until the string had passed on, led by some veteran charger who knew perfectly well where he was going.

The roads twisted considerably, as I have said, by reason of the wanderings of the horses, but as moors and waste-lands were gradually taken in and enclosed, they twisted more and more, because the old trackway would often in such cases be disregarded by those who were enclosing, and the traffic would consequently have to go round the angles of the newly-made fence until the old road could be resumed. There was practically no such thing, on any but a very few of the main roads, as a public conveyance. Every-thing was done on foot or on horseback Even the very farmyard manure, and lime, and the earth from the bot-toms of the steep fields, were carried upon horses' backs.

The fathers of two intimate friends of mine, contempo-raries of my own father, used to ride together from North Devon to Oxford, and back again for the long vacation. Their fathers would purchase a horse for each of them, to be sold, if possible, at a profit on reaching Oxford, and they would buy another at the end of the term for the return journey; or they would buy at Oxford, keep the horse through the vacation, and ride him back again. Imagine these youths with valises strapped in front of them, and heavy bell-mouthed pistols in their belts, riding away over the central moors of Devonshire through Tiverton to Oxford!

When communication was in this primitive condition, the manners and the customs of the people corresponded therewith. Hospitality was general among all classes of the community, a hospitality rough and ready. In those days Sir Thomas Acland and Lord Fortescue alternately kept the staghounds, and on the evening preceding a meet near the master's house, that house was thrown open to all comers; some had beds, but more did without them. Horses were quartered everywhere, and a good deal of wine was, I imagine, consumed in the course of the evening.

After the stag was killed – and it took many hours to hunt him down with the aid of the slow old hounds – anyone who pleased might return to the house, and after dinner a long silver cup was inserted in the animal's mouth and secured with a cord round the nose. Each guest then in turn grasped the horns, raised the head, and was expected to empty without spilling the contents of the cup.

The clergy were very primitive in their ways. One of them, a Fortescue, said to me in my youth, speaking of the smugglers of his youth in a kindly way, 'Poor fellows, they had a rough time of it. It was a nuisance, certainly, when they took one's carriage horses from the stable for a midnight run; but then, you see, they always left a keg of something extra good in the stable straw in return for the liberty they had taken.'

Yeomen farmers were common in those days. They rose early, sported much, dined at three o'clock, and then drank hard until they went to bed at a correspondingly early hour. Very often card-playing was a terrible evil. Fields frequently, farms sometimes, changed hands in an evening over whist. I have very often been told by farmers who were riding with me that where a farm has outlying fields belonging to it, they have been thus acquired. I know an old man now who would in my North Devon days sometime play at whist for thirty-six hours at a stretch, and without intermission.

When the approaches were so difficult, visits were apt to become visitations, for people had no idea of leaving a house quickly after they had undergone much labour and hardship in reaching it. The host, moreover, was not overdone with too much society, and liked to retain his guests.

In those days the pillion was in fashion, a horrible contrivance, occupying the whole body of a horse from his neck to his tail,with galligaskins, or huge leather projections, between the legs of the male rider and the horse, attached to it. The lady sat behind, with her hand in a loop of leather tied on to the girdle of the man. The roads were in the condition already described, and the over-weighted animal would stumble among the rocks and plunge up to his knees in the 'pucksy' holes, as the soft places caused by upright springs were then called. It is no wonder that under these circumstances when once they had arrived they prolonged their visit. A University man would often keep his friend through the whole of a long vacation, and a Christmas party would last for a week.

Listen, good reader, to the utterances of a Barnstaple M.D. so late as the year 1820:

> Did two pounds of mutton, an ounce of cheese, a glass of ale, a pint of Madeira and a bottle of port ever yet hurt a man at his dinner? Or the wings and breast of a fowl, two plates of custard pudding, four glasses of Madeira and four of port ever yet do injury to a woman? If they will cram melted butter upon hot plum-pudding, and stuff down muffins, crumpets and coffee, why should they complain to us of having heart-burn?

I am afraid that the drinking customs were sometimes very bad, but only with certain classes. I have heard the two-bottle men lament the departure from among them of the three-bottle heroes, and have seen them shake their heads sadly over the degeneracy of the times. It is not long ago that an old farmer came up to a great friend of mine in the streets of South Molton and took him warmly by the hand.

'Oh, Sir,' he said, 'I am glad to see you once more. I am not long for this world. I know I am not, and I am right glad to shake hands with you once again. Good-bye.'

My friend told him that although he was undoubtedly an old man, yet that he was looking extremely well, and they might hope often to meet again; but the old farmer could not agree to this, and continued, 'No, Sir, I have attended market here for more than fifty years, and I have never gone home until I have had twelve glasses of grog, and now eight are enough for me. I am a failing man, Sir, I know I be.'

He was a late survivor of the old sort, but I am not sure that the young people are generally much better than the old ones, although they drink in a different way. In most houses the consumption of whisky is ten times as great as it used to be, and yet I do not find that my wine bills grow any smaller. There is, I am afraid, much more general drinking now than ever there was, if there is less particular. In old times young men were kept under restraint in a manner that is scarcely conceivable now. I can remember houses in which the sons were expected to take only one glass of wine after dinner, and the ladies as a rule did not drink stimulants at all. The older men drank a good deal of wine after dinner, but they did not drink before dinner or at night.

And now we come to the consideration of the condition of the poorer classes of the community one hundred years ago. They did not, I fear, fare well in the later half of the eighteenth century and the earlier years of the nineteenth, before railways had given them an opportunity to escape from the surroundings of their youth. Cottages were insufficient and bad, and wages were very low. I have known seven shillings a week given, with cider and a cottage and a garden, but with no other privileges except extra food in harvest time, and everything was dearer than it is now.

Children were put out as apprentices at seven years without having received any previous education. Mr Vancouver, writing in 1808, expresses himself horrified at the way young girls were treated. He saw them loading dung-pots and wading deep in clay driving horses through the

furrows, etc. The labourers were very poor, very superstitious, very ignorant, and the country was thinly populated;
there was, consequently, a good deal of crime committed.
Mr Vancouver conversed with one farmer who had lost
one hundred and eight sheep in five years on Exmoor by
thieves. I knew some of these people – deer-stealers, pony-
stealers, sheep-stealers, poachers, smugglers, and have
heard them tell of the days of their youth and boast of their
deeds and performances.

As if the roads were not bad enough by reason of neglect
and bad management, the government used to add to
their horrors by hanging its malefactors up in chains until
their bodies dropped rotting to the ground. How many
gibbet posts are there in Devonshire, or forche's crosses
preserved in the names of the cross-roads? I have heard
old people tell how their flesh would creep when, perhaps
unexpectedly and at night, they heard a corpse creak on a
gibbet on some lonely common; and this was not all.

Some of you may know Farley's grave near North Tawton, or Jay's grave near Manaton, or half-a-dozen other
similar tombs. In each of these there is resting the body of
a suicide which was left there at dead of night after the
neighbours had, with the help of a big stone, driven a
sharp stake through and through the poor cold breast.
Poor Farley! I do not know his history, but he evidently
preferred to remain at three cross-roads staked down, to
prolonging an existence which his own fortunes, coupled
with the conditions of his day, had rendered too irksome
and unpleasant to be endured.

The roads were bad enough to travel upon, but to make
things as unpleasant as possible our fathers deliberately
scared in this abominable way those who had to crawl
painfully along after dark out of the very few wits with
which a kind Providence had endowed them. Rocks and
pucksy holes were nuisances, but to have to go for miles
out of your road, and on worse paths, in order to avoid a
clanking highwayman, or the pale ghost of a girl suicide,
was worse.

Do not imagine that my picture of the period is in this
respect overdrawn. The grandfather of one of my sons-in-
law, who commanded an East-Indiaman in the early years

of the present century, as hard a seaman as ever trod a quarter-deck, informed me that a man on horse-back accosted him on Hounslow Heath when he was a boy. The man asked him in a stern, short way whether he had met a coach upon the road, and then galloped off. Some time afterwards the child saw a dead body swinging in the air, but very near the ground, and impelled by a strange fascination went to it, and recognised in the blackened and distorted countenance his acquaintance on the Hounslow road. That boy was possessed of exceptionally strong nerves, as in later life he abundantly manifested, and he must that afternoon had use for them.

In those days, my father's days, almost my days, there was very little money in the County of Devon, and a small income went a long way. I can remember a time when five pounds would purchase a pony and twenty a good horse, when a good cow and calf could be bought for ten sovereigns, and wages were very low.

There were two worlds in those days, the world of what men call civilisation, and the world of the country, in which you could preserve some sort of individuality, breathe, and think, and be quiet. It was pleasant to live in the latter world, with an occasional excursion into the other, the world of expenditure, rattle, and smoke.

In the country there were many people of a high order of intelligence, more of them, I think, than you will meet with now, and in country libraries there were books of a much higher character than most of those which are popular today; but there was delay in transmission of news. But then even in London in those days people depended a good deal upon gossip picked up in coffee-houses, and the newspapers were few and small, and afforded but scanty information. I do not know how they fared in the West Country in this respect, but I daresay that they went on praying for George II in Selworthy church for many weeks after that somewhat stolid Hanoverian monarch had passed away to his grandfathers, and that without any injury to or violation of their Protestant principles.

But the change, although tardy, came at last, came with the railways at railway speed. It was a great change. Prices doubled and became similar to those of London. Population increased. Foreigners from other counties, aye, even from the black coal country itself, thronged in. Wealth quadrupled. Excellent roads, but little used, except for pleasure in the summer time, were everywhere constructed. Everybody became acquainted with everybody else. Nobody wanted to live, but all wanted to grow rich. Rest and peace, and quietness, became well-nigh impossible. The whole world was uneasy, and ever on the move, for the most part for no reason at all save restlessness.

Newspapers, good, bad and indifferent, found their way into every cottage, and heart disease and brain disease increased by leaps and bounds. Class distinctions, wealth distinctions, professional distinctions, race distinctions, became much less marked than formerly, and men, women and children were rapidly gaining ground down to a dead level of most uninteresting uniformity.

With the railways have come much wealth, large households and ever-increasing luxury, and it is scarcely an exaggeration to assert that many an employer now does not recognise his own servant when he meets with him in the street. In every direction alike we have expanded enormously. When I was young a single indulgence was thought to be quite sufficient for a man of means. If he hunted, he did not keep a yacht. If he had a Scotch moor and was fond of shooting, he did not hunt or race. If he travelled greatly, and bought pictures and antiquities, he curtailed his expenditure at home. But now one expensive indulgence follows hard upon the heels of another, and a man is considered to be nowhere in the race of life if he is not spending his money lavishly in a hundred different channels at once.

People in all capacities and grades are engaged to serve him at home, and others in numbers serve him abroad. He takes them on for the season and dismisses them again. The bond which should exist between master and servant is now often reduced to a mere money obligation, and carries with it no single sanctifying element of human regard and mutual affection.

We are becoming refined, unbelieving, free-thinking modern philosophers, people whose conception of wisdom is not that of the good old Book, but, as we think, vastly superior to it. Yet notwithstanding all our progress, is there not value to be assigned to such antique virtues as loyalty in its many and attractive forms, to friendship, piety, constancy, faith and hardihood? I confess that, with all their faults, I can see many things to regret in the passing-away of the old-fashioned, inconvenient ways of the past – ways which were typified and partly caused by the condition of the roads, which we are all very busily engaged in improving off the face of creation.

CHAPTER FOURTEEN

A Little Farming

MANY PEOPLE KEEP hunters, and yachts, and game, and have gardens, without expecting an equivalent money return. Why not carry on the principle and farm for pleasure? I have done so for a long time, and to the best of my belief I have made my income meet my expenditure, and I have not expected to do more. Just now I farm about forty acres, and it is possible that readers may like to know why I do so, and what pleasure I can find in the process.

In the first place it gives me *ease*. I am a poor man, and it always sadly grieves me to part with my money; but when I have my own hay, and oats, and carrots, I sometimes think I can afford to buy a likely-looking young colt if I see one to be sold at a moderate price. It is very illogical, I know, but we are all creatures of sentiment, and I do not mind parting with money's worth, although I should shrink from expending money. So it comes to pass that the useless colt gets the superfluous oats, and presently I obtain a good horse without having to put my hand into my pocket to extract those few sovereigns with which it is always so painful to part.

Then, again, the pursuit of farming tends to relieve that fearful tedium which, as my lay friends think, is the bane of the country clergyman's life. I am always interested. Either the rain is going to spoil my hay, or there is no rain, and consequently no hay; or my favourite cow has caught cold, or something or other interesting occurs, and I am very philosophical. The rain clears off and the hay is saved, or the rain comes down and the grass grows, and the old cow has a bran mash and eventually recovers.

I always behave by my farm as I do by my money invest-
ments, and endeavour to do by my saddle. I sit tight and
hold on, and so far the system has answered; but then as I
have only tried it for seventy years, I have clearly no right to
express an opinion on the subject one way or another.

Farming is, moreover, a very healthy occupation, and it
brings a man into amiable intercourse with his fellow-
creatures, and it makes him sympathetic. Here I am, with
forty sheep and a clip of say four hundred pounds of wool.
I used to obtain eighteen pence a pound for my wool, and
this year the value is fourpence. That makes a difference to
me of from £30 to less than £7, entailing a loss of £23 on
my small flock.

Do you suppose that this fact, so cruelly brought home,
does not make me sympathise with my parishioners?
Indeed, it does so. 'A fellow-feeling makes us wondrous
kind' – and I do not, moreover, like to lose my £23.

My farm amuses me very much. My sheep are not nearly
so stupid as people commonly imagine sheep to be. I have
an outlying farm of seventeen acres, which I have recently
purchased. The land has not been so well done by as the
land nearer home, and the sheep, consequently, do not
like the herbage. If I want them to go out to turnpike (as
we phrase it), it is wonderful how stupid all those sheep,
aye, even down to the most innocent-looking lambs, can
be. They do not know the way, they run in all directions
except the one that leads to the turnpike. They display an
amount of gentle, woolly obstinacy which is quite surprising; but if I go outwards and open the gate of the field in
which they are feeding, I have no trouble. They know the
way home perfectly well, and shaking their fleecy hindquarters and prancing they run off home much faster than
I care to follow them.

They are able to reason perfectly well. When with my
dogs I go to drive them outward they say to each other, 'He
is going to take us to those horrid turnpike fields again,
and we won't go if we can possibly help it.' If, on the
contrary, I open the gate by the turnpike, they seem to cry,
'Hurrah for home! Now we are off' – and away they go at a
gallop.

How do they know that they are going to the turnpike? Sometimes I send them to the claylands for a change, and they like that well enough, but they are aware that more frequently they are sent to the turnpike, and they believe in the doctrine of chances. They are very inquisitive, as well as very friendly. If I go into a field where they are they will come to me and inspect me most minutely. My feet are now rather gouty, and I am, consequently, apt to wear 'old shoes and clouted', to which naturally enough I do not wish attention to be drawn; but my sheep *will* notice them, and, marvelling at their shabbiness, they look up at me with wondering and reproachful eyes. 'Well! I never! There's a master for you! A beggar man would not accept his boots: you had better go home and change them.'

They are very gentle, very helpless, and pitifully patient. If you do not look to them daily in summer-time they are apt to get fly-blown, and then they will go into a corner, and in a day or two will be eaten alive and perish like King Herod. They never complain, they suffer silently, horribly, and die.

There is generally one very naughty one in a flock, a ringleader. As soon as I let my sheep into a new field of good grass I see this bad sheep walk quietly all round the fences, looking up, and I know what he is thinking about. Expressed in words, it amounts to this: 'Oh, very well, quite nice, I dare say, but there is no harm in just finding out at once where I can break out if bye-and-bye I should desire to do so.' And I know that all the rest will jump as soon as he does, and at the same place exactly.

I know them all. If I call them they will come galloping, and be only too confiding and familiar. I cannot bear to have them killed; indeed, nothing troubles me more than to have to kill an old horse or dog, or even a sheep. But what else can be done? I keep my sheep as long as it is possible to keep them, and then I sell them to a dealer, but it is a hollow device, for I know that ultimately they will go to the butcher.

As a farmer I frequently see many curious things which interest me. The larvae of daddy long-legs, for instance, are very stupid-looking green grubs, with tough skins. They always, when found, curl themselves up and seem to

be dead; and our ordinary earthworms are not supposed
to be particularly active and intelligent. But one day in the
very hot dry weather I was walking with my old gardener in
a mangold field, when I saw a marvellous phenomenon.
The earth opened, and out came many dull green grubs
and stupid earthworms with surprising alacrity. They wriggled, they jumped, they extended themselves on the surface of the soil.

'Look there, Collins,' I cried. 'What is the meaning of
that?' And he told me that a mole was running near to us
underground. Stupid as they may seem to be, dull green
grub and brainless earthworm knew enough to know that
the rumbling subterraneous sound which they heard fore-
boded danger, and that safety was to be found on the
surface of the ground.

One of the finest swordsmen in the English army, a man
renowned for his single-handed encounters with many
and warlike enemies, once told me that men often get
killed in action by people whom they do not see. They are
engaged with a particular foeman, and they are unconscious of all save him, and another man cuts them down. It
is the same with the lower animals of creation.

Some time ago I lost some half-grown ducks, which were
killed by rats. One day I was in my garden with a hoe in my
hand when I heard a duck cry out, and looking I saw the
bird running, flapping, with tail spread out and drooping
near the ground. Behind came a lean, fierce-looking rat,
which overtook the duck and ran up its tail, on to its back,
and fixed its sharp teeth in the bird's neck. I went forward
and stood over the pair, which seemed to be unconscious
of my presence, and I killed the rat on the duck's back. I
have done the same thing with stoats, and frequently with
snakes. They seem to be completely absorbed in that
which they are doing.

But what are birds and beasts to the civilised man?
Nevertheless, I will put in my plea. I will say to those who
have money and leisure, 'Dear friends, a few of you are
savages at heart, even as I am. Come out of the horrid
town. Take a farm and work it. It will not cost you much
more than you spend on your wretched urban amusements. The plan has its advantages. You will in the country

soon be a personage, and not as at present number one thousand nine hundred and sixty-one and nothing more. The smell of the newly-turned earth is very wholesome, and new-made hay is very nice.

'You will make friends with your neighbours, and form a lasting connection with your labourers. You will soon cease to object to wetting your feet, and your children will, consequently, cease to be ricketty. You will learn to love bird and beast and plant. You will develop some sporting instincts, and will feel pleased when you see that your crops are heavier than those of your neighbours. You will take an interest in your cows, and learn to know every sheep in your flock as well as you know your own children.

'You will develop new interests of the old and healthy kind, interests in nature and in agriculture. You will experience in some respects great ease, be able to pull a turnip for your dinner, and eat your own partridge or even your own sucking pig. After a while you will, perhaps, be able to sit upon a horse without falling off, and ten years will probably be added to your term of existence.

'You will learn to distinguish barley from oats, and you will become generally more observant. If you have a little money and can purchase the land which you farm, you can begin to plant trees and to watch their growth. No employment is more fascinating, and I have, indeed but seldom known a man who beginning to plant did not become devoted to his woods.'

My desire has been to write nothing that is inconsistent with a reasonable Church of England Christianity; nothing that a good woman is unable to read aloud to her family by an honest English fireside; nothing that, if antiquated, is otherwise than honourable; nothing that, if unpopular, is not absolutely straight from my heart, spontaneous; nothing that a presbyter of the old school has cause to be ashamed of; nothing, perhaps, that is more dull than my nature necessitates. Nothing that is not kindly; nothing that is inconsistent with a fervent desire that Israel may be saved, far as Israel in general may be from that desirable consummation.

I end as I began. It is all to me a tangled puzzle, and, in this world, a puzzle that I shall never understand. I see excellent people everywhere, most lovable people, even sometimes trustworthy people, all these in conjunction with an apparently increasing national falling-away from inconvenient rectitude, and a very general abandonment of religious conviction. Now many will follow the law, but few will be guided by the Bible.

There is much of particular goodness and more of general ungodliness. I cannot unravel the mystery, but I know that in town, parish and crowded city, in barracks and battleships alike, aye, even in country parsonages, it is still possible to walk by faith and not by sight, to act from principle and not for popularity, and from a long distance behind to endeavour to keep the skirts in sight of the ten honest men who yet, perchance, may save the city.

CHAPTER FIFTEEN

Finale

MY WIFE AND I are beginning to grow old, and the serious question arises whether a clergyman ought to hold on to his benefice in old age, or whether he ought to resign it. The bishops seem to think that a rector should resign at seventy years of age, although they do not carry out the principle by applying it to themselves. This oversight I cannot understand, except upon the supposition that the care of a diocese is less onerous and less important than the care of parish – and that is a proposition which no one will admit.

The question of resignation is a vexed one, and difficult to decide. In my case, my wife and I have had pretty much our own way in one place for more than thirty years. It may therefore be said that our last bolt is shot, and our last word spoken. We have had our say. We have done our work. We have left upon the population some marks of our individuality. It is perhaps time to put up the shutters, and to put out the lights before retiring finally to bed.

The world, also, during the last thirty years, has been going on much faster than ourselves, No one can possibly feel more strongly than I do that the type which I represent, and in this book have been describing, is that of the clergyman of the past; but I am not absolutely certain that the laity are acting in accordance with their own interests by entirely improving it away.

Whatever were his shortcomings, at least the old clergyman was generally a man, which is more than can be truly said of some of those who are succeeding him. He was capable of doing some work, of standing some exposure, of getting about. Above all, he was generally in touch with the laity. They really trusted to him in most matters, spiritual, educational, pecuniary, recreational. He may yet be regretted, but nevertheless he is gone, or going.

Whatever the faults of the old men, they were not generally self-seeking. They did not come of the self-seeking class. They did not, to use St. Paul's phrase, when speaking of his friends, 'Seek their's but them.' And the longer they lived in a place, the more genuinely attached they became to the inhabitants, the deeper the interest they felt in their well-being.

The question arises, whether it is always desirable to substitute a young man, fresh and vigorous, for a veteran of this sort, whether it is desirable to do so in the interests of the parishioners. It is not all gain either way. A clergyman after thirty years spent in one place may be rather stale, but then, on the other hand, his parishioners know him; they have, we may hope, acquired confidence in his kindness, his straightforwardness, perhaps in his judgment.

And he knows *them,* every man, woman and child of them, and he has a personal regard for them all. It is hard, if under such conditions some sort of human affection has not sprung up, mutual, on both sides, taking in both him and his.

Thirty years is a long time upon which to look back! Its ministrations ought to have produced some fruit. And yet thirty years, although a long time for a man, is a short time for a parish. But there has been, in this parish at least, some progress in the direction of good. For instance, it is a fact that within the memory of living men a North Bovey farmer has dared to say in open vestry that he proposed to turn the old church into a barn, as no one longer required it. There is no living soul who would say *that* now, or be listened to for a moment if he did.

At the time that speech was made there were three celebrations of Holy Communion in North Bovey church in a year; now there are six-and-twenty, twelve in the early morning, and at the last early celebration there were fifteen communicants. There are more than sixty communicants in the parish of four hundred people. It was formerly a most quarrelsome place: it is now most peaceable. There is hardly a house in the parish into which the clergyman is unable to go with the assurance of receiving a hearty welcome. No parent ever objects to the religious instruction given by the rector. No children are withdrawn from the school teaching under the conscience clause. No sick person refuses church ministrations. There has never been a Nonconformist funeral in the parish. The rector baptises, and teaches in school, catechises, prepares for confirmation, visits, marries, churches, communicates and buries well nigh the entire population of the place.

In this parish there is positively no serious crime committed. One boy once stole three sovereigns from the box of another boy. That, for thirty years, is our criminal record. There is comparatively speaking very little drunkenness, and not much of any kind of immorality. All classes join with the rector in the condemnation of sin. All will back and support him in any endeavour to check its exhibition. The children are very good. During thirty years nothing very bad has occurred at the school. Boys and girls are educated side by side, and very few complaints of their behaviour to each other are heard. There are often two Sunday schools in different parts of the parish, and both are well attended, as well as a young men's class.

Thirty years ago the churchwardens were afraid to leave the gates of the churchyard open, lest terrible things should occur. Now you can enter churchyard or church without difficulty during most hours of the day. In other words, a building which was until quite recently regarded as the private property of a few unpopular individuals, is felt to be the valued property of the whole of the population, who have become its affectionate guardians.

I for my part am full of hope. We shall go on from good to better. No man can teach a nicer, better-behaved set of children than now come to North Bovey school. They are gentler, more refined, and much more in touch with me than were the children of thirty years ago. They have never been mercenary, any more than their elders are mercenary, where the church is concerned. They will decorate, or subscribe, or do what they can for a church which they claim very properly as their own.

We all help each other willingly. We do not ask to be paid for every trifling service which we render to God's house, or to each other, in our interlacing and constant relationship as clergyman and parishioners. There has been improvement, but the level is not high, and the attendance at church is inadequate.

When my successor arrives, I trust that he may raise the standard to a higher degree than I have been able to accomplish. Everywhere money is being spent upon our churches; nearly one thousand pounds has been laid out in this place during the time of my incumbency, and the renovated buildings and less slovenly ritual are outward and visible signs of a generally improved life in a better educated population.

I would conclude these reminiscences with the expression of a fervent hope that the mutual relations of the clergy and laity may continue to improve, that both orders may amicably transact together all public business, spiritual and secular, until they go to fresh endeavours to be mutually undertaken in that more perfect place, which their great Master has gone to prepare for all those who in this life have in any capacity served Him well. For it is the acceptance or rejection of His service which makes the difference between man and man, both in this world and the next.

END

Lightning Source UK Ltd.
Milton Keynes UK
07 March 2011

168830UK00001B/107/P

9 781900 318389